The Secret Life of Bacon Tait,
a White Slave Trader
Married to a Free Woman of Color

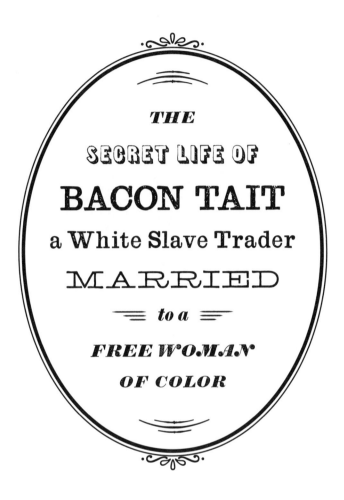

THE
SECRET LIFE OF
BACON TAIT
a White Slave Trader
MARRIED
to a
FREE WOMAN
OF COLOR

HANK TRENT

Louisiana State University Press
Baton Rouge

Published by Louisiana State University Press
Copyright © 2017 by Louisiana State University Press
All rights reserved
Manufactured in the United States of America
First printing

DESIGNER: *Mandy McDonald Scallan*
TYPEFACE: *Whitman*
PRINTER AND BINDER: *McNaughton & Gunn, Inc.*

Library of Congress Cataloging-in-Publication Data are available at the Library of Congress.

ISBN 978-0-8071-6521-8 (cloth: alk. paper) — ISBN 978-0-8071-6522-5 (pdf) — ISBN 978-0-8071-6523-2 (epub)

To my wife, Linda Tope Trent,
with my eternal gratitude for her love, research, care, and assistance

Contents

The Secret Life of Bacon Tait,
a White Slave Trader
Married to a Free Woman of Color

INTRODUCTION

As slave trader Bacon Tait passed forty still unmarried, he sat in his Richmond home and wrote to his business colleagues of loneliness. Among his many paragraphs about shipping arrangements, financing, politics, bill collecting, and the condition of the market, these were the themes he returned to: love, marriage, rejection, being alone. Nearby, in his private jail, the men and women whom he kept caged awaited their forced passage from friends and family to a life of labor in strange states. In 1834 he had constructed a new and larger complex of buildings at Fifteenth and Cary Streets, "to insure the safe keeping, and, at the same time, the health and comfort of the negroes who may be placed thereat." Over the years he occupied various locations, but he kept a presence for thirty years there in dank Shockoe Bottom. It was the lowest part of the city and the heart of the slave market, conveniently located along the James River to load human cargo bound down the coast to New Orleans.

Waiting to hear the result of Rice C. Ballard's marriage proposal in 1838, he revealed his own disappointment at age forty-two as he recited, as if from personal experience, the usual excuses for genteel rejection of a suitor: "She said she was very gratefull for the good opinion you expressed for her and that she would always respect you and would be glad to hear of your marrying some young lady who would make you happy but that she herself had no inclination to marry &c. and a deuce more of such flummery." He was writing late in November, during the busiest time, so he spoke also of loans and collections, adding the happy news that "unless Boudar & myself are very unfortunate we will make out to ship 150 negroes this winter perhaps 200." In the postscript, though, he returned to the old theme, hopeful again: "Mr. Grimm sends his respects to you, I think that he and Mrs. Spaulding will make a match."[1]

The next summer, in the quiet of a Sunday morning during a lull in sales, he reported he "had not been engaged in love affairs of any kind." "Ballard my friend," he wrote, before concluding with a brief note about business, "when you shall have numbered as many years and mishaps in affairs of gallantry as I have you will find that many ladies have hearts as hard as the steel pen with which I now write."[2]

He was headed out in the morning for a short holiday, alone. Two weeks later, after he returned, he related a marvelous occurrence in Alexandria: "Untill last Saturday I had not sat at table in a private house with ladies for more than twenty years." The bittersweet occasion transpired at the home of John Armfield, who had been selling a thousand people south each year. It reinforced Tait's belief: "Happiness my friend is only to be found in the domestic circle . . . I glory in the happiness of others even tho I am myself shut out from it forever."

Then he made a confession, in dramatic contrast to the other letters now preserved as the Rice C. Ballard Papers at the University of North Carolina. Historians have used the collection to document the sexual exploitation of enslaved women, as prominent slave dealers bragged candidly to each other about rape, sexual predation, and prostitution.[3] In this masculine, sexually charged atmosphere, Tait admitted his own frustration: "I beg you sincerely not to become an old bachelor, I speak from experience and declare that his is an insipid life. I could not wish my greatest enemy so great a curse as that he should be avowed to celibacy." The letter was actually about financing for upcoming purchases of men and women to send south. He had enclosed some banknotes to be endorsed.[4] Not only was he failing at love, he was failing to make male friends outside of commercial acquaintances. He stopped writing Ballard in 1842 when their business partnership ended.

Bacon Tait's long life, from 1796 to 1871, began when slavery was weakening due to unprofitability, continued through the renewed surge of greed and power during the cotton boom, and ended after freedom came. He toiled at the heart of the interstate slave trade, in Richmond, where he first built the slave jail that would later become famous as Robert Lumpkin's.

Tait sold it to construct his Cary Street Jail on a lot six times as big. When he died, he was one of the wealthiest residents of Richmond, according to his obituary. Professionally, he chose a career that was notorious even among slave owners, and he not only profited from it, he protected his profits through the Civil War. His personal life illustrates an even stranger journey, which would start less than three years after the letters in which he resigned himself to bachelorhood.

His isolation was not unique among Richmond slave dealers. Despite their wealth, others struggled with loneliness and, like him, at last turned to black or mixed-race women not only for brief encounters but for marriage-like commitment, dedicating slave-trading profits to them, relinquishing a share of their affection and wealth to them even as they exerted cold-hearted control over hundreds of others. Historians have discussed the interracial families of Richmond slave dealers Hector Davis, Silas Omohundro, and Robert Lumpkin.[5]

Until now, historians have overlooked fellow Richmond trader Bacon Tait, who was as wealthy and prominent as the others, but whose loneliness and frustration drove him to an unexpected and remarkable second life in Massachusetts. Some white men sent their interracial children north to be educated, and others even sent their purported spouses to free states, visiting them and claiming to be legally married. In that sense, Bacon Tait was typical, and one can use a full biography of his life as an example of how a man first got into a distasteful business, embraced it, and eventually found himself trapped in loneliness. In another way, though, Tait's life was unique. His journey deep into antislavery territory began at the request of a free woman of color, whose family had ties to the Underground Railroad and to the black abolitionist community.

Tait took Courtney Fountain as his mistress in Richmond, but when their children reached school age, they moved to Salem, Massachusetts, where he bought a home in 1852. "This family, consisting if I am right in my memory, of a wife, three daughters & a son, was always recognized in Salem, as the family of Mr. Tait," a Salem lawyer recalled in 1875. "They were reputed to be the wife & children of Mr. Bacon Tait of Richmond, just as much and exactly as my wife & children were reputed to be mine." The 1865 state census taker recorded the family as Bacon Tait, white, Courtney Tait, mulatto, married, with four mulatto children. Mrs. Tait surely suggested the destination. Some of her siblings and extended family had already immigrated to Massachusetts from Virginia, including James W. Fountain, who represented the county along with Salem's noted black abolitionist Charles Lenox Remond at antislavery meetings during the time Tait lived there. While Tait spent part of each year with his family in Salem during the 1850s, returning to Richmond for a few months to take care of business, his longtime manager Sidnum Grady took care of the slave jail. To the 1860 Massachusetts census taker, Tait was merely a "merchant," but the Virginia census taker reported Grady's occupation more specifically: "buyer & seller of slaves." When war came, Tait stayed in Virginia while his wife and children remained in Salem. James W. Fountain enlisted in the 54th Massachusetts, and Grady found new business for the old jail punishing slaves for the Confederate army. Husband and wife died within two weeks of each other in 1871, five hundred miles apart, he alone in Richmond with a hired caretaker, she near her family in the North. Both had benefited from the marriage, and Tait passed on a substantial estate to their son and three daughters.

Full-length biographies of American interstate slave traders are rare. Isaac Franklin was the subject of one by Wendell Holmes Stephenson in 1938. More recently, Kari J. Winter wrote *The American Dreams of John B. Prentis, Slave Trader*, published in 2011. Historians have written papers and shorter chapters tracing the lives of others.[6] Bacon Tait would not seem an obvious subject for an extensive biography. No collection of his papers survives, though some might yet be lying undiscovered in an attic or archive. The Rice C. Ballard Papers contain the largest number of his letters, a couple dozen over only six years. Even without a central collection of documents, though, one can gather enough information to follow his life through newspapers, lawsuits, letters about him, and other diverse sources. Rarer evidence sheds light on the free black Fountain family, but unfortunately information about them is limited, so the Taits' story must be primarily Bacon's rather than Courtney's. Still, the Fountains, originally from Winchester, Virginia, can be connected through scattered records that show members of the extended family gradually leaving for abolitionist enclaves as hostility toward free blacks increased in the South. Courtney's own decision to relocate from Virginia to Salem fit the family's pattern, but she was the only one to use the money and influence of a white slave trader to accomplish it.

The extraordinary facts of Tait's life challenge stereotypes. The wife he chose was a free woman of color, so although he had legal control over thousands of black women at different times, he had none over her. No less remarkably, Courtney received the benefits of Tait's wealth while remaining close to both him and her family, bringing him into her world more than she entered his. Their lives illuminate the many complex ways that whites and blacks interacted, controlled, manipulated, hated, denigrated, loved, and respected each other within the larger context of a society that revolved around the enslavement of one race by another.

Chapter 1

DOING A GREAT DEAL OF BUSINESS

In the eighteenth century, the sprawling Tait family struck westward from the crowded eastern edge of Virginia toward the Blue Ridge Mountains. This was before the cotton gin, and therefore before the incessant demands for more black men and women to work the cotton fields in the Deep South, so a path to wealth through interstate slave trading was not yet obvious. Ambitious families like the Taits prospered by judging which trail or clearing would become the next road or city. At the fringe of Virginia's settled areas, the many descendants opened land for plantations, claimed town lots, built mills, and stocked supplies for the coming masses. A dozen or so enslaved people might do the hard work for a family, but the profit came from their labor itself, rather than what their bodies would fetch on the market.

By the end of the eighteenth century, the Taits had shouldered their way to the second tier of status in central Virginia, behind the city founders and statesmen. Caleb Tait—or Tate, as the family was beginning to spell it—had concentrated more than most of his kin on the mercantile business. After his family came west from Louisa County, he sold wares as a young man in New London, Virginia, a village that mushroomed into a bustling center for military supplies during the Revolution. Using his older brother Edmund, a captain in the militia, as an agent on the front lines, he profited by sending wagonloads of necessities and luxuries to soldiers.[1]

After the war, he expanded beyond land-locked New London a dozen miles northeast to Lynchburg, where prospects seemed better. Though the community was hardly more than a few buildings clustered near John Lynch's ferry, goods could glide easily between there and Richmond on the broad back of the James River. Trading with the help of his influential brother-in-law, Colonel James Callaway, Caleb invested his profits in gristmills, land, and buildings as the town grew.[2]

In 1796 he was about forty years old and married to the former Nancy Cooper. She and Caleb lived on a plantation along Blackwater Creek near Lynchburg, close to his older brother Edmund and also near his widowed mother, Sarah, who still resided on her late husband's plantation. Caleb and his brother would inherit it when she died.[3] In six years of marriage, Nancy already had borne Caleb four children—Caleb Jr., Netherland, Patrick, and Charles—when she gave birth to a fifth son in the spring of 1796.[4] The new parents needed to decide what to name him. Netherland had been named for his paternal grandmother; Charles for an uncle.

Coincidentally, a different Caleb Tate about the same age, perhaps a cousin, lived in Lynchburg, and he *also* would marry a woman named Ann, nicknamed Nancy, though this other Nancy came from the Whitlock family rather than the Coopers. The name "Bacon" was peppered throughout the Whitlock clan, prompted by the other Nancy Tate's mother, Fanny Bacon Whitlock, who probably descended from Captain Edmund Bacon of England.[5] All the Tates had a habit of reusing names of uncles, cousins, parents, and grandparents, and from these Whitlock in-laws, or soon-to-be in-laws, Caleb and Nancy chose the first name of their new son: Bacon. Over the next few years two sisters, Celine and Eloisa, would complete the family.

Bacon Tait spent his youth on his father's small plantation, growing up on the outskirts of Lynchburg as the son of a well-known mill owner and landlord. When he reached adulthood, he would break away from his family and move off, never to return, but the unique time and place in which he was raised left an indelible mark. Although he spent decades as a slave trader, the conflicting scenes, messages, and arguments about people of color that he was exposed to in his boyhood may have opened his mind enough to allow him the second secret life he would lead forty years later.

A Collision of Cultures

In the early 1800s, Lynchburg was characterized by a collision of cultures in regard to slave ownership. The Quaker founders promoted emancipation, while other investors scrambled to buy and sell enslaved people for the booming local tobacco trade. Plantation owners, meanwhile, felt a duty to give their family servants lifelong care. In the volatile early years of the community, Tait could have met blacks who were educated or degraded, heard the shouts of slave sales or antislavery sermons, and seen some whites emancipating their slaves and others eager to bid on newly arrived coffles. As a slave trader, Tait would emulate the coldest masters, disregarding the humanity of the hundreds of people he shipped south and put on the auction block to further his own interests. Yet in Lynchburg he also must have seen how whites could treat blacks with respect and kindness, not as creatures to be pitied but as equal human beings, because that was a lesson he eventually acted on as well.

A budding center of trade for central Virginia, Lynchburg perched above where Blackwater Creek flowed into the larger James River. An encyclopedia described it in 1803, when Tait was seven: "Here are about 100 houses, and a large ware-house for the inspection of tobacco. There is also a printing-office which issues a weekly gazette. In the vicinity of the town are several valuable merchant mills"—some of which Tait's father owned. Caleb also had erected Tate's Brick Row on Main Street, a landmark and "one of the largest brick buildings in the Corporation, well calculated for the accommodation of a number of mercantile gentlemen." The rent added to the family income, along with profits from the farm and mills.[6]

Schools were few in this thinly settled area, but Tait's father lacked neither money nor desire to educate his family. He owned a personal library of over 150 books, not a small feat when each cost as much as the daily wage of a common laborer.[7] For those who wished to pay, private teachers sporadically held small classes in Lynchburg or tutored in homes. The largest slaveholder of the area, Thomas Jefferson, the absentee owner of Poplar Forest, endorsed New London Academy nearby in Caleb's old hometown. There is no available record of how Tait received his education, but there is no reason to suppose it was deficient in the skills any gentleman needed, either to keep accounts and handle correspondence, or to mingle profitably with those of higher social classes.

Tobacco

Soon after Tait turned ten, new structures began appearing in Lynchburg—as imposing as his father's Brick Row, but presaging the area's future source of riches. With land cleared and fenced, and enough food crops and cattle in production, farmers could now focus more on the most profitable commodity for export: tobacco. The James River would be their highway, but they needed central markets for buyers. John Lynch, the town's founder, built two brick tobacco warehouses, while Dr. George Campbell added a stone one with a slate roof. Other investors, recognizing the potential for profit, built or planned more. Lynch and Campbell laid out new lots on their empty land, and the village became incorporated.

Circumstances had not yet created the key incentive for an interstate slave trader: a difference in price between slaves who could be bought low in Virginia and sold high in the newly acquired or newly opened lands of Georgia, Alabama, Mississippi, and Louisiana. If young Tait expected to repeat his family's success, he could follow his father's example and start out as a storekeeper, or, if he wanted to find a path better suited to his generation, he might recognize the opportunity symbolized by the new warehouses.

Over the next few decades, the community would explode as a center for tobacco production, with its black residents performing most of the labor. Prices surged for a few years after the War of 1812, then stagnated, but by the 1840s the booming market would make Lynchburg among the wealthiest cities in the state for its size.[8] Looking back, *Niles' Weekly Register* of Baltimore reported in 1815, "The town of Lynchburg, that ten years ago was quite an insignificant place, now has a population of 2500 souls; doing a great deal of business."[9] Two-thirds of the souls owned the other one-third, according to an 1816 city census. Less than 10 percent of the residents were free blacks, a proportion that would fall over the decades as the total population of whites and enslaved blacks rose.[10]

Young Tait thus discovered, when he became aware of the world around him, that this was the natural order of things: wealth came from buying and selling, from tobacco—a commodity as natural to humanity as bread or meat—and from black enslaved people who toiled for whites. If circumstances had not led him to slave trading, he might have sought his fortune as a tobacco broker.

Calvin Tate

Calvin Tate, his first cousin, did just that. The son of Colonel Edmund Tate, Calvin was only about four years younger than Tait, and they grew up near each other on their fathers' plantations. In the years ahead, Tait would isolate himself from his Lynchburg kin and most of his youthful acquaintances, but Calvin's livelihood drew him closer to his family and neighbors. Calvin partnered at various times with Linnaeus Dupuy, the husband of Tait's younger sister Celine; with G. B. Tate, another of the Lynchburg Tates; and later, with Charles Lewis Dupuy, Tait's nephew. Though Calvin lived most of his life in far-off New Orleans, he relocated there to represent his hometown, advertising tobacco grown by all the prominent Lynchburg families in the *New Orleans Daily Picayune*.[11]

Occasionally the cousins' paths crossed during their careers, as Tait's occupation also required close attention to the New Orleans market. They even served a few of the same plantations, when Calvin dabbled in brokering cotton for Deep South growers, but their worlds only rarely overlapped. Calvin generally sold nonsentient commodities, no worse than any businessman, while Tait bore the stigma of brokering and shipping human beings, a constant reminder to his Virginia peers of the worst side of slavery.

Calvin prospered modestly, not nearly as well as Tait, but unlike his cousin's steadily increasing wealth, Calvin's road to comfort was rocky. In 1842 he endured a spectacular bankruptcy after the failure of Luke Tiernen's Baltimore shipping company, in which he was a partner, and was forced to write off hundreds of thousands of dollars in debt.[12] He caught the boom in the tobacco market in the 1840s, only to suffer from a devastating fire at his New Orleans warehouse in 1854, but recovered again.[13]

Like Tait, he spent most of his life as a bachelor, traveling and socializing with other men to make the endless contacts necessary for buying and selling. One family historian said Calvin "is not known to have married," but at fifty he wed at last to a New Orleans widow in her thirties and enjoyed a few years of marriage before his death after the Civil War. Unlike Tait's choice of a partner late in life, Calvin's wife, Mrs. Elizabeth Flower Chase, was the respectable daughter of another white New Orleans merchant. She was the widow of Colonel George E. Chase, formerly of northern Massachusetts (now Maine), who had succumbed in 1844 to the ill health that had driven him south.[14]

Calvin may have occasionally kept a few slaves, but he also used white Irish servants. His free mulatto warehouseman in New Orleans, Robert Henry Steptoe, also formerly of Virginia, accomplished more of enduring worth than Calvin himself. In the 1850s, Reverend Steptoe founded the Fourth Baptist Church of New Orleans, which lasted into the twenty-first century.[15]

Calvin exemplified what Tait himself might have become: a merchant like his father rather than a planter like most of the Tates. He could have dealt in Lynchburg's most lucrative commodity and moved away only to further the interests of his old friends and his hometown. Instead, Tait diverged from that path and chose a vocation that appalled even those who had reconciled themselves to the idea of owning human beings.

Justifying Slavery

Tait's grandfather Henry had set an example of a paternal slave owner by ensuring his enslaved people would remain with kin rather than be auctioned to strangers at his death in 1793. The elder Tate willed them by name, one or two to each of his many offspring, including a man named James to Tait's father. The others were to stay on the farm until Henry's widow died, when they could be sold—but only if they could be purchased within the family.[16]

Owners like Henry Tate avoided deals purely for profit, but such sales nonetheless abounded, though more scrupulous owners still felt the need to disguise their motive. Agents bringing a hundred slaves to Lynchburg in 1806 explained, "All the infirm and sickly people, are directed to be left to be supported by their master's humanity." The rest were being offered only due to unspecified "imperious circumstances."[17]

In the 1830s, when Tait had become a trader himself, he recognized owners' reluctance and tried to appeal to those who felt guilty selling for profit. Advertising the virtues of his slave jail for those "who may wish their negroes safely and comfortably taken care of," he promised "the health of the Negroes [shall be] so promoted, that they will be well prepared to encounter a change of climate when removed to the South," making the act of selling enslaved people downriver sound like a visit to a spa. While such words may have allowed potential sellers to ease their remorse, undeceived abolitionists would blast him with sarcasm in northern publications.[18]

Even before Lynchburg's tobacco boom, Quaker Stephen Grellet saw through the veneer of paternalistic care and recognized how the lowest workers became cogs in a money-making machine. "The slaves in that part of the country are treated with more cruelty than I have seen elsewhere. I felt deeply for them, whilst beholding their ragged and emaciated condition," he wrote in his memoir. "I saw the anguish of some of them, whilst passing through the market place of Lynchburgh, as they were publicly selling them, like so many cattle. O the distress they manifested when separated from their nearest relations!"[19]

As the profitability of tobacco increased, so did the demand for human property. "Lynchburg, for a dozen or 15 years back, has proved to be the best market in Virginia for traffic in human blood," a local correspondent wrote to a Boston newspaper in 1811. "Negroes have been sought and purchased with astonishing avidity, whenever the purchase could be effected by the high price of tobacco or otherwise." The writer witnessed a sale that probably took place on March 4, 1811:

> This market has been glutted during the week with Human Flesh and Tobacco, set up to the highest bidder; and otherwise offered for sale, barter or computation, particularly the first article, in every possible shape or form. . . .
>
> The cargo of Monday embraced the range of color, by varied tints, in gradation between the jetty black of the native of the banks of Gambia; and the hardy, durable, home made color of a lowland Virginian.

From the bills of the day, one parcel consisted of one hundred and ten. There were others besides. . . .

Merciful God! what a sad picture of human wretchedness was here presented to the eye and soul of sensibility, on beholding the street crowded with those devoted victims of avarice on the one hand and obduracy on the other. Men, women and children, doomed to the last breath, to serve they [know] not whom, a tyrant, a tiger, a murderer or a man.[20]

Those who bought and sold considered neither themselves nor their wares to be wretched. Josiah L. Deans, one of the wealthiest men of Gloucester County, brought the 110 men and women from beyond Richmond for that sale. He advertised in the Richmond papers for weeks: "NEGROES FOR CASH. One Hundred and Ten, will positively be sold in Lynchburg, Campbell County, Virginia, consisting of Men, Women and Children in families whose extraordinary value and qualities ought to attract every purchaser's attention—Two COOKERS, a BLACK-SMITH and WHEEL-WRIGHT, are in the number."[21] The talents of slaves did not go unrecognized, even when performing ordinary labor. The boatmen had "skill, courage and strength in a high degree," one white man recalled.[22] "The skill which those negroes, who have been accustomed to the business, display in managing the tobacco-casks, and in hoisting them on board the vessels destined to carry them to Europe, is very great," another noted.[23] But the work was unhealthy. Nicotine seeped into the skin and lungs of workers constantly handling the leaves and breathing the dusty air. And, worse, when the two races were in proximity, "collisions could not be prevented," as Reverend Steptoe, Calvin Tate's former warehouseman, wrote with deep understatement after the war, explaining why he did not want white children at his postwar school.[24]

Collisions

During Tait's early teens, several such collisions reached the local courts. Bob Hawkins was accused of beating his slave Milley to death on his Bedford County plantation. Another woman died while her overseer,

Tom Johnson, was leading her home with a rope around her neck, but he was found innocent. A man named Sledd tied up and savagely whipped a rented slave woman, who succumbed while crawling to a creek to find water afterward. Sledd received only two years in the penitentiary because, as his lawyer argued, a master had a right to correct his slave, so the crime did not amount to murder. Outraged northern papers circulated a graphic description of the whipping, giving Lynchburg brief infamy.[25] But the most spectacular Lynchburg trial, the one that "called the attention of a considerable number of citizens, of both town and country," involved the death of Dr. John Lynch Jr., the son of the town's well-known founder, when Tait was thirteen. It also illustrated a third, and dramatically different, path that white people took. Rather than apply paternalism or abuse, Quakers like the Lynches tried to treat black people fairly, as humans.

Dr. Lynch's slave Bob "had, with malevolent curses, wished for his [master's] dissolution" and apparently taken steps to hasten it. Around Christmas of 1809, Dr. Lynch ate soup that Bob offered and suddenly became ill, but recovered. Three weeks later, Bob served him hominy. Dr. Lynch immediately began vomiting again and after a few days suffered "great anguish of body, anxiety of mind, faintings, convulsions, delirium, mania and death." Officials took Bob into custody. "After some violent treatment," as the Richmond newspaper casually related, he confessed to murdering his master and repeated the confession uncoerced to several other people.

John Lynch Sr., the deceased man's father, was a Quaker. True to his humanitarian beliefs, he obtained two attorneys—both to defend Bob, so "the slave might have a fair and impartial trial." They did their work well, even though the father himself, some of the justices, and much of the town believed he was guilty. The court acquitted Bob.

But there was still the question of Bob's fate. Legally, his ownership passed to the next of kin, who happened to be John Lynch Sr. and the murdered man's brother. Rather than sell him away, John Lynch Sr. set him free, "being fully persuaded that freedom and liberty is the natural law of mankind . . . notwithstanding the injury done to me and mine." A cynic might say that manumission would accomplish the same as selling him out of state, because an 1806 law required freed blacks to leave Virginia within one year or be sold back into slavery, but the surprising public gesture of benevolence stood in contrast to the other sides of slavery that were shaping Tait's perspective.[26]

Despite the area's increasing emphasis on slave labor, local Quakers had been setting the opposite example for years, and they were hard to ignore. In the era before both sides had hardened their positions, Quakers mingled easily with slave owners, their names intermixed on lists of town officials and business partners. In the eighteenth century they had owned slaves themselves, but by Tait's youth that had changed. They pressured fellow Friends to adopt the church's new antislavery stance, appointing individuals to encourage those who were reluctant to emancipate. By 1806 the local meeting reported, "We know of none among us who hold slaves. Some are concerned to instruct the black children under their care."[27]

Some apparently took their concern further, at a time when the Underground Railroad could not even be called by its metaphoric name, because no real railroads existed. In 1798, a Lynchburg citizen offered a reward for his escaped slave Salley and her two young children, "seen a few days after her elopement [escape] near the Quaker meeting house, in this neighbourhood, where she is probably consealed [sic] among the free negroes."[28]

Factions with such different views of slavery could not coexist for long. By the 1820s, most of the Quakers would leave for Ohio and other free states, but until then Tait had an opportunity not only to hear discourse on the topic of slavery, but to see the transformation of enslaved people themselves after they were freed.[29] One who stood out, literally, was Reverend John Charleston. "Jet black, between six and seven feet in height," energetic and powerful, he was as likely to be addressing a crowd as to be part of it. Born in the 1760s, he had converted to Methodism in Hanover County. In the early 1800s, he belonged to an equally active and controversial white Lynchburg preacher, Stith Mead. The Methodist Church had not yet split on the issue of slavery, so although the local Methodists were not as opposed as Quakers, they leaned strongly against it even in Virginia. Reverend Mead and Samuel K. Jennings, another local Methodist preacher and doctor, both took credit for raising funds and securing Reverend Charleston's freedom, but legally Reverend Jennings purchased him, then formally manumitted him, "believing that God hath of one blood made all nations of the earth, and—according to our excellent bill of rights—that all are equally entitled to the blessings of liberty." The imposing black preacher continued to minister in the area, but Reverend Mead admitted, "during his ministry he has been severely persecuted."[30]

Despite the presence of sympathetic whites, there was a steady undercurrent of fear, because blacks could not know how any particular white stranger felt until it might be too late. When two sympathetic whites paused among a group of slaves to listen to an open-air funeral conducted by another enslaved preacher, one reported, "every eye seemed fixed upon us with tremulous anxiety, and their expression told me that the company was agitated with the fear that we came to disturb them. . . . Although humbly seated as we were in the midst of them, all seemed yet distrust, not unmixed with dismay." The experience, published in Stith Mead's *Lynchburg Press* in 1822, affected the anonymous writer: "I feel unable to do justice to the discourse of this venerable black man, and have ever since been haunted by the reflections it has given birth to. It has redeemed, in my estimation, the whole unfortunate race from the unmerited prejudices of my early years."[31]

The writer's message came too late for Lynchburg. Spreading an abolitionist message was hopeless in the midst of a booming tobacco market and escalating profits from slavery. But six hundred miles away, the *Salem (Mass.) Gazette* picked up the same newspaper article and printed it for a more receptive audience, in the antislavery town where Tait and his mixed-race family would live twenty-five years later. A prescient verse by abolitionist William Cowper headed the article in both newspapers:

> Fleecy locks and black complexion
> Cannot forfeit nature's claim;
> Skins may differ, but affection
> Dwells in white and black the same.

The community's reaction to men like Reverend Charleston, in contrast to other black men bought and sold at auction, may have taught Tait how to compartmentalize what he thought about black people. Whites needed to classify men like Reverend Charleston as exceptions, or else they would have to treat everyone equally. They could not deny the potential of those who had been given education and freedom when there were living examples around them.

Religion

Aside from the Quakers, sustained religious organizations played little role in early Lynchburg. Protestant revivals swept through, lighting righteous fires that burned out quickly. Famous preacher Lorenzo Dow claimed that as many as five thousand people came to an 1804 camp meeting he held nearby in cooperation with Stith Mead and Tait's uncle by marriage, Colonel Callaway. Reverend Dow managed to gain fifty converts, but he complained that Lynchburg was "the seat of Satan's kingdom" and "a deadly place for the worship of God," with few Methodists closer than twenty miles.

Like many residents, Tait and his family probably did not attend any church regularly, primarily due to a lack of opportunity. Splintered denominations failed to attract enough followers to build churches of their own, so they shared the Masonic Hall, courthouse, or other buildings and held services sporadically until they gained enough membership. Both the local Baptists and Methodists, following the usual customs, accepted black and white worshipers, and when they could afford buildings, accommodated them under the same roof, seated separately.[32]

At their big camp revivals, the Methodists would "stamp and clap and tremble, and wail and cry and scream," as a hymn in Stith Mead's 1807 songbook described it.[33] Such an emotional display would have shocked Tait's grandfather, who had sworn allegiance to the staid Church of England before the Revolution when he served as a vestryman. But that was no longer a practical option in an independent nation that shunned all things connected to the former regime. The local Anglican preacher, Pastor Charles Clay, simply stopped preaching after the Revolution, leaving the church building vacant.[34]

The Episcopal Church was the natural descendant of the Church of England, offering a sober, authoritarian alternative to the emotional revivalist religions, and it was most likely the church that Tait leaned toward, even if he had no opportunity to attend regularly. His uncle Edmund Tate was married by an Episcopalian minister in Charlotte County in 1792, and so was his sister Celine in 1831. A relative donated money to help construct an Episcopal church in neighboring Franklin County, but with the local Church of England building abandoned and finally burned, Lynchburg offered no facility for Episcopalian worship until 1817, when a visiting bishop performed the first nearby service in the Methodist church building. There was no serious effort to form a regular congregation until a few years after that.[35] Decades later, St. Mark's Episcopal Church in Richmond conducted Tait's funeral, but sectarian religion did not seem to play a role in his relationships, either in youth or adulthood. Over the years, one of his closest friends, Solomon Myers, was Jewish and another, Thomas Boudar, was Catholic.

In fact, no man would influence Tait's personal and professional life more than Thomas Boudar. Around 1815, the Boudar family would arrive in Lynchburg fresh from overseas, with hair-raising tales of gruesome insurrections, life-saving loyal slaves, and near-death escapes from foreign lands. The conflicting views of slavery and people of color that Tait had already encountered in Lynchburg, and what he would hear of during the War of 1812, paled in comparison to what the Boudars had seen. But first, as a young man, Tait had to tackle his generation's war.

Chapter 2

A YOUNG GENTLEMAN OF VERY RESPECTABLE PARENTAGE AND DEPORTMENT

The residents of Lynchburg lived safely back from the coast, but they had been following news of Great Britain's naval belligerence since at least 1807, when a British warship attacked the USS *Chesapeake* off Norfolk. In January of 1812, the state General Assembly passed a resolution affirming what most Virginians already realized: they were about to be embroiled in war with England.

Enthusiasm ran high in Lynchburg. As soon as word came calling for soldiers, young lawyer Powhatan Ellis "immediately sallied out, attended by fife and drum, himself bearing a flag, beating for recruits through the streets of the town." Recruiting Sergeant Colin Buckner, although "unaided by martial Music, Colors, Clothing, Blankets, or the other essential incentives to military ardor," enlisted twenty-six volunteers, but he was calling for men aged eighteen to thirty-five—too old for Tait, who was only fifteen. The local newspaper suggested that Lynchburg might even hold the place that nearby New London had in the previous war, as a central rendezvous site for troops.[1]

The early passion waned quickly. After President James Madison signed the official declaration of war in June, Lynchburgers discovered that the government had no special plans for their city and their part would consist primarily of drilling at home and reading news reports about naval battles. When Tait turned sixteen, he may have trained with the local militia riflemen, but for a while any chance that they would see action was slim. In the late winter of 1813, British ships set up a blockade and sporadically threatened to land along the Virginia coast. Tait's older brother Netherland was serving as a private in a local artillery company and received the call to take the field on March 16. Militia companies rotated through quickly, so Netherland returned home in August, his uneventful service completed just five months after he left. He had been too far from the coast to see the major events of the summer, the British landings at Craney Island and Hampton.[2] The next request for soldiers from Lynchburg came the following summer, on June 22, 1814, when the governor called up Captain Samuel J. Wiatt's Lynchburg Rifles, including eighteen-year-old Private Bacon Tait.

Tait had grown into "a young gentleman of very respectable parentage, and deportment" and was old enough that society expected him to begin looking for a wife and to enter a career.[3] Until now, he may have been helping his father, learning how to make profitable investments in land, buildings, and mills, seeing the intricacies of collecting rents and storekeeping, and perhaps drawing the attention of young ladies in town. But whatever future he pictured for himself, events beyond his control would buffet and frustrate him for the next year, shaping his life in ways he could not have predicted. One can only speculate whether such loss of control and failure may have spurred him soon afterward into a career where he could exert complete domination over the lives of others. It certainly started him on almost thirty years of loneliness.

The Tates and War

War disrupted Tait's daily life, but he knew that it also could bring opportunity. His father and uncle had both been young men when the Revolutionary War broke out, and they capitalized on it for the rest of their lives, though in very different ways. His father, Caleb, barely twenty when his generation's war started, had been a merchant in New London and took advantage of the rendezvous of troops there to boost his business. If Tait had asked his father what he did in the war, the only adventure that Caleb could tell was the time he had several wagonloads of goods impressed and had to wait for the Virginia legislature to reimburse him.[4] Though exciting enough for a young merchant with his livelihood on the line, such a story perhaps did not rouse the imagination of teenage Tait sufficiently to make him yearn for an army sutler's life.

Nearby, his uncle offered a different perspective. Colonel Edmund Tate had been twenty-one at the start of the Revolutionary War. Fifty-eight now, he made a living investing in buildings and mills, had received permission to build a toll bridge over Blackwater Creek in 1807, and farmed with a few slaves on his plantation. For years, he had wrangled with John Lynch in the courts over the ownership of some land. But more than that, he was the kind of larger-than-life uncle that most boys would find irresistible. A spring on his property contained iron and sulphur, and his grand dream was to develop it as the central feature of a fashionable health resort, envisioning "a ball-room, extending from one hill to another, across a ravine; an elegant dining-hall; and a company of musicians, who were to play as near as possible to perpetual motion." He was also a fount of knowledge about machinery and the latest inventions. After reading of experiments that showed messages could be sent by electricity and people could be carried by steam-powered locomotives in England and Europe, "he clearly prophesied railroad and telegraphs, and those steps proposed by him to advance the cause, though to all others they only seemed vague and imaginary, were clearly to his mental vision a glorious ascent to the very summit of the hill of Science."[5]

If all that was not enough to excite a teenager's imagination, Colonel Tate could bring out his treasured possessions, his old Revolutionary War sword and cocked hat. Years later, Tait's brother Netherland remembered those occasions. "But young at the time, yet he recollects distinctly, that his uncle Edmund would relate to him and others his encounters and skirmishes and battles, that he was engaged in with the British and also against the Tories in North and South Carolina—he being a Captain of a volunteer Company at the time which he raised." Colonel Tate was "fond of military life, brave, and patriotic, and was no doubt in every enterprise against the enemy, that he would be admitted in by his superior officers." After the war, in the 1790s, he served as a lieutenant colonel in the Campbell County militia and earned his lifelong title, but his memorable achievements came when he was still a captain.[6] While Caleb fretted back in New London, Edmund risked his life to get supplies through. "At one time, [Edmund] had charge of the provision train of waggons . . . which he succeeded in getting safe to our army without being intercepted by the British and Tories."[7]

His stories were both heroic and tragic. Sometimes he was sick and "underwent great privations, having on one occasion, to eat wheat, instead of bread." He nursed a wounded man, who was a neighbor from home, "with his own hands" until the wounded man's death. He fought at Guilford Courthouse and Eutaw Springs before marching his men home late in 1781 after the close of the war.[8] Tait also had other relatives who achieved military rank in wartime, including his uncle Nathaniel Tate, no longer living, and two uncles by marriage, the Callaways.[9]

Steeped in such family history and now prepared to do his part, he boarded the batteaux in the summer of 1814 with about fifty other members of the Lynchburg Rifles and floated down the James River to Richmond. The captain of his company was a relative of Colonel John Wiatt, a distinguished veteran of the Revolutionary War, but Captain Samuel Wiatt's men had no opportunity for heroism. Assigned to the 4th Virginia Regiment, they camped first at the peach orchard in the rear of Fort Norfolk, then a month later moved to the area between there and Lindsay's Garden.[10]

Tait's infantry life was nothing like his uncle's. Though the Lynchburg Rifles prepared to defend the city of Norfolk, there were no enemy incursions. The Norfolk troops began to believe, correctly, that the enemy had no plans for their city. The Lynchburg Rifles' lieutenant, Powhatan Ellis, recalled the disappointment at Norfolk when the soldiers realized they were not to be a target, "and their vehement indignation when they heard of the vandalism of the enemy in burning the Capitol and archives of the nation" in August of 1814.[11]

While Tait endured the tedium of daily drill, news of larger events swirled around him. The first great excitement happened at the mouth of the Potomac a hundred miles to the north, starting July 20, where enemy soldiers landed several times, pushing back the militia, wreaking havoc, and confiscating silver, tobacco, cattle, and over a hundred slaves. The loss of the slaves meant more than just the loss of property. During this war, the enemy was turning the slaves into soldiers. After years of seeing Quakers emancipate blacks, white Lynchburgers had become accustomed to watching the transition from property to humanity, even if they chose not to facilitate it themselves. Former slave Reverend Charleston lived a life as exemplary as any white man, and in cases like his, even slave owners could grudgingly admit that setting him free in their midst was a blessing to him and no harm to the community. Tait now saw the dark side of freedom. He was surrounded by stories of trained, drilled, armed black men, some of them former slaves, invading their native Virginia soil and driving off or killing white men like himself. The British supposedly had set up camp on Tangier Island in Chesapeake Bay, seventy miles to the north across the water, where they were uniforming, arming, and training seven hundred escaped slaves.

The August 3 enemy attack on the Yeocomico River in Northumberland County proved the danger. General John P. Hungerford reported from neighboring Westmoreland County: "I must not omit to mention that several platoons were uniformed negroes. . . . Our negroes are flocking to the enemy from all quarters, which they convert into troops, vindictive and rapacious—with a most minute knowledge of every bye path. They leave us as spies upon our posts and our strength, and they return upon us as guides and soldiers and incendiaries. . . . From this cause alone the enemy have a great advantage over us in a country where the passes and by-ways through our innumerable necks and swamps are so little known to but very few of our officers and men, and through which they can penetrate and be conducted with so much ease by these refugee blacks." Men like Reverend Charleston offered one model for slaves to follow, but this showed another: "The example too which is held out in these bands of armed negroes . . . must have a strong effect upon those blacks which have not yet been able to escape."[12]

Before the war, rumors had already spread from Henry County, a hundred miles southwest of Lynchburg, that the British arrival would cause a slave uprising. A black man named Tom, arrested for murdering his master, gave a chilling confession to his captors in April of 1812: "The negroes in the neighborhood said that these British people was about to rise against this country, and that they intended to rise sometime in next May. That they were buying up guns for the purpose. . . . The negroes in the neighborhood said they were glad that the people were burnt in Richmond [in the famous accidental theater fire of 1811 that killed seventy-two], and wished that all the white people had been burnt with them. That God Almighty had sent them a little Hell for the white people, and that in a little time they would get a greater."[13] The slaves followed current events by getting news from poor people and from overhearing newspapers being read. May of 1812 came and went, and although the British war arrived, the slaves had not risen up of their own accord, but they had used the opportunity to become soldiers and spies, and to take revenge on their former masters. The war drove home that white Virginians had to be vigilant against not only a distant enemy, but a potential menace from within, and the danger would not disappear after a British defeat. It would trouble slave-owning Virginians like Tait as long as slavery lasted.

Lynchburgers may have felt that God was smiting them already, however. In May of 1814, the month before Tait left, "the severest hail storm ever known in this quarter of the world occurred with thunder, lightning, and torrents of rain." Hail shattered all the windows facing west.[14] The storm was only a prelude. In August, the area was "visited by a most unprecedented fall of rain. . . . The damage was incalculable. Mills, Bridges and Fences in the adjacent counties were swept off and injured to an extent never before known."[15] Tait heard that his family's property had not been spared. His father, Caleb, and Uncle Edmund had spent a year and a half building a dam and new mill house on Blackwater Creek. Now, before they could earn a cent to recoup their investment, it was gone, and his father owned a two-thirds interest. Edmund was too discouraged to rebuild, but Caleb wanted them both to sink more money in it. They were arguing.[16]

Bad News

If Tait already felt frustrated at being too far from home to help, new rumors in September 1814 only added to his guilt. Stories circulated from Lynchburg "that a general rising of the blacks in this quarter has lately been the subject of frequent conversations amongst them." The cause was twofold: the war, but more specifically, "the exposed condition in which this part of the country has been left by the repeated calls of the Militia which have been made upon it, leaving scarcely any other population than that of old men and boys."[17] Yet Tait could do nothing; he had been legally required to go.

Fear of insurrection paled in comparison to the worst news he received that month. On September 2, his father died. No one was prepared; he had been ill only a few days. Caleb left a widow, five sons, two daughters, no will, and the ongoing fight with his brother Edmund over the mill, as well as some Kentucky land without a properly recorded title.[18] He was about fifty-eight years old. His obituary in the *Lynchburg Press* recalled him as "a most useful & respectable member of society . . . [who] effected more for the advancement of Lynchburg than any other of its inhabitants"—a claim that the Lynches and other influential citizens might quibble with, but the obituary did note the mills and the Brick Row that benefited farmers and businessmen. His wealth gave "a high testimonial of what prudence, industry, perseverance, and economy can accomplish. In all his various transactions with mankind, for strict justice, honor, honesty, and integrity, few men could be found equal and none to surpass him."[19]

Though Netherland was probably not the oldest child, he plunged into managing the estate. Only he, Caleb Jr., and Patrick had reached their majority, so although he was only twenty-two himself, he acted as legal guardian for his four younger siblings: Charles, Bacon, Celine, and Elouisa. He also had to deal with ongoing lawsuits, including the one involving the washed-away mill, which would drag on into the 1830s, and another trying to collect rent from an 1812 contract their father had made with the Kyle brothers and James C. Moorman, which would last into the 1840s.[20]

Little information about brothers Caleb Jr., Patrick, or Charles is available. Patrick had died by 1841, but Tait would buy out his share of the estate in 1819.[21] Sixteen-year-old Celine, next to the youngest of the siblings, later married merchant Linnaeus Dupuy and eventually moved to the Deep South.[22] The youngest child, Eloisa, never married and died on February 25, 1830, at the home of "Mrs. Dabney" in Campbell County, according to her obituary. The home was probably Vaucluse, the isolated plantation mansion of Susannah Dabney, who was the wealthy widow of Judge John Dabney and owner of fifty slaves. Eloisa wrote her will on February 14, less than two weeks before she died, leaving her debt-free estate to her sister, Celine.[23]

The estate of Tait's father consisted of the modest plantation along the Blackwater, with its cattle, sheep, hogs, horses, corn, and wheat. There were three slaves—Cue (worth $700), Esther ($200), and Hannah ($100)—a carriage, side saddle, the usual household items, and all his books. When the estate was combined with the real wealth of the family—the scattered farmland, mills, and buildings that Caleb had purchased over the years—the total inheritance came to $25,900, a significant amount. Most of the property lay locally in Lynchburg or the neighboring counties, but Caleb also owned some land in Bourbon County, Kentucky, which he had received as partial payment for a downtown building he sold to fellow Lynchburger James Moorman.[24]

His father's death left Tait suddenly rich enough that money was of no immediate concern. He was far away from home, though, and in fact by December had no childhood home to return to. Netherland authorized the sale of Caleb's "mantion [mansion] house" for $2,379.67 on December 20. The now fatherless family owned many other buildings they could move into, in Lynchburg and the surrounding area. Caleb's widow, Ann, and the two daughters may have lived in an apartment in Brick Row, for which they held an insurance policy in 1822.[25]

A Military Career

Tait was ready to leave his old home by now anyway, and he had plans in Norfolk for his future. He apparently enjoyed the idea of army life, if not the tedium of being an enlisted man, and had no strong attachment to Lynchburg. In November, the Norfolk newspaper carried articles about the ongoing Congressional debate over the need for more officers and men. Tait had served most of his time in the 4th Virginia with the Lynchburg Rifles, but when some of the 21st Virginia Regiment from Gloucester had been stationed at Norfolk, he was assigned briefly to that regiment. He had earned a promotion from private to corporal, but now he set his ambitions higher: an officer's commission.[26]

His chance of being chosen as one of the officers of the Lynchburg Rifles at the next militia election was slim, because such officers usually had qualifications far exceeding his. The current captain, Samuel J. Wiatt, benefited from being a well-known attorney whose strong reputation had motivated John Lynch to choose him as one of the two lawyers to defend Bob in the murder trial. Wiatt had military experience as well, previously serving as the company's ensign. The captain before him, William Radford, equally prominent, happened to be the other lawyer paid to defend Bob. The current lieutenant, Powhatan Ellis, though younger and less well-known, was also a lawyer. He had recently arrived in town with a college education and an abundance of ambition and self-importance. In the present scramble for rank, Ellis was angling for major in the state corps, with Norfolk's commanding general, Robert B. Taylor, as his sponsor.[27]

Tait possessed neither the persuasive skills of an attorney nor any experience as an officer to help him at the next election. Though people knew his family, he was too young to have been noticed much himself. However, running for election in the militia was not the only way (nor even the best way) to become an officer. He chose another strategy: requesting a commission from the War Department as a lieutenant in the U.S. Army itself.

Rather than a popularity contest, this was a test of connections, but he was prepared. He actually knew someone, who knew someone, who knew the secretary of war—or at least the previous secretary of war who had just resigned in September, but perhaps the new one also. The man who helped him was Dr. Samuel K. Jennings, a respected Lynchburger already noted for assisting deserving people in need. A few years earlier he had raised money to purchase and set free John Charleston, the black preacher, as well as an enslaved man named Toby and a woman named Sally.[28] Besides being a Methodist minister and former teacher at New London Academy, he also served Lynchburg as a doctor, picturing himself as an undiscovered genius in medicine, and that was the source of his connections. For several years he had been developing a new theory of treatment. His ideas paralleled those of Samuel Thomson in New Hampshire, whose similar system of medicine, based on steam baths and maintaining the body's vital heat, would soar in popularity over the coming decades. Since Jennings had received a patent in January, he had been promoting "a discovery which promises much for the alleviation of the sufferings of humanity": a portable hot bath. Dr. Jennings had already used his connections for his own benefit. In the spring, he had sent a pamphlet about his invention to Thomas Gholson, the current congressman from the 18th District of Virginia, which included Brunswick, Lunenburg, Mecklenburg, and Greenville Counties, but not Lynchburg.

The choice was a strategic one. Dr. Jennings had hoped to attract the attention of the army, and he knew that Surgeon General James Tilton "happened to lodge in the same house with Mr. Gholson." As Dr. Jennings hoped, Gholson told his fellow lodger about the invention, and the surgeon general told the secretary of war. The two military men invited Dr. Jennings to Washington, then allowed him to show off his portable hot bath at the hospital in Norfolk. There, earlier in the summer, he had demonstrated it on thirty patients, harvested more endorsements for a future pamphlet, and received a guarded recommendation from the hospital's surgeon.

Dr. Jennings might not have been as willing to commend Tait's character had he been able to divine the young man's future. The doctor's insight into medicine was blinded by the ignorance of his day, but his observations on slavery were accurate and farsighted. A steadfast abolitionist, he was unable to resist a jab at the slave trade even in a medical pamphlet about his bath. He criticized "false fears of future loss" that made people afraid to accept new ideas, such as his invention or the end of slavery. He complained that people would "rather witness destructive scenes of sickness, pain, and death, than hazard the possible loss of sordid gain." Yet there was always hope. "Truth is necessarily imperishable. It may be opposed and even suppressed for a season, but it will ultimately break forth in all its native splendor, and enlighten the world. Such was the fact in the memorable Wilberforce's motion before the parliament of England, to put an end to the slave trade. 'It fell dead from his lips.' Some thirty years afterwards it was taken up and this odious trade in human souls forever abolished."[29]

Dr. Jennings knew the Tates were not abolitionists, but unable to guess at Bacon Tait's future career, he apparently felt the family had been responsible enough as masters. Tait also had more pressing concerns than either the greed of slave traders or the suffering of slaves: his commission, and he did not mind cooperating with an abolitionist to get it. At Tait's request, Dr. Jennings wrote Congressman Gholson, praising Tait's suitability as an officer. He, or someone else, also circulated a petition among the leading men of Lynchburg, recommending Tait. Twenty-three signed it, as further evidence of the young man's worthiness. Like most congressmen, Gholson was used to receiving such requests. This one seemed reasonable, so he forwarded it on January 2, 1815, to James Monroe, the newly appointed secretary of war, with the explanation: "In behalf of Mr. Bacon Tait now in service at Norfolk, I take the liberty of transmitting to you the enclosed letter. I recd a letter from Dr. Jennings requesting me to introduce Mr. Tait to you, whence I infer he is a respectable man. He is desirous of obtaining the appt of Lieut & I expect he is worthy of it."

The letter he enclosed was the one with all the signatures, and the list of names really was impressive, if one knew who mattered in Lynchburg. There were old war heroes, doctors, lawyers, businessmen, several Lynches, even a Wiatt, of the same family as Tait's captain. Many of the men had rented rooms in Tate's Brick Row as storekeepers, bought property from Caleb or sold it to him, or otherwise knew Tait's father. All could afford to be generous, because there was no competition among the other sons of Lynchburg for this rank.[30]

The last signature on the list, "C. Clay," belonged to Reverend Charles Clay. When the letter came around for him to sign, whoever presented it must have realized that he also had connections, perhaps even better than those of Dr. Jennings. Parson Clay, almost seventy, had represented the Church of England in Lynchburg before the Revolution, but he enthusiastically supported the new country and gave up preaching when the Church of England's local influence dissolved. He owned over a thousand acres in Bedford County, where he resided with his family and maintained a wide circle of friends. A chance encounter with Thomas Jefferson had ripened into a solid friendship, and he also knew Secretary of War James Monroe.[31]

He did not know Tait, though he had known Tait's father and grandfather. The request for a letter of introduction for the hopeful young man put him in an uncomfortable position. On the one hand, he owed a favor to his recently deceased longtime friend, Caleb. On the other hand, he did not really know anything about this teenager. The awkwardness of the situation showed in the letter he wrote, addressed to Monroe on December 12, 1814:

> Application is made to me by a friend of Mr. Bacon Tait's for a letter of introduction to you in his favour as a candidate for a subaltern commission in the Army of the United States. It seems they are pursuaded because I am personally known to you that my signature might have some weight in drawing your attention, to their & the young mans application—his Father was an intimate acquaintance

of mine, I always considered as a candid upright man, he was in the mercantile line in the town of Lynchburg & of respectable connections, & has lately deceased,—his son the bearer of this I have but small acquaintance with, but his testimonial signed by most of the respectable citizens of Lynchburg,—a number of whose honour & integrity I can have no hesitation in saying are indesputable will be handed to you with this I therefore presume that should you see cause to indulge him with a commission that he will conduct himself in the discharge of it with propriety.[32]

Apparently the plan was for Tait to have an interview in person with the secretary of war, bearing letters of introduction from Clay and Gholson and the endorsement of all the important men of Lynchburg. Whether it happened that way, or whether the letters were mailed separately, they wound up filed with all the correspondence the secretary of war received. Unfortunately, the timing was horrible. The Virginia legislature had recently passed an act offering state militiamen if the federal government would equip and pay them, but other state legislatures rebelled at putting their militias under national control, so the need for federal officers was uncertain. Meanwhile, the president had negotiated peace with Britain and was already looking ahead to the postwar reduction of military expenditures. Appointing another lieutenant simply was not practical until the chaos sorted itself out, and by then the army would undoubtedly be smaller, with less need for new officers. No offer of rank came. The governor released the Lynchburg Rifles from service on February 9, 1815. While the majority marched home in high spirits, arriving in March to a public dinner in their honor, Corporal Bacon Tait surely was not overjoyed to see the end of his chance at a military career.[33]

He came home to a community devoid of his father, but he was rich at nineteen, even with only his fraction of the estate. Already he may have been planning how to leverage it into more. Netherland seemed willing to let him manage his own portion with minimal interference, despite being his legal guardian. A life as a merchant and investor appeared to be his lot, though the lingering military fanfare served as a reminder of his frustrated plans, and it did not end quickly. Months later, Lynchburg welcomed the hero of New Orleans, General Andrew Jackson, who stopped on November 7, 1815, to visit Thomas Jefferson at nearby Poplar Forest Plantation on his way to Washington. "The Artillery and Rifle Companies, with their usual order and brilliancy, marched out beyond the hill to salute him as he advanced. . . . The two companies in a style which would have graced veterans, performed their task, and fell in the rear of the General and his suite."

When the entourage reached town, the militia joined other guests at a dinner for three hundred people in one of the tobacco warehouses. The self-important young lawyer Powhatan Ellis, who had also failed to get his commission as a major, had now risen from lieutenant to captain of the Lynchburg Rifles. He made sure to insinuate himself into the festivities, standing beside Jefferson when the former president gave the toast, "Honor and gratitude to those, who have filled the measure of their country's honor." General Jackson offered his own simple toast, to the man who had disappointed Tait: "James Monroe, late Secretary of War."[34] The parallel to the celebrations feting General Washington at the conclusion of the Revolution was too obvious for the newspapers to overlook, and so the festivities became the final postscript to the War of 1812.

Tait's chance for military glory had passed, and unlike his uncle, he would never have an officer's sword or heroic tales to share with his descendants. So far, he had seen no indication that he would have descendants at all. His luck with women had not been the best. Financially, though, he was well off for now. But the perilous decade after the War of 1812 broke some investors and enriched others. It would be a test for a young man with capital.

Chapter 3

FOUR DOORS BELOW THE BELL TAVERN

Lynchburgers enjoyed a boom just after the War of 1812, when western trade shifted in their direction, as sellers used the James River and its canal to funnel goods to the eastern seaports. Nicely situated with an interest in buildings, mills, and farmland, Tait rode the crest, coming into maturity at the same time as his hometown.

"Lynchburg is, perhaps, the most flourishing town in the state, certainly the most flourishing in the interior of Virginia," a traveler wrote in 1818.

> There are few towns increasing more rapidly in wealth and population. This child of the mountains, (as it may be called) has scarcely emerged from her teens, and, (can you believe it?) she has upwards of 5,000 inhabitants; about 700 houses, perhaps more; among which are two banks, three churches, viz. a Presbyterian, a Methodist and a Baptist; a spacious and elegant hotel. . . . These are fine brick buildings, as, indeed are most of the houses here. There are ten subordinant taverns, about sixty stores, two printing offices, from which newspapers are published, and three stationers and book-sellers. There are also seven tobacco warehouses, and three merchant mills. . . . The advantages Lynchburg derives from its situation are immense. It has no rival, nor can it ever have. Its resources are incalculable.[1]

Tait raised money by selling part of his father's Brick Row in 1817, then purchased some of his brother Patrick's share of the estate in 1818. In 1819, the nationwide expansion turned to a temporary economic panic. At the same time a drought hit local crops. The joyous mood swiftly changed. "Business is at a complete stand in Lynchburg, many respectable merchants have been compelled to shut up their stores," a newspaper reported. Shrewdly, Tait bought out the rest of Patrick's inheritance that year, positioning himself for the next upswing in business. Those who had over-invested in real estate before the panic spent years digging themselves out of debt, but the trade in tobacco and other commodities recovered quickly. The following year, a resident reflected on "the speculating mania that pervaded," but noted, "Now the trade, the real business of the place, continues very great."[2]

Tait's older brother Netherland had set his sights on Tennessee, where some of the new western trade was coming from. He began traveling there soon after the war, returning periodically to deal with the estate and finish up business in Virginia. On December 9, 1819, he married Frances Park Cooper, probably a distant relative, in Maury County, Tennessee, fifty miles southwest of Nashville. While back in Virginia, he allowed one of her kin to hire out his slave Cupid to a man in Nashville, but after the wedding Netherland took Cupid back for his own use and settled more permanently in Tennessee. In 1820, he and his wife and their enslaved man lived in Franklin, halfway between Maury County and Nashville, with some members of another family, but by 1830 they had moved closer to her relatives in Maury County. The first of their children appeared exactly nine months after the wedding, on September 9, 1820. They named him Charles Bacon Tate, after his two uncles.[3]

Tait also was spending more time away from Lynchburg. At the end of his long life, his death certificate stated that he had lived in Richmond for fifty-five years, which would indicate he arrived there in 1816. That does seem to be about the time he first temporarily lived and worked there, though not when he became a permanent resident. In 1817 he was identified as "of the city of Richmond" on a Lynchburg deed, but he appeared in the 1820 census as a resident of Lynchburg again, and in 1821 he served jury duty locally in Campbell County.[4] Had his life continued as it was going, he might have become a moderately successful landlord and real estate investor like his father, either in Lynchburg or the larger city of Richmond, but accidental circumstances placed him in what would soon become the heart of the interstate slave trade, where he could be tempted by far more potential for profit.

An 1818 newspaper gives a clue not only to why he wound up in Richmond, but how he came to the specific area of the city where he would make his mark. In August of that year he advertised in the *Richmond Commercial Compiler* that he had for sale three hundred acres and a mill house in Campbell County on Flat Creek, part of the estate he had inherited. He wanted either to sell it or exchange it "for real property in the city of Richmond"—an indication that he already expected to settle there, or at least invest there. He asked those interested to "please apply to the subscriber, at the store of Messrs. David & Wm. Kyle."[5]

The Kyle brothers actually operated two stores in Virginia, but because this ad was in a Richmond newspaper, readers could safely assume which one he meant. It was located near the foot of Richmond's Market Bridge, the well-known passageway across Shockoe Creek. On the other side of the bridge, buyers gathered to haggle over the wares in the stalls of the massive public market house. This was the economic center of the city, located in the lowest section close to the James River. Another store owned by the same Kyles had long been a familiar fixture in a building at the heart of another Virginia town: Tate's Brick Row of Lynchburg. David Kyle had been among the signers of Tait's petition for lieutenant and "was the acting partner of the firm in Lynchburg," but his brother William and cousin Jeremiah Kyle announced in the summer of 1816 they were "now opening in the house formerly occupied by Messrs. F. A. Mayo & Co. four doors below the Bell Tavern" in Richmond and would have "a pretty general assortment of Dry Goods."[6]

Tait now had a natural connection with Richmond through the Kyles. In fact, their new store was within a block of the district where he would make his fortune and trade in the lives of thousands of enslaved people, but he scarcely could have envisioned such a future. The slave trade between Virginia and the Deep South was still in its infancy even in the late 1810s. Traders used taverns, hotels, or other natural gathering places as auction sites, not expecting there to be enough money in the business to build dedicated complexes of auction rooms and jails. Richmond, though, already was growing quickly. The mercantile district had spread across Shockoe Creek and into the surrounding streets that were now crowded with stores like the Kyles', but old-timers could remember when the area around the market house had been a broad green where laundresses spread out clothes to dry.

Watching Slave Auctions

The Bell Tavern sat on the corner of Fifteenth and Main, just a block from the site of Tait's future home at Fifteenth and Cary. Since its opening in 1803, it had been a convenient place for crowds to gather. Citizens had met there to raise money for charity, organize a school, found a bank, and to enlist for the War of 1812. Land and other items had already been auctioned there, so when auctioneers needed a place to sell gangs of slaves, the tavern was a logical choice.[7] Heron, Sinton and Co. advertised on December 30, 1817, that they "will sell, for cash in front of the Bell Tavern . . . from twenty to 30 very likely Negroes."[8] The auctioneers were not slave traders specifically. They also advertised sales of building lots, sugar, and coffee, and they had an office on E Street, near the Kyles.[9] Other notices abounded for slave auctions at the tavern, as did requests to buy: "Cash and a liberal price will be given for a few likely Young Negroes, by applying at the Bell-Tavern," one trader advertised in 1817.[10]

Tait, watching the sales from the Kyles' store nearby, was no fool. He could estimate what shopkeepers and landlords netted in Richmond based on his father's experience in Lynchburg and compare it to the increasing profits earned by those he saw buying enslaved people in Virginia and selling them for the southern market. Regardless of the tempting potential return of slave trading, he was hardly situated to enter the business himself. He had never even visited the Deep South and had no contacts where a slave trader would need them on the other end, in New Orleans or Natchez. However, a solution to that problem also lay nearby, in the Boudar family.

The Boudars

While Tait was preparing to relocate permanently from Lynchburg to Richmond, another family, the Boudars, was undertaking the opposite move. Across the market bridge and one street further back from the river, at the corner of Seventeenth and F, the widow Constance Boudar—or Madame

Boudar as people called her—kept a modest grocery to support herself and her three children. Born in France, the widow of a count, "she was a polite, well-bred lady, truly French in appearance, with her large hoop ear-rings and her handsome snuff-box . . . an excellent, honest-hearted woman, well-cultivated in the literature of her native land."[11]

Though her son would remain in Richmond, she and her two daughters would soon move to Lynchburg and support themselves there, offering music lessons and selling toys and candy. It is unclear exactly when they relocated, though probably around 1819 or 1820. Longtime Lynchburg resident John D. Murrell said he had known them since about 1814, while others claimed the family arrived in Lynchburg at the start of the War of 1812, but the city directory still listed Mrs. Boudar's store in Richmond in 1819 and her landlords paid fire insurance on her store and dwelling in Richmond in 1818 and 1820. Another Frenchman, Paul Pascal, said he had lived beside them for five years in Richmond, probably starting around 1813 or 1814, so the most one can conclude is that Tait met them sometime during the late 1810s, either in Lynchburg or Richmond.[12]

Madame Boudar's son Thomas was sixteen in 1818, six years younger than Tait, but they would form both a personal and professional bond that lasted decades. Tait named two of his daughters after Boudar's family, while Boudar named his son after Tait. Twenty years later, when Tait was considering a new business strategy that would end their partnership, he wrote, "This idea of a separation from Boudar is painfull to me but then we would be as good friends with each other as ever."[13]

Madame Boudar's two daughters at home were Marie Rosalie, two years older than Thomas, and Mercie Hyacinth, somewhat younger. After they moved to Lynchburg, Mercie, "possessing considerable musical talents, aided her mother by giving instructions in that accomplishment" on the piano in their small parlor.[14]

There was also a fourth child, Josephine, a source of anxiety to the family. When the rest had fled from Havana, they had left Josephine behind, though she was probably no more than eight or nine years old. Paul Pascal recalled, "Altho frequent enquiries and researches were made by the family in the city of Havana where she had been left some time in the year 1812, no news or information about her, could ever be procured, which circumstances seemed very much to distress the family." Yet the family never gave up hope. When Madame Boudar wrote her will in 1854, she split her estate four ways, still allocating an equal share to the missing daughter.[15]

The Boudars' entire exotic past became a thing of legend in Lynchburg, resulting in confused and contradictory tales. One resident recalled hearing years later that Madame Boudar was in Santo Domingo "at the time of the insurrection, having been for several days concealed in a large brick oven," adding, "This was always told and believed, but the writer does not vouch for the truth."[16] According to the rumors, they had survived every slave owner's nightmare—a major insurrection. Whatever horrors of slave uprisings that Tait could imagine, they had lived firsthand.

The core of their remarkable story, as near as it can be pieced together, actually lay not far from the tales. Madame Constance Boudar was born in 1783 in France, the daughter of Marie Constance Simonette and Edouard Garreau. In 1791, when she was about eight years old, the family was visiting their landholdings in Santo Domingo when the slaves rebelled in the massive Haitian revolution, giving rise to one story: "Monsieur Garreau was entertaining a party of gentlemen when a slave warned them of the uprising, and they hurriedly sought safety, their host being shot while standing in his doorway. The faithful slave rescued the wife and children, concealing them under the sweet potato vines until he could get them aboard a vessel leaving for Spain."[17]

The now-fatherless daughter eventually married Count Joseph Boudar on November 13, 1798, or 23d Brumaire of the year seven of the French Republic, as the marriage contract described it. Not quite a year later, Napoleon Bonaparte staged the coup of 18 Brumaire, installing the new French Consulate. The Count and Madame Boudar, who was now sixteen years old and five months pregnant with her first child, had to flee. She left first for New York City, followed by her husband, prompting the second story: "He encountered many difficulties in making his escape, being driven into the sea by his pursuers, but was rescued by a passing vessel and brought to the United States, where his wife had preceded him, and given birth to their eldest child, Marie Rosalie, who was born March 2, 1800."[18]

The Joseph Boudar family showed up in the 1800 census in New York City's Sixth Ward. Joseph earned a living as a silversmith or jeweler there, but they did not stay long.[19] In the fall of 1801, the couple left the United States for Cuba, perhaps choosing that location because thousands of French refugees had fled directly there after the Haitian Revolution. The Boudars may have felt comfortable among others of their countrymen who had been driven from Santo Domingo like Mrs. Boudar's family. In 1802, Madame Boudar gave birth to a second child, her son Thomas. Because of his birthplace, he was a Spanish citizen, and would not become a naturalized U.S. citizen until 1853. While in Cuba she had two more children, Mercie Jacinthe (or Hyacinth, as she would later anglicize her name) and Josephine.

Their safety was short-lived. In 1808 Napoleon invaded Spain, and anti-French sentiment rose among the Spanish Cubans. Joseph Boudar fled for the United States once again, this time leaving behind his wife and children. Using his six-year-old son's name, Thomas Boudar, he boarded the brig *Niagara*, which had just arrived in Havana from Philadelphia and was preparing to return there. He landed in the United States on July 28, 1808, with one trunk, bedding, and the clothes he was wearing. In the next Philadelphia city directory, J. M. D. Boudar appeared on the corner of Third and Lombard Streets, and the following year, 1810, he was listed there again as "J. Boudar," operating a china store.[20]

Madame Boudar and the four children continued to reside in Havana until trouble struck once more: another slave revolt. In February of 1812, a free black man, José Antonio Aponte, attempted to start an antislavery revolution in Cuba that he hoped would become as great as what had swept through Haiti. Officials captured the conspirators quickly and executed them, but Cuban slave owners were stunned by the depth and breadth of the conspiracy. In April, the Boudar children witnessed the unforgettable scene of black human heads impaled on sticks being displayed around the city as a warning to others who would plan such a revolt.

One writer, combining the mother's experience in the Haitian Revolution of 1791 when she was eight years old, and the daughter's experience in Cuba in 1812 when she was twelve, described what he thought was the daughter Marie's tale of her youth:

> Although she was but ten years of age at that time she always retained a distinct recollection of the terrible scenes. She remembered

seeing the mob from the garret window, where she and her brother, Thomas Boudar, had been concealed by the porter. Madam Boudar was away from home when the mob was forming and knew nothing of it until she met the governor driving rapidly down the street, who took her into his carriage and drove her out of the city, and out of the way of harm. The scene that Marie Rosalie witnessed from the window as she looked out upon the mob was horrible beyond description. The streets were running with blood, and the ground was nearly covered with the bodies of the slain; maddened negroes were going about with human heads impaled upon sticks, while some of the rioters were dressed in the handsome silks and jewelry of the murdered women, and all were shouting and screaming as loud as they could.

As soon as possible the Boudar family returned to the United States. They first located in the city of Philadelphia, Pennsylvania, then in Norfolk, Virginia, and then in Richmond, the same state.[21]

Lynchburgers understandably misunderstood the Boudars' history, because both the mother and her children had lived through different but similar slave uprisings. The Aponte attempt must have reminded Madame Boudar too much of her childhood, because as soon as she could make arrangements, she and the children boarded the *Apollo,* a ship bound for Philadelphia with a cargo of sugar and coffee plus four other women. She and the children, with two trunks, bedding, and two boxes, landed in Philadelphia on June 15, 1812, the year that Thomas later recalled arriving in the United States on his naturalization papers.[22] For some unknown reason, the child Josephine was left behind.

Reunited again except for their lost child, the Boudar family may have moved from Philadelphia to Norfolk, but the next sign of them is in Richmond in the spring of 1814, when the post office advertised a letter for "Madam Boudar." Her husband, still not content to settle down, traveled to New Orleans, but there his journeying ended. He fell ill, made his will, and died five days later on June 18, 1815, being cared for by a hired "negress" named Jeanne.[23]

Unlike the substantial inheritance that Tait received the year before, the estate of Thomas Boudar's father provided enough for a respectable burial, but little more. When Tait met the family, he found Madame Boudar leading a shabby genteel life, supporting herself and her children with her store. It is even possible that he encouraged them to resettle in his hometown, though Thomas remained in Richmond and would later figure largely in Tait's life.

If Tait had any romantic interest in the eldest daughter, Marie, his opportunity was short-lived. In the summer of 1818, at the age of eighteen, she wed an Irish immigrant about twice her age, William Dornin. They were married by Catholic priest Roger Baxter in Richmond, but moved to Lynchburg about the same time as her mother and siblings.[24]

Alone

This was the beginning of a long, lonely period for Tait. Despite attempts at courtship, he failed miserably whenever he tried to win the heart of a woman. In 1839, looking back, he reported that he had suffered many "mishaps in affairs of gallantry," and this was the long period in which he "had not sat at table in a private house with ladies for more than twenty years."[25]

At the age of twenty-four in 1820, he was not particularly overdue for marriage, but still he must have been disheartened to hear reports of matches back home—even unusual ones, such as the three Lynchburg sisters who married on the same day in June of 1819, or the seventy-year-old man who married a fifteen-year-old girl in Lynchburg in December. Not only had his brother Netherland wed in Tennessee in 1818, his first cousin Alice Tate married Lynchburger David Gamble Murrell on January 19, 1820.[26]

One can only speculate where, if anyplace, he received sexual gratification as a young man. When he did have children much later, he doted on them as if he had no others, and no blood relatives contested his will. He already owned one young enslaved woman and would have the chance to exploit any of the hundreds of others who would pass through his jail in future years. Unlike his friends in the slave trade, who openly wrote about intercourse with their wares, his few surviving letters avoided their bawdy references. The one and only woman he is known to have loved was almost certainly free. Shortly before he met her, he wrote, in another context, "If you can not have the kindness or friendship of others without paying for it, 'twere much better to be without either."[27]

Racial Loyalty and Tension

Aside from the angst of trying to find a wife and establish a career, there was always the tension of race. If Tait planned to manage a household with slaves, as any wealthy bachelor had the opportunity to do, he needed to figure out, like all white people, how to associate with them. The contrast between loyal slaves and insurrectionists was not only a tale from far-off lands that Tait heard from the Boudars; it was happening in real life around him. A slave owner could categorize blacks in general as a potential threat and, out of fear or anger, exploit them physically, mentally, and sexually. But a slave owner would also know that his safety in a real insurrection might depend on not only appeasing his slaves, but developing genuine loyalty through a bond of mutual trust and fondness. The fear that made owners dehumanize their slaves also was an incentive to build an emotional connection with at least some of them. Such a dichotomy may help explain the seeming contradictions in the lives of Tait and other whites, as they related to the blacks around them.

In 1816, an enslaved woman, Lucy, turned against her own race and revealed to her master that a white man in Spotsylvania County, George Boxley, planned to incite a general insurrection. Lucy's husband, Simon, belonged to Spotswood Crenshaw of Lynchburg, and Simon claimed the slaves there also were calculating insurrection. Officials questioned other Louisa County blacks, offering them immunity, and uncovered the plot, arresting several slaves. They were hampered from arresting Boxley by the laws they had put in place to protect themselves: their black informants could not testify in court against a white man, even if they knew he was plotting an uprising. Boxley incriminated himself finally, though, and turned himself in, but he escaped from jail with the help of his wife and fled the state. The excitement divided blacks more than whites. Investigators urged that Lucy's identity be kept secret. "We suggest this course to protect the woman from the rage of the people of her own colour, as we have been informed that the life of a negro man in Louisa who informed of the conduct of Boxley in assembling his associates there, has been endangered."[28]

If that was not lesson enough about the individuality of blacks and the importance of gaining their trust, a December 4, 1818, attack in Campbell County emphasized it even more. At 2 A.M., a black stranger arrived at the detached kitchen of slave owner Meredith Lambeth's home. He told Lambeth's male slave, whom he found there, "that he came from the Alabama territory, whence he had fought his way; and that he had killed several persons: seated himself and asked for a drink of water." Racial ties did not win out. "Mr. L's negro said he would go to the spring, but instead of doing so, went to the house and called up his master, telling him there was a runaway in the kitchen. Mr. L. went down to assist in taking him." The runaway shot Lambeth, wounding him, but Lambeth's enslaved man jumped the runaway. Another of his slaves came to help. "The negroes would have taken [the runaway's] life but for the interference of Mr. L., who by this time had recovered from the immediate effect of the shot," producing the strange result of a white man saving a black runaway from the attack of two slaves. The runaway died in jail, while Lambeth, although seriously wounded, apparently recovered.[29] In 1820, Tait was living in Campbell County with five enslaved people, including two males. Had the runaway shown up at another kitchen, his own slaves might have been put to the test.

Yet racial tension continued. Some whites and slaves, as in Lambeth's home, pictured themselves as part of the same household and therefore united in their goals. More found themselves in an adversarial relationship where whites used their power to control and punish blacks as they saw fit. In February of 1819, Joseph Cohen of Lynchburg shot and killed another man's slave. He was found guilty of manslaughter, served a term in the penitentiary, but eventually returned to live near the city. Later that year, "Reuben, a negro man, was executed at Lynchburg, Va. . . . for committing a rape upon a respectable female," and in 1823 "Charles, the property of Mr. Jas. Cardwell," was hanged at the Campbell County courthouse for the same crime.

In the summer of 1821, two black men ambushed and murdered two white women riding together, though people speculated the slaves had no motive of their own and "were only the instruments of another's vengeance." One named Tom was caught, convicted, and hanged in Lynchburg a few weeks later. Though as a slave he could not legally marry, in his last words he chastised whites who did have that privilege but failed to respect it, and confirmed the rumors: "He particularly besought those who were married, to cherish for each other that affection which had been mutually pledged at the altar. A departure from this sworn duty by another person, had led him to the scaffold."[30]

Despite evidence that the word "lynch" had its origins in the area, these were court-based sentences and "lynch's law," as the phrase was used then, implied neither a racial motive nor death for the victim. "Thirty-nine lashes, inflicted without trial or law, on mere suspicion of guilt, which could not be regularly proved," was how one of the earliest writers explained it in 1817. The phrase probably originated with the action of one of John Lynch's relatives to keep the peace against Tories or criminals in the eighteenth century.[31]

Looking Ahead

In 1820, when he was twenty-four years old, Tait had no marriage vows to uphold yet, but he already had attempted the start of a career as an army officer, a real estate investor, and a planter, all common paths for a white man of his generation. His greatest success seemed to come from buying and selling. The purchase of his brother Patrick's share of the estate, at the exact low point of the market in 1819, was looking like a wise decision. So was the deal with the Flat Creek land that he had wanted to sell or exchange for property in Richmond. The land wound up going to two local men: Chiswell Dabney, a Lynchburg lawyer, and Samuel Harrison, another real estate investor who had just built Lynchburg's new Franklin Hotel. In this case, Tait had sold at just the right time, in the summer of 1818 when prices were high. The panic of 1819 hit Samuel Harrison hard, and he "lost in a breath the fortune which he had patiently accumulated," including his new hotel.[32] With his eye for profit, Tait could not escape seeing the growing interest in slave trading in both Richmond and Lynchburg, nor fail to notice that prices had soared 50 percent since the end of the War of 1812. Even after the 1819 panic, slave prices remained high and would not dip to their prewar level for another two or three years, when they would start a steady climb once more.

Whatever psychological effect a friendship with the Boudars had on Tait, it had an important practical one. Thomas Boudar spoke both French and English fluently, and maybe some Spanish as well—just the languages a slave trader in New Orleans would need to know. He would be comfortable traveling to the Deep South and interacting with the different cultures there, and even at a young age he already had a connection with at least one influential Louisianan, Magloire Guichard. The guardian of his father's pitiful estate in New Orleans, Guichard had helped frame Louisiana's constitution, had been speaker of the state's House of Representatives during the War of 1812, and was a slave owner himself as well as the father of several mulatto children.[33]

If Tait had been concerned about finding a trusted partner before he could engage in the interstate slave trade, his friendship with young Thomas Boudar solved that. Boudar was only eighteen in 1820, though, not yet old enough to command the respect a slave trader would need in New Orleans negotiations. For several years, apparently neither he nor Tait acted on the possibility. In the 1820 census Boudar remained alone in Richmond, while Tait showed up again in or near Lynchburg, probably on some of the family land, living with five enslaved people, four of whom were engaged in agriculture—two men a little older than himself, a woman about his age, and two girls under fourteen.[34]

The panic of 1819 probably unsettled him, but in hindsight it may have given him enough confidence to believe he could judge markets as well or better than even older, more experienced investors. Soon he would embark on the business that he would stay with for most of his life.

Chapter 4

ANOTHER DEALER IN HUMAN FLESH AND BONES

By 1828, Tait had left Lynchburg permanently and settled in Richmond, living with his household servants in a rented three-story brick home with a detached kitchen. They resided just a block northwest of the Bell Tavern, on the corner of New Street and an alley. He also owned a modest little dwelling across Shockoe Creek, a couple of blocks behind Madame Boudar's old store, but he was leasing that out for income. In addition, he continued to receive rent from his properties around Lynchburg.

In the 1830 census, Tait's household included himself, a white male aged fifteen to nineteen, and his four enslaved servants: a man and two women aged twenty-four to thirty-five and one girl aged ten to twenty-three. Later, when censuses named all free individuals and their occupations, one younger white man in his household served as his clerk, so the white male in 1830 may have been a teenage clerk as well. The household slaves had decreased by one male since 1820, but it is unknown whether the remaining ones were the same. The age ranges are not an exact match.

Tait needed the extra space of a larger home, and this one also happened to be close to what would become the future slave trading heart of the city. Before long, the area would be overrun with slave jails and traders' offices, but for now the neighborhood was a mixture of dwellings and small businesses clustered on the hillside leading up from the lowland along Shockoe Creek. Tait's house was probably about ten years old, one of the new ones that had sprung up after the demise of the old Falling Garden. James Lownes, an elderly Quaker, had developed the terraced ornamental garden on the hillside above the creek, offering public baths there in 1805, but by the 1810s the demand for homes had become great enough that he divided most of it and sold lots. Tait's landlord, plantation owner John Sheppard, held homes in the area as an investment, as did others.[1]

Richmond traders still typically used local hotels or taverns as gathering points for sales, though in Baltimore Austin Woolfolk had built his own private jail—a symbol of the greater profits to come. The trade along the East Coast was beginning to take the form it would for most of the antebellum period. White men worked in pairs, one scouring the Upper South for excess slaves to purchase as cheaply as possible, then shipping them to a partner waiting in the Deep South, who would market them to plantation owners there. Traders forced many enslaved people to make the long journey overland on foot, but coastal shipping, though more expensive, was faster, more certain, and less wearing to the merchandise.

The ads for "negroes wanted," which would become ubiquitous a decade later, had already begun to appear in Virginia papers. As the population and the need for slave labor increased in the Deep South, Virginia commission merchants, who had begun by selling a few slaves besides cattle or groceries, realized the potential for profits and began to specialize. The panic of 1819 had finally forced slave prices lower, but traders cared more about the *difference* in price between the Upper South, where slaves were in excess, and the Lower South, where planters needed them for labor. That difference put money in their pockets, and it was still significant. For an investor like Tait, slave trading was looking like a first-rate opportunity.

Thomas Boudar still lived in Richmond in a rented home, though his mother and siblings had moved to Lynchburg. In 1828 he was twenty-six, old enough now to act with authority in New Orleans as a seller. He and Tait already may have begun purchasing a few slaves and reselling them in a small way. The business was seasonal, with shippers sending most enslaved people south starting in the fall and continuing through spring. A letter dated September 10, 1825, to Tait in Richmond asked him to take care of a real estate deed "before you go to the South as you speak of doing," perhaps a hint that Tait might have traveled to the Deep South at the start of the slave-shipping season that year.[2] But Tait's major entrance into the interstate trade came in the winter of 1827–28.

Deep South states were becoming concerned about the new influx of what they feared were the worst slaves of the Upper South. The Louisiana legislature had passed a law banning traders from importing slaves in 1826, but planters needed labor. The legislature repealed the ban on February 4, 1828, and barely a month later Tait sent a shipment of slaves to New Orleans, his first shipment for which any record survives.

He speculated on the purchase of at least thirty-seven people that year, probably costing him well over $10,000, but thanks to his choice of mostly young males, he could expect to sell them for one-third more than he had spent, enough to cover the expense of holding and shipping them plus a profit of 15 or 20 percent. On March 18 he took them to the schooner *James Monroe* in Norfolk and signed the standard declaration that he had not imported them from Africa. Walter Bush, the schooner's master, crowded them on board with 143 others, some of whom had been loaded the day before, consigned by half a dozen different shippers. The process went smoothly, even though it was new to Tait. Bush had been hauling slaves for years, and this was already his second round trip since January.

The slaves, "shipped by Bacon Tait and consigned to himself," were twenty-nine males and eight females, chosen carefully to maximize profit. The majority were in their late teens or early twenties, the age most in demand for field hands, though one was a two-year-old girl named Lucinda with her mother. Each was recorded by name, sex, age, height, and color. Tait probably joined them on the trip so he could arrange for their sale, or at least he arrived in New Orleans about the same time they did. The schooner started on March 18, was put back the following day, and finally left for good on the 20th, sailing south along the coast for two and a half weeks before arriving at the mouth of the Mississippi on April 7. There, at Balize, the boarding officer checked the paperwork again to make sure none of the cargo had come from Africa, then signed them on to New Orleans. On April 9, New Orleans residents read in the newspaper that the *James Monroe* had just arrived from Norfolk with one barrel, four packages of merchandise, and a cargo of slaves.[3]

Tait's first business was to find buyers to liquidate his investment, but he was a newcomer in an increasingly lucrative but competitive field. He must have realized that if he wanted to succeed, the help of more experienced traders would be invaluable.

Partnership

While in New Orleans Tait made a bold move. Two older traders, both orig-inally from Cumberland County, Virginia, were also in the city that spring of 1828, and Tait took the opportunity to propose an equal partnership with them. James P. Wilkinson and Henry De Ende had dabbled in the business separately, but on May 11, 1822, six years earlier, they had "entered into articles of agreement and partnership for the purpose of carrying on a trade in slaves from Richmond and New Orleans." Wilkinson bought in Virginia, while De Ende sold in Louisiana.[4]

Like many wealthy Virginians, thirty-six-year-old Wilkinson maintained a plantation in the country, staying in Richmond when he needed to take care of business there. He and his wife, Catherine, had a home at the corner of C Street and Sixth near the James River Canal—not particularly close to Tait, but anyone interested in slave trading kept an eye on other buyers, and Tait had been acquainted with him for a while. In the spring of 1828, Wilkinson had come down to New Orleans to see De Ende, perhaps to wrap up business for the 1827–28 season and plan the following year.[5]

Henry De Ende, forty-four, had ventured to New Orleans right after the Louisiana Purchase, when he was nineteen, and had prospered as a merchant there. Neither he nor his four siblings had married. His three maiden sisters still lived in Virginia, while his much younger and poorer half-brother, Francis, a bricklayer, also lived in New Orleans.

For the last six years, Wilkinson and De Ende's partnership had gone well. Wilkinson increased the number of slaves he purchased and sent south, until they were marketing fifty or more a year. He and De Ende "continued to trade without difficulty or disagreement until the month of April in the year 1828."[6] That was when Tait approached them.

Tait explained that he was planning to increase his purchases and sales, but he had a proposition for the two more experienced traders. He would invest $10,000 with them if they would admit him as an equal third partner. He offered a persuasive argument: "It would put him out of the markets of Richmond and New Orleans as a competitor thus giving greater control over those markets and of course benefitting each party." Slave trad-ing tied up capital because buyers needed to hold slaves in inventory until they were sold, so having extra funds would allow expansion and more profit for all. The proposition sounded attractive to the other two traders. The three "entered into a verbal agreement of partnership, for the purpose of carrying on the Domestic Slave Trade—in other words, for the purpose of purchasing slaves in Virginia and transporting them to Louisiana for sale." Tait suggested putting the contract in writing and proposed that all "give security for a faithful compliance with the agreement, but the other parties deemed it unnecessary and [he] acquiesced." He described the partnership:

> This agreement was, by express stipulation, to continue for one year only, and by its terms, each was to advance ten thousand dollars, so as to make the entire capital thirty thousand dollars. This capital was to be laid out by [Tait] and Wilkinson in the purchase as near as practicable of a specified class of slaves in Virginia and elsewhere, which were to be sold by De Ende at New Orleans, whither they were to be sent, and the proceeds of sales made by De Ende to be remitted from time to time to [Tait] and Wilkinson, to be again invested from time to time during the year, in the purchase of other slaves, so as to continue uninterruptedly the business for the whole year, reserving however to Wilkinson and [Tait] the discretion of reselling or otherwise disposing of any of the slaves purchased with the partnership funds in Virginia. At the end of the year, the profits, if any, were to be equally divided among the three partners, or if a loss had been sustained, each was to bear his equal proportions.[7]

De Ende realized in hindsight that Tait had not explicitly promised to avoid trading in competition, but believed it would clearly be "in direct violation of the spirit of the contract."[8]

To pay his $10,000 share, Tait handed Wilkinson "bills of exchange payable sixty [days] after sight for the sum of $20,000 . . . drawn on persons in New York and Philadelphia and Baltimore." The amount was far more than enough to cover his required investment, even if the bills were discounted, but Tait, being a relative newcomer to the business, wanted "to shew his entire ability to comply with the engagement into which he had entered."

He returned home via Norfolk, probably again on the *James Monroe,* which arrived back in port on May 29. He wasted no time. Starting June 7, he began purchasing slaves in Virginia for the partnership, as he had promised. Wilkinson sailed to New York and made his way down to Richmond through Philadelphia and Baltimore, presenting the bills to Tait's debtors. They were probably bankers or investors to whom Tait had loaned some of his real estate profits in order to earn interest. Following typical prudent business practices, Wilkinson had the bills accepted, which proved that the debtors acknowledged they owed the money, but Wilkinson could not actually collect the money because the bills were payable sixty days after sight. Wilkinson arrived in Richmond later in June, and Tait immediately asked if he and De Ende had put up their shares too. Wilkinson replied that he had received $10,000 from De Ende and that his own share of $10,000 was ready as well.

Tait trusted him and spent the summer buying more slaves and shipping them to New Orleans, paying with his own money, occasionally asking Wilkinson to reimburse him from the partnership's funds. Wilkinson did the same, reimbursing himself also, but he kept the transactions confusing enough that eventually Tait objected, pointing out that Wilkinson sometimes "obtained two vouchers for the same money, and some times a voucher where the money was drawn for [Wilkinson's] own use."[9]

Wilkinson explained he had always done things that way. "To depart from this practice, might subject him to inconveniences," and the "due bills and memorandums" that Tait was giving him for each transaction "would always show how much of these orders were properly chargeable to [Tait]."

Tait reluctantly acquiesced, because, as he explained later, he had "unbounded confidence" in Wilkinson and naively did not suspect "that any fraud was intended, or could be practiced by one with whom he had confided so much, and by whom he had long known." Wilkinson felt the same way, equally naively, about Tait. He and De Ende did not discover until later that Tait had "entered into another copartnership with another person viz one Thomas Boudar and was secretly engaged in shipping slaves to him." This undermined one of the main reasons they had accepted him as a partner. His side business with Boudar was "increasing the competition and lessening [their] profits."[10]

But that was not all. In hindsight, Wilkinson realized that Tait had offered the original $20,000 in due bills as his portion of the partnership's capital, but when the creditors paid the bills, the money was not necessarily making its way into the partnership's funds. Though Tait was buying slaves with his own money, the periodic reimbursements he requested seemed to be greater than the amount he was spending. Worse yet, he may have been using the partners' funds not only to pay for slaves he bought for them, but for slaves he was sending to Thomas Boudar as well.[11]

Still, at the time, Wilkinson trusted Tait. They continued scouring auctions, estate sales, and plantations for young, healthy people who could be bought cheaply, until they had gathered about seventy, which they shipped on the *James Monroe* again to De Ende in late September. Their purchases had used up most of the $30,000 capital that the partnership had agreed to risk. They might not receive it back from sales for several months, but the buying and shipping season had barely begun. "Wilkinson expressed a wish that each partner should augment his stock $5000, so as to make the whole capital of the concern $45,000."[12] Tait agreed. Both partners assumed that De Ende would consent as well. So, while waiting to hear from him, Tait continued using his own money to purchase more slaves, until November 27, 1828, when he felt he had invested a total of $15,000, the overall sum to which he had agreed.

At that time he added up what he had spent buying slaves minus what he had been reimbursed and discovered, as Wilkinson had suspected, that he had indeed taken out more than he had put in: $3,035 more. But that hardly mattered now, because the purchasing season was ending. As soon as De Ende finished selling their wares in New Orleans, the partners could each withdraw their funds anyway. Tait expected that the $3,035 would be deducted from his third.

He was still waiting to see evidence, though, that De Ende actually would put up the extra $5,000 capital. The Virginia partners had not heard back from him yet, although eight weeks had passed, allowing plenty of time to reply. The mail took a little less than three weeks each way. Finally, when De Ende wrote to say that he had sold the slaves in the last shipment for $6,181, he enclosed a check to cover his $5,000 contribution, but he did not send the $6,181. Tait realized that De Ende had sent the partnership its own revenue back, and had not contributed $5,000 of new money. Already frustrated with Wilkinson's sloppy accounting, Tait was ready to be done with the whole arrangement, and he applied to Wilkinson for a final settlement late in February of 1829.

Not surprisingly, the records that Wilkinson showed him were a mess. According to their best calculations, Wilkinson and De Ende together had invested only $13,147 of the $30,000 they should have, and Tait suspected that even some of that, like De Ende's extra $5,000, came from recycling the partnership's funds rather than adding actual capital. Tait had been doing the same thing, of course, though he minimized that point when discussing the other partners' investments. Reluctantly, he agreed to the figures that Wilkinson provided, but both Virginia partners wanted to see a record of what they had grossed in New Orleans and Tait wanted to be paid his share of the profits.

Around the middle of April 1829, Tait left for New Orleans with Wilkinson's brother Tom "for the purpose of obtaining an account of the affairs of the partnership from De Ende who had made all the sales." They arrived about May 1 and asked for a clear accounting, which De Ende at first "declined and finally refused." De Ende tried to dodge by telling Tait that Wilkinson still had $6,000 back in Virginia that was due Tait.

Tait reported: "After incessant applications by [myself,] De Ende finally furnished a sketch of what he denominated a statement of the partnership, but which is nothing in the character and hardly form of an account, from which the least satisfactory information of the business could be obtained being without form, without dates and not shewing when or to whom the slaves of the concern had been sold." Frustrated, Tait returned to Richmond and approached Wilkinson again, demanding the money he was due. Wilkinson brushed him off with another vague financial statement, but no money.

Although Tait seemed to have come out ahead by withdrawing $3,035 more than he had spent, he knew that the actual profits were "very considerable," estimating that he was due at least "one equal third part of the profits, a sum not short of nine thousand dollars." He also suspected that the other two partners "never did furnish at any time as much as $30,000 of stock," so if he was to get his share based on the amount he contributed, he should get even more than that.[13]

The three partners were maintaining a strained politeness. De Ende wrote Wilkinson on July 24, 1829, sending another $2,500 that had trickled in from sales and promising to remit more "'to you,' in order that you may reimburse Mr. Tait and yourself for the amount of your purchases towards Mr. Tait's $9000, or thereabouts, which he says he was out when here; it will be recollected that I advanced him $3000, you will therefore only have about $6000 to refund him, to all which he is not yet entitled, because I have not yet received as much, over and above the expenses here." As far as whether each partner had contributed his equal third to the capital, De Ende wrote, "we will enquire . . . and endeavor to make the thing right."[14]

By the end of the year, both sides realized they lacked records adequate to prove their claims, but each stalled by refusing to supply documentation until the other did. The veneer of politeness had disappeared, and even the original two partners were squabbling. De Ende wrote Wilkinson in December: "You must leave off scolding . . . and Mr. Tait must discard the very indecorous language in which he delights to indulge, or our intercourse must cease—on its present footing it is extremely unpleasant."[15] Tait saw that any friendly resolution was hopeless. The one-year partnership had ended anyway, and he was moving on into his own business. He abandoned trying to collect directly and, as the new decade began, started planning a lawsuit to salvage what he could.

Lessons Learned

Tait's first partnership with experienced traders confirmed the enormous potential for profit in buying and selling slaves. He also learned the importance of keeping accurate records and working with someone in whom he could have complete trust, which affirmed the value of his friendship with Thomas Boudar. He had discovered how to purchase profitably for the southern market, met other traders in both Virginia and New Orleans, and, despite the monetary frustration, left the venture prepared to invest and succeed on his own.

Not all purchases produced a profit, but he noticed how even losses could be ameliorated. For example, the enslaved man George, about twenty-five years old, suffered from severely inflamed eyes in the summer of

1828—a temporary condition, everyone hoped, from the smoke of firing tobacco on the Powhatan County plantation where he worked, but there was some concern he would become permanently blind. As if George's fear of going blind was not distressing enough, he and his wife, Elvira, were now for sale in Richmond. When Wilkinson purchased the couple for $700, he required the seller to agree to pay the "depreciation" in value if George lost his sight. Despite providing $11.50 worth of medical treatment, Wilkinson had to send George to New Orleans still not cured. De Ende sold him the following year as defective in one eye for $63.50 less than the purchase price, rather than $200 more, as the traders had hoped. Tait saw that his partners minimized the loss two ways. Wilkinson could—and did—sue the original seller for $125, the appraised loss of value. De Ende also received a higher price than he might have, by careful marketing. Experienced traders knew that if they included an ill slave in a lot with healthy ones, "it frequently happens that by that means a defective negro is sold for much more than the same negro could be sold for single, or alone."[16]

If Tait had not known before, he also learned that slave trading required close attention to condition and cost. As the season's purchasing wound down, De Ende wrote, "If you can buy two or three female servants that are perfect, and will bear the town, don't let them pass into other hands, and a good carpenter or mason will never come amiss, if likely and of good character. . . . Of field negroes, or indeed any other description, I want none, till I see farther." Sickness was also a problem to be avoided. De Ende explained why he had not yet sold all the slaves at the end of the season: he had "4 men and 1 woman of ours, three unwell, but mending, and two of Langhorne's, in no condition for sale."[17]

Such calculated selling of human beings bothered even other slave owners, although they saw it as a necessary service in the slave states. As Tait sank deeper into the business, the social repercussions may have concerned him, but he had little to lose. Without a wife, and isolated from his family in Lynchburg, he needed to find new associates in Richmond anyway, so he could make friendships among those connected with the slave trade without losing an already-existing social network. If he had any doubts about how others viewed his new profession, a scandal hit the newspapers during the presidential election year of 1828. Candidate Andrew Jackson's political rivals accused Jackson of being a slave trader, based on an incident years earlier. Andrew Erwin published a pamphlet, "Gen. Jackson's Negro Speculations, and his Traffic in Human Flesh, Examined and Established by Positive Proof," and anti-Jacksonian editorialists jumped on the opportunity, writing lurid condemnations of those who engaged in interstate slave trading. As Erwin explained:

> The practice, even where tolerated by law, is becoming exceedingly odious. The humane slave holder in those states where this species of servitude is recognized under the constitution detests it as cruel and subversive of the dearest ties of domestic affection: but the non slave holder of the free states, condemns it, as war with human rights, republican principles, and every feeling of the human heart. What then shall we say of those who follow this ignoble traffic? Are not private citizens, to say the least, liable to the reproach of all good society and of christians, who are guilty of this odious practice? Such we find to be the light in which those who are termed "negro buyers," and "negro sellers," are viewed.

Tait might have cringed when he read such insults about his new profession in the Richmond papers, but he plunged into the business anyway.[18] The competitive nature of slave trading required keeping a closer eye on profits than ethics, but Tait seemed to be comfortable with that. He lied to Wilkinson and De Ende, while treating Boudar fairly. As with blacks, he separated whites into two categories: those he needed to exploit and those with whom he wanted to develop a bond of trust.

An Example in Henry De Ende

Tait may have expected to find a man who was cruelly indifferent to people of color when he met Henry De Ende in New Orleans, but like many traders De Ende had found a free woman that he could love across the racial divide. He lived on Louisa Street. Like Tait, he was single and owned a few servants for his household. Just over half a mile to the west, at the corner of Casa Calvo and Espagne Streets, he also kept a home for his "concubine,"

Victoire (or Victorie) Cavelier, a free woman of color, and the five children they had together: Eliza, Emily, Harriet, Simon Bolivar, and Benjamin Franklin. One more child, Marion, would be born in 1831 before both De Ende and their mother died in 1832. The children, who ranged in age from newborn to about thirteen when Tait visited the city, were born free and colored because of their mother, but they would become wealthy and educated due to their father. De Ende openly acknowledged his relationship with their mother in his 1832 will, hiring a tutor for his "natural children" and leaving them as much of his large estate as he could by law.

In their youth, when people remembered the children's parentage, they were deemed to belong to their mother's race, but that changed. The baby, Marion, was categorized as colored when he died in 1832, but his older brother, Simon Bolivar, was considered white when he died in 1851 at the age of twenty-six. As the other children became adults, they took the last name De Ende. Emily married Timothy Donnellan, an Irishman, and they moved to Houston, Texas, about 1839. She claimed to be the daughter of "French General de Adendy of New Orleans," though a modern writer unsurprisingly admitted "no other sources, as yet, can confirm that." Her siblings Harriet and Franklin were living with her by 1850, none marked as black or mulatto on the census.[19] Benjamin Franklin De Ende, like any other white person, ran for office and was elected assessor and collector of Harris County, Texas, in 1862, later served as county clerk, and handled legal matters for various estates.[20] De Ende's children had successfully transitioned into white society. Loyalty to the race they had been raised in did not define them any more than it had defined De Ende.

The profits from De Ende's slave trading had, in part, gone to a family of color—a theme that would be repeated with surprising regularity in the coming decades by other traders in both Richmond and New Orleans. Though Victoire Cavalier might have accepted the funds at arm's length from their slave-trading origin, she was involved in the daily management of Mary, an enslaved woman whom De Ende provided her, and she was apparently successful at controlling Mary. When Mary began to behave too much like a free woman, the children sold her as one who overstepped her social and legal position. Whether that decision was truly their own or influenced by their white tutor and lawyer, they embraced it as they moved forward into the white middle class. Emily De Ende kept a black enslaved woman in her household as late as the 1860 census.[21]

The racial culture of New Orleans in the 1820s, with its mix of foreign backgrounds and shades of color, was a world away from Richmond. But when Virginia slave traders like Tait began dealing with Louisianans, they found reinforcement for the idea that people of color could be—and must be—dealt with in a variety of ways, from the cold-hearted treatment of slaves for trading to the pampered acceptance of loved ones, such as De Ende's family.

Auctions

Enslaved people themselves also reacted in diverse ways as they negotiated the challenging and often brutal world into which they were born. A Swedish onlooker at a Richmond slave auction, typical of those that Tait attended in the early 1830s, expressed surprise at the behavior of the participants, who did not fit his idea of a sharp divide between cruel whites and noble blacks. After vilifying white buyers who would "divert themselves [with humor] at the expence of the slaves, and indulge in *bons mots*, as piercing to the heart of every feeling man as the point of a dagger," he turned his attention to the other bystanders:

> In the crowd I discovered at least a dozen Negroes and Negro women, who stopped in passing to gratify their curiosity. They appeared to listen with an extraordinary degree of attention to the progress of the sale. I could not avoid sympathizing with them, in witnessing the expression of feeling they showed toward their fellow-creatures. . . .
>
> At that moment, I heard, to my horror, a burst of laughter from the crowd. I looked round, and observed all the surrounding Blacks indulging in so hearty a laugh, that I was nigh being smitten with the same fit. . . . Full of surprise, I inquired the cause, and was informed that one of them had happened to make a most striking and ludicrous remark, respecting the mother then about to be sold. Can there be anything more unfeeling, more unbecoming, than that persons, themselves slaves, who have often gone through the same ordeal of being sold like beasts, and who are consequently

thoroughly acquainted with its iniquity, that these persons should jest and laugh at the natural horror and timidity felt by a mother at the time of sale?

A buyer and seller like Tait was not presented with relentless scenes of misery. Blacks in eastern Virginia, as well as whites, lived in a world permeated by slavery and racism, without the luxury to step outside, compare it to how things should be, and feel continuous moral outrage. Their priority was survival with the least psychological and physical damage. The result produced incongruous behavior, which the writer went on to describe, as the auction proceeded. Among the three adults being sold, "the only one of these Blacks who appeared to feel her degraded situation was poor Betsy. Her eyes were constantly fixed on her infant. . . . This, however, was not the case with the other slaves: they laughed good-naturedly at every jest, looked upon the inspection as extremely foolish, and their large white eyes sparkled like brilliants in their heads with delight at the lively and witty talk of the 'Gentlemen' who had come all the way from the country for the purpose of purchasing human creatures!"[22]

The enslaved men and women whom traders shipped to New Orleans handled their fate with all the range of human emotional displays, from the anger, fear, or depression that one would expect, to grim good humor or even the naive bravado of youth, as Solomon Northup observed in his fellow voyager Maria, "a rather genteel looking colored girl, with a faultless form, but ignorant and extremely vain. . . . Assuming a haughty mien, she declared to her companions, that immediately on our arrival in New-Orleans, she had no doubt, some wealthy single gentleman of good taste would purchase her at once!"[23] Seeing the range of reactions, a trader like Tait could convince himself that the suffering he caused, though unfortunate, was not universal.

The Coming Decade

The late 1820s led up to the 1830s boom, when demand for labor in the Deep South soared. The familiar faces at the Richmond auctions would change also within a decade or so, as older traders retired or died, some leaving the trade by the 1830s, others in the 1840s. Abner Robinson, John C. Saunders, Henry King, and D. and E. Woodward would fade from the scene to be replaced by Robert Lumpkin, Silas Omohundro, and Hector Davis. James P. Wilkinson dropped dead at the Bell Tavern one summer day in 1845, but his widow, Catherine, married Nathaniel B. Hill of the slave auction firm Dickinson, Hill and Co., which kept selling through the Civil War.[24] The 1820s were also, in retrospect, a time of relative tolerance for another class of blacks: those who did not need to fear sale, unless they were kidnapped or convicted as criminals. Free blacks, either born free or manumitted and allowed to remain in the state, had been steadily increasing.

The Jacksonian era, with its emphasis on the worth of the common man, encouraged an attitude worrisome to many whites. An anonymous letter writer to the *Richmond Enquirer* in 1825 warned how far zealots might go: "if '*all* men be free and equal,' and 'taxation and representation be inseparable,' why not now, as formerly, permit free negroes and mulattoes to vote, and even slaves . . . ?" The writer, identifying himself only as being from the Northern Neck, northeast of Richmond, warned that "the spirit of the times is very favourable," and "the preservation of our rights and the safety and happiness of our children, will greatly depend on a jealous watchfulness of certain artful and plausable politicians" who would take the principle of equality too far, into "a subversion of the principles by which Virginia has been so long distinguished."[25]

Such fears were not entirely unfounded. At Virginia's constitutional convention in 1829–30, representatives from the eastern and western halves of the state argued whether voting should be expanded to include white men who did not own land. The wealthier easterners eventually compromised to allow more white males to vote, but the question of extending other rights even further, to both free and enslaved blacks, naturally arose. Elder statesman John Randolph complained of the "fanatical spirit" of abolitionism "growing up in the land." He hinted at secret plans: "Do you not know—that petitions were preparing for the purpose of being presented to this body on that subject? . . . The abolitionist is as free to hold his opinions as I am to hold mine. . . . But I never will suffer him to put a torch to my property, that he may slake it in the blood of all that is dear to me."[26]

Plain-spoken Samuel McDowell Moore, representing Rockbridge

County at the convention, asked rhetorically, if all men are created equal, why not slaves? He said what many thought: "The answer to this question is so easily given, and is so obvious, that I am surprised it should ever have been asked. The answer is, that we do not choose to . . . because we believe that they would not make good citizens, or because we are prejudiced against their colour; or if you please, because we think proper to disregard their natural rights, and to hold them in slavery, that we may reap the benefit of their labour." Though he did not necessarily agree, he accepted the consensus of Virginia's white men.[27]

Threats of insurrection increased, especially in the summer of 1829 as white men elected delegates for the convention. Enslaved people spread rumors that they all were to be given their free papers in August, or that an insurrection was to begin then. The state militia went on alert, but August came and went without incident. Although the governor had not actually expected anything to happen, he issued extra arms to the militia, acknowledging the underlying problem: "The number of slaves is so great in some parts of the Commonwealth as to give cause at all times for apprehending danger, or adopting measures of precaution."[28]

The interstate slave trade produced an outlet for excess slaves, but there was none for free blacks, who continued to raise their families and multiply. Whites considered them as dangerous as slaves, if not more so, because they had freedom to plot undetected. Colonization—the plan of offering them passage to Africa or elsewhere—had its advocates, but was still in its infancy and generally considered unworkable. Although Virginia's whites acknowledged the increasing problem, they dithered about a solution. Nat Turner had not yet lit the powder keg that would motivate them to action.

Personal Life

By the close of the 1820s, Tait was successfully managing his trade in enslaved people and could use the courts to extract his missing partnership profits, but he still could not find a woman who would say yes to marriage. Thomas Boudar, a bachelor when Tait met him, had already found a wife, fifteen-year-old Mary Ann Girardin. Although also bearing the stigma of a slave trader, Boudar succeeded where Tait and others failed. Besides being of French Catholic heritage, Miss Girardin fit naturally in the crisis-ridden Boudar family. Her father, educator and writer Louis Hue Girardin, had fled France during the Revolution. They wed on October 19, 1825, in a Catholic ceremony conducted by Father Thomas Hore of Richmond.[29]

The marriages that Tait saw occurring around him seemed to come from natural connections that he could not access. Thomas Boudar and his wife shared both an uncommon religion and a French refugee heritage. In 1824, two daughters of the Kyle mercantile family, cousins both named Harriet, married men who worked for the Kyles, but Tait might not have had a chance with them. The new husbands, John and William McCausland, came from a family that had intermarried with the Kyles even before they emigrated from Ireland.[30]

Otherwise, Tait did not seem to have any particular faults. Much later, a visiting couple described him as "another dealer in human flesh and bones, but in every other respect a man of good standing with his fellow-citizens, quite a gentleman in his manners, and of good moral conduct." Indeed, a few days before Christmas of 1829, Tait came upon a Dickensian scene. William Howlett had a wife and two young daughters, but he was deep in debt. All their household furnishings as well as their "old negro woman named Rose" were to be sold by order of the local hustings court, to pay his creditors. Tait attended the sale on December 19 and bought a long list of things he did not need for a total of $225.42, including the slave for $15, probably the least he had ever paid for one. Then, "in consideration of the natural love and affection which I bear to Lucy Francis Howlett and Elizabeth Catherine Howlett"—the two young daughters—Tait gave everything to them, including their old servant Rose. Presumably, because the two daughters were not liable for their father's debts, this would protect the property from ever legally being lost again. Thanks to his generosity, the Howletts could keep their belongings and Rose could spend Christmas with the family she was used to.[31]

Yet, despite such shows of humanity, men of Tait's profession were inevitably outcasts. The visiting couple who met him much later noticed that another slave trader, Hope Slatter, who had recently arrived in Richmond, was endeavouring to gain the respect and attention of the citizens, so as to be admitted to their society. But it appeared to be all in vain. . . . [T]hey stand aloof from the man who makes it his business to traffic in them, and look down upon him as it were with abhorrence. . . . Although the slave-holders unhesitatingly deal with these traders when their convenience requires it, yet will they not associate with them, scarcely live in the same neighbourhood, nor even allow them to worship with them at the same altar. This is one of the anomalies in human nature which it is difficult to solve, at least for those who are not participators in the system, and are disposed to consider the slave-holder and the slave-dealer as standing on one common platform.[32]

Tait was isolated from family connections in Lynchburg, though it is not known if the choice was his or his extended family's. He also had no particular religious or ethnic group for bonding. Tait now spent time at slave sales bargaining with unsavory men—an association that lowered his chances with women whose social status would depend on their husband's occupation. Plunging further into slave trading during the next decade, he became less desirable as a husband even as he grew wealthier and lonelier.

Chapter 5

A SPACIOUS COMFORTABLE JAIL

Tait had threatened to become a serious competitor in the Richmond slave market, and as the 1830s began he focused on doing just that. With Thomas Boudar to help him sell in New Orleans, he continued purchasing and sending people southward. Traders moved hundreds of slaves each year, using experienced men to lead them in coffles overland or transport them on ships down the coast, but in the winter of 1829–30 Tait saw how quickly things could go wrong, and how narrowly he and his fellow traders escaped disaster.

Boudar was waiting in New Orleans for just one black man, twenty-seven-year-old Sampson, to arrive on the schooner *Lafayette*, but the ship was packed with additional human cargo when it left Norfolk on November 14, 1829. Most of the 197 slaves belonged to one of two large lots being shipped between two pairs of traders, C. W. Diggs and James B. Diggs, and John B. Prentis and William Priddy, though there was a smattering of other slaves in smaller groups. The schooner also carried 150 kegs of pickled oysters, which some of the slaves had been ordered to load, and a white passenger, longtime Norfolk merchant Thomas L. Balls. He dealt in groceries rather than humans and owned none of the people on board.

The captain, Benjamin Bissell, shipped slaves regularly, having just returned from a previous trip to New Orleans. To separate the men from the women at night, he overturned a small boat across the deck, left out a cask of water for them to drink, and let them sleep crowded on the planks. The third day out, he was sitting on deck a little before midnight, talking to his white passenger, when three of the male slaves jumped over the upturned boat, saying they wanted to get some water. According to a newspaper report, after they spent some time at the water cask, the captain got up to investigate. "They seized him, threw him down and commenced fight, with handspikes, knives, billets of wood, &c. Mr. B[alls] immediately jumped below and awoke the mate, armed himself with a cutlass, and soon as possible rushed to the assistance of the captain, and as good luck would have it, just in time to save him from the death blow aimed at him with a handspike by one of the mutineers, while others held him."

The crew managed to regain control and trap the mutineers in the hold until the next day, when the captain questioned each of the thirty or forty men individually. "On the examination it was proved that one of the leaders had induced the others to join in by telling them that he had assisted to stow away one hundred and fifty thousand dollars," spreading the rumor that the kegs on board actually contained money, not oysters. The men had planned to hijack the boat and "force the crew to take them to St. Domingo or New York." Their hope of freedom was short-lived. The captain sailed the *Lafayette* into New Orleans on December 7 with the twenty-five most dangerous insurrectionists ring-bolted to the deck, where they had spent the last three weeks of the journey. The rest of the slaves presumably were delivered successfully, including Thomas Boudar's Sampson.

According to the captain, the mutineers had hatched their plot on the brig *Ajax* in Norfolk harbor before they were transferred to the *Lafayette,* and the same uprising was to take place on the *Ajax.* The *Lafayette* had been saved by the actions of the white men on board. Newspapers reported that on the *Ajax* the plan had been "discovered by one of the slaves who was faithful to his master, in time to save the lives of the whites by securing the leaders." Whether the story of the *Ajax* was true, whites again reminded themselves of the life-saving value of keeping the confidence of some slaves, even in the midst of interstate trading.[1]

With so many enslaved people being moved through Richmond and south each winter, an eventual successful mass escape seemed inevitable. Though Tait was not in charge of slaves during transportation, he had to house them after purchase and prior to shipping, so he faced a similar problem of control, as did other traders. He decided to construct his own private slave jail that summer, similar to the other private jails that dealers had begun to use. Traders held their own slaves before transportation south or for display to local buyers, but such jails also brought in extra income. For a daily fee, travelers, buyers, or slave catchers could secure slaves temporarily. The jails also evolved to provide whipping services for local residents. Though private jails generally were not used by courts to confine slaves convicted of crimes, owners could pay to imprison their own slaves for punishment, without recourse to the law.

The site Tait selected was on three adjoining lots controlled by Charles Copland, an elderly Richmond lawyer. It was not far from where Tait currently lived, on the other side of what was still left of the old Falling Garden. In the low part of the city, it fronted on narrow Wall Street, also called Birch Alley, and extended back to Shockoe Creek. Most important, it was a couple blocks north of the Bell Tavern, close to the area where slave traders gathered. The lawyer who owned the site lived and worked near the city hall and state capitol, a few blocks from Tait, but he had also invested in other real estate, including the building occupied by Tompkins and Fisher's grocery store, diagonally across from Tait's home on New Street, so Tait had several chances to become acquainted with him. Copland, seventy-four years old, exemplified the previous generation of Richmond's elite. He had lived in the city since before Tait was born, had served in the Virginia House of Delegates, and, like Thomas Boudar's father-in-law, had been attending the Richmond Theatre the night of the fire, losing a daughter. His parsimonious temperament matched Tait's own. In 1833, Copland would pay off his debts and make a resolution never to owe more than a thousand dollars again. In 1838, Tait expressed a similar philosophy: "I will never go in debt unless I can see clearly how I am to pay with certainty. . . . Thank God I owe nothing to Banks or to individuals."[2]

Tait purchased lots 63 and 64 from Copland and Copland's wife, Heningham, for $354 on May 24, 1830, and on June 11 paid $200 for adjoining lot 62, which Copland controlled as executor of the estate of his late son-in-law, John H. Brown. The resulting site was almost square, with ninety feet fronting Wall Street, the back sloping lower toward the creek.[3]

Tait Builds a Jail

Tait developed and lived on the property, but he would own it only three years before he sold it to another slave trader, Lewis A. Collier. When Collier ran into financial trouble, it passed to yet another slave trader, Robert Lumpkin, who would hold it until the close of the Civil War. The property is the only real estate connected to Tait that has been studied extensively by archaeologists, due to its more famous use in the decades before the Civil War as Robert Lumpkin's slave jail.

The old cobblestones of the yard saw daylight for a few weeks in 2008, when investigators from the James River Institute for Archaeology excavated the area. The original surface is now buried again under a parking lot near Interstate 95. As expected, most of the recovered artifacts dated from long after Tait occupied the lots, but the report stated: "Interestingly, a small but still significant proportion of the ceramics consisted of Pearlware, which first appeared in the United States in the 1780s and continued in popular use until ca. 1830. The presence of this earlier ware type suggested that certain cultural strata and features at the site might pre-date Lumpkin's ownership, possibly representing the occupation of his predecessors Bacon Tait and Lewis A. Collier."[4]

Historians agree that Tait built the two-story brick home that once stood on the lot fronting Wall Street. The house, twenty-two by twenty-six feet with a wooden-shingled roof, had a porch that overlooked the back of the lot. Based on evidence from land records and fire insurance policies, the archaeology report concluded that Tait probably used the lots for his slave-trading business, but suggested that he *did not* build the well-known jail itself: "In fact, there is compelling evidence to suggest that it was Collier who built the two-and-a-half-story brick structure that ultimately became known as 'Lumpkin's Jail.'"[5]

The James River Institute for Archaeology report, prepared by Dr. Matthew R. Laird for the Richmond City Council Slave Trail Commission, made its case based on the value of the buildings, noting structures worth only $400 were on the land when Tait bought it, so the jail was not there yet.[6] A fire insurance policy dated July 18, 1833, twelve days after Tait sold the property to Lewis A. Collier, indicated Tait was occupying the brick dwelling house worth $1,500 dollars, but the jail was not mentioned on the policy. A notation on the policy said, "There is one wooden building within 30 feet of the building described on this plat," but the jail would have been brick.[7] The archaeological report stated, "It was not recorded what additional buildings Tait may have erected on the lots, but any other structures would have been fairly insubstantial, as the total assessed value of his buildings, including his dwelling, never exceeded, $2,200."[8]

However, there is significant evidence that Lumpkin's now-famous jail was actually built by Bacon Tait, not Collier. The key evidence is an advertisement that Collier ran in the *Richmond Enquirer*, August 23, 1833, seven weeks after he purchased the property from Tait, which the archaeological report did not include:

> This is to inform the citizens of Richmond and the public generally, that I have recently bought of Bacon Tait his Negro establishment, which consists of a spacious comfortable strong jail, and which is convenient and suitable for the reception of slaves, as it is within a few yards of the Bell Tavern, where the sales of slaves are generally made.
>
> This establishment will be kept open for the accommodation of the public generally; and gentlemen wishing to deposit negroes in jail, for sale or otherwise, is [*sic*] respectfully requested to give me a call. Every attention that may be necessary will be rendered, to have them carefully and well attended to; and I will at all times pay a fair market price for slaves, and can at any time be seen, either at the said place, or my old stand on Shockoe Hill, which will be kept up as formerly. I shall constantly keep on hand, for sale, a great many slaves; and gentlemen from the Southern States, or elsewhere, will be well to call on me, as I shall be able at any time to furnish them with a suitable lot, as I generally have on hand the use of one hundred, and will at all times sell at a small advance on cost, in lots, to suit purchasers; and gentlemen in the Southern States, or elsewhere, wishing to communicate with me, either in buying or selling, will please forward their wishes to me, and all letters, post-paid, will be duly and promptly attended to.
>
> LEWIS A. COLLIER.

The advertisement indicates that Tait had indeed already built a substantial jail as part of his "Negro establishment" on the property, consistent with the structure that Lumpkin later used.

Neither Collier nor Lumpkin included the jail when they insured the dwelling in 1837, 1844, or 1851, so the lack of insurance on the jail in 1833 is not surprising. The lots extended far enough back from the street, even before Shockoe Creek was channeled farther east, that the brick jail may have sat more than thirty feet from the dwelling if it was located on the back of the lot, and therefore was not noted as a nearby building for fire insurance purposes like the wooden one that was listed.

If the jail was already standing when Tait sold the lots, one must then explain why the $2,200 total valuation of Tait's buildings was high enough to include both the house and jail. If the house was valued at about $1,500, the same as its insurance appraisal, then $700 would remain for the jail. Collier insured his two-story brick jail on Shockoe Hill for $750 in 1832, so a valuation of around $700 for Tait's similar jail would not be unreasonable.

Tait purchased the lots for $554 and sold them for $5,750, reflecting substantial improvements, and his deed to Collier was also more specific than most, stating he was selling the lots "together with all and singular the houses, dwellings, buildings, walls, enclosures and erections thereupon," as if both men wanted to be clear the entire jail complex was included. There does not seem to be any compelling evidence to eliminate the possibility that Tait built the jail, and several strong indications that he did. Tait's construction of the jail also fits with a statement in a postwar Richmond city guide, though he would have built it no earlier than 1830: "The most noted of these [jails] because the largest and, therefore, able to accommodate the largest number, was the one known as Lumpkin's.—This house was built some time about the year 1825, by Bacon Tait, for this purpose."[9] An article prepared for the National Register of Historic Places also indicates, without further sources, that "Lewis A. Collier and Bacon Tait operated jails on this site before it was purchased by Lumpkin."[10]

Tait v. Wilkinson and De Ende

In May of 1830, just before Tait bought the lots from Copland, he made another trip to New Orleans, perhaps to tie up loose ends of that winter's sales. While there, he tried one last time to learn the fate of his profits from his former partnership with Wilkinson and De Ende, without success. He was "furnished in the same loose and uncertain and unsatisfactory manner with another rough statement, without dates to the entries or the terms on which the slaves were sold. This ended every effort or attempt by either

Wilkinson or De Ende to disclose to [Tait] the true state of the partnership business."[11]

Though he continued with his own trading, Tait never gave up trying to collect the money. Later that year, he hired the Richmond law firm of Johnson, Stanard and Scott and filed suit on December 10, 1830, in the Superior Court of Chancery for the Richmond District, requesting the court to decide "the nett [sic] profit and who is entitled thereto . . . and to render in favour of your complainant a decree for the amount due him."[12]

Judge Creed Taylor collected statements from the other two partners. De Ende replied with a sworn statement on March 4, 1831, from New Orleans, while Wilkinson gave a similar response from his rural residence in Goochland County on April 28, 1831. Both pointed out the withdrawals Tait had made from the partnership funds and how he had been trading secretly with Thomas Boudar in competition, violating their agreement. The suit dragged on, and stagnated entirely after De Ende died in 1832.

The following summer, not yet ready to admit defeat, Tait decided to pursue a different, underhanded, and ultimately successful strategy. Secretly, he "combined and confederated" with his former opponent, Wilkinson, so that both could get their hands on some of the money in De Ende's estate—to "defraud" the estate, as the beneficiaries later claimed, though Tait probably would have used a less harsh term. According to the plan, success would be easier for both Wilkinson and Tait if the estate were less guarded.[13] De Ende's unmarried sisters, who received the bulk of his estate, lived about fifty miles from Richmond in Cumberland County, Virginia. Tait managed to convince the Cumberland county court that De Ende had died without a will while living in New Orleans, even though De Ende actually had a will there, and that the estate should be administered in Virginia, even though De Ende had not lived there for decades. Tait asked the court to appoint the Cumberland sheriff, Charles Womack, as executor of the estate, and on July 3, 1833, the court agreed.[14]

The sisters knew their inheritance was involved in Tait's Richmond lawsuit, but Wilkinson now performed his part to lull the sisters into a false sense of security. He "quieted the apprehensions" of the sisters by assuring one of them, Caroline, that their late brother "was only a formal party" to the suit and that "the whole controversy" was between Tait and himself, so there was actually no claim against the sisters' part of the estate.[15] Publicly, and perhaps privately to some extent as well, Tait and Wilkinson were still enemies. Henry King, who had been shipping slaves to New Orleans even before Tait entered the business, testified in 1835, "I have no doubt that for several years last past, those gentlemen have entertained toward each other, sentiments and feelings of a strong and decidedly unfriendly character, and that such enmity still exists, as I believe, between them."[16] Lulled into a false sense of security, the De Ende sisters spent little time worrying about the suit and for a while did not even hire an attorney, so the only person left guarding the old partnership profits was the disinterested—and uninterested—Cumberland County sheriff. The partnership records were in such disarray that both Tait and Wilkinson could claim De Ende had kept some of the money due them. Both managed to get a judgment on March 16, 1839, against De Ende's estate, which was not just a formal party to the suit after all, but their specific target. Tait received a decree for $3,761.85 with interest from March 31, 1831, while Wilkinson, who had withdrawn less money originally, made out better: $7,402.42 plus interest.

The money was Wilkinson's reward for helping Tait, but Wilkinson was a native of Cumberland County and still had connections there. He did not want to alienate himself more than necessary from De Ende's remaining extended family, so he tried to distance himself from Tait's scheme. Speaking confidentially to William Rickman Coupland, a first cousin of the De Ende siblings, he praised the late Henry De Ende as "a gentleman" who "had fulfilled all of his contracts," and said that De Ende did not really owe either Tait or himself anything "and that Tait was a damned rascal."[17]

Although both Tait and Wilkinson now held successful judgments against the estate, they still needed to collect. Despite what he said to the Cumberland members of the family, Wilkinson moved first against the actual executors of De Ende's estate in New Orleans, filing petitions on March 30 and June 25, 1839, requesting payment of the money he was owed by the Richmond court's decree. Tait did the same on April 30, 1841.[18] Now that they realized what was happening, the entire De Ende clan in both Virginia and New Orleans united in refusing to pay. Tait's clever strategy to get an easy judgment in Virginia in the 1830s shifted to a new struggle to collect payment that would last through the 1840s.

Slave-Trading Legalities

Tait showed his loose sense of business ethics in other ways, too. As early as the 1820s, some residents of the Deep South worried that the Upper South was flooding their states with the least desirable slaves, all while siphoning their cash northward. As a result, Mississippi, Alabama, and Louisiana passed various laws in the late 1820s and early 1830s restricting or regulating the importation of slaves. Other residents, though, wanted the source of new labor and successfully pressured legislators to lift the restrictions, but the respite was short-lived. Nat Turner's rebellion in Southampton County, Virginia, in the summer of 1831 struck new terror not only in Virginians, but in slave buyers in the Deep South, who feared a new wave of rebellious slaves would be dumped on them by frightened Virginians.

Louisiana law discouraged commercial importation from 1831 to 1834, so traders shifted their main market to Natchez, Mississippi. When cholera swept through the crowded slave jails, the city of Natchez banned traders there. The market moved to a site nearby that became known as the "Forks of the Road," competing with New Orleans as a major slave dealer's destination and buyer's market, even after Louisiana reopened to importation.

Mississippi's constitution had given the legislature power to ban commercial importation of slaves, but the legislature had never acted. When the constitution needed updating in 1832 to deal with judges and newly opened Native American lands, the framers of the new constitution went so far as to include the statement: "The introduction of slaves into this state as merchandise, or for sale, shall be prohibited from and after the first day of May, 1833," but the legislature still took no action to provide for enforcement, and for years sellers ignored the restriction. Richmond traders, therefore, had to deal with a patchwork of complex and shifting regulations.

A friend of Thomas Boudar, Paul Pascal, had begun slave trading in Virginia also, working out of Norfolk in partnership with Bernard Raux and Nathaniel Currier. Pascal, also a French immigrant, had lived near the Boudars in Richmond before most of them moved to Lynchburg, had been "intimately acquainted" with them, and remembered their distress as they tried to locate their missing sister in Havana. When Pascal wrote his will in 1836 a few days before he died, he named Boudar the executor of his estate.

Like Boudar, Pascal divided his time between Virginia and Louisiana, facilitating the sale of his partnership's slaves in the Deep South. Born about 1785, he was almost old enough to be Boudar's father, but slave trading was relatively new for all those who had jumped into the boom of the last few years, and all needed to figure out the business.[19] In 1832, Pascal asked his Virginia partner, Nathaniel Currier, how to deal with a Mississippi law that required each slave to be accompanied by a certificate of good character. Currier was not sure either. Although the partnership of Tait and Boudar was a competing firm, Boudar's friendship made them mutual colleagues, so Currier asked Tait for advice.

Tait replied on October 4, 1832, that the certificates were "more trouble than profit," but he advised "friend Pascal" to take one south with his slaves anyway. "He may not have to use it at all, but the laws of Mississippi demand it and to prevent the possibility of a difficulty I would advise them to take one along—you can put as many negroes as you please in *one certificate*." Tait explained, "I have never traded to Mississippi & therefore have never had use for these certificates, but if I was going to trade there I certainly should be prepared with one." He was not suggesting scrupulous compliance with the law, however. He described "the usual way as I understand of obtaining these certificates." It involved finding "two freeholders to go & look at your negroes. You then tell them the name of each negroe. The freeholders then say they know the negroes & give the certificate accordingly."[20]

The Taint of Slave Trading

Like his secret trading with Boudar during his partnership with Wilkinson and De Ende, and his scheme to defraud De Ende's estate, Tait's willingness to create false certificates showed his aggressive dishonesty in business, even while he maintained a veneer of respectability. Such behavior was stereotypical of slave traders and led to their poor reputation as scapegoats for all that was wrong with slavery, but even among traders there were levels of acceptability. By building a private jail, investing heavily, and becoming wealthy, Tait was gaining a grudging respect that would later allow him to win a seat on the city council and cooperate with other investors in enterprises unconnected to slavery. But like others of his class, he still carried the taint of the trade.

Thomas Jefferson Randolph noticed a distinction between men such as Tait and the even worse men they employed:

> Should it be asked what is the character and standing in society of the men who are actively engaged in the slave trade, variously called "soul-drivers," "slave traders," "speculators," &c., we would reply that there are two classes of them, who are held in very different estimation by the community generally, though their characters and deserts are intrinsically the same.
>
> One class is composed of the slave merchants, who have large establishments or factories in Washington City, Alexandria, Baltimore, Norfolk, Richmond, Petersburgh, &c., and keep slavers constantly plying between those ports, and Charleston or New Orleans. Their slave advertisements are blazoned in the most influential secular papers in the union, and to their service the national and state prisons are most obligingly devoted, when their private jails chance to overflow. These are men of large capital, and conduct the traffic on the broadest scale. They hold an honorable rank among the heavy capitalists and extensive merchants of our southern cities, and move in the highest social circles.
>
> The other class consists of the agents and pimps of these gentry, who are constantly scouring the breeding states to gather fresh supplies for the slave-prisons and slave-ships; and also of traders of limited capital, who buy up small gangs and drive their own coffles. The latter class are generally despised even in the slaveholding states, and they are doubtless horribly base wretches of vile origin, and viler lives.[21]

Tait most likely did work surrounded by such men. One piece of evidence comes from a slave, Madison Henderson. Though "Tait & Boudar" always operated as their own partnership, Tait corresponded and dealt with a network of other traders in the 1830s. Henderson belonged to a buyer for Tait's friend and colleague Rice C. Ballard, and he also named other men associated with Tait in the 1830s: Samuel Alsop and James Franklin. Sentenced to death for an unrelated murder, Henderson published his confessions of the slave trade, which included details of how he assisted the unnamed buyer:

> We went to these places to buy, and if the negroes whom we wished to purchase, were unwilling to be sold, it was my duty to overcome their objections, and by false tales of what my master would do for them, or the purposes for which they were wanted, induce them to agree to be sold. But the most important part of my duty was to coax off, and harbor negroes: in other words, to aid in stealing them. As the sequel will show, this required a good deal of courage and skill, and was generally accomplished by representing my master as from a free state, generally from Philadelphia, and that his purpose in getting them to run off was to set them free; that he would take them to Canada, or some other place out of the reach of their masters. To the men I represented that they would become rich and own plenty of property—to the women and girls, I held out the prospect of marrying rich white men, and of living in style and splendor.

Henderson also described forging a bill of sale while traveling with a coffle from Richmond to New Orleans: "Once a man demanded of my master to see his bill of sale of a certain negro. He appeared very indignant, at what he said was an insult, and spoke of the long time he had been engaged in the business. The man apologized, and then my master showed him a bill of sale, apparently properly executed; but it was one that *his clerk* had made out."[22]

Tait was enmeshed in a dirty business, yet by becoming rich at it, he could buy his way out of some of the poor reputation that clung to the trade. The same would prove true as he and others crossed the color boundary with his family. De Ende's children, and Tait's own children, and even Tait's wife in Massachusetts, became rich enough that they would be accepted in a racist society with at least some of the privileges of being not-black, just as Tait bought some of the privileges of being not-a-slave-trader.

Chapter 6

SUCH DIABOLICAL MISCREANTS AS BACON TAIT

The clamor for slaves continued through 1836 as prosperity and land speculation soared. Though none of Tait's account books survive, other records suggest the extent and profitability of his business. A shipping manifest shows that the brig *Adelaide* left Richmond in September of 1835 for New Orleans with 144 slaves packed on board, almost all of whom were his, headed for Thomas Boudar or Henry Davis in New Orleans. He forced others to walk the thousand-mile journey. In August of 1836, he wrote Rice Ballard, "In your letter you say it is 120 miles from Alexandria to where my road will fall in—do you mean at Charlottesville?" He was probably planning to link his slaves with a Franklin and Armfield coffle traveling from Alexandria through Tennessee to the Forks of the Road in Mississippi. Traders started such groups early so they could arrive in time for the beginning of the selling season.

Tait reported in August of 1836 that he had already spent $35,000 that year, with about $2,000 more on hand to invest. He was "pretty certain of obtaining ten thousand more immediately or as soon as necessary, after expending this ten thousand, then I will try upon the letter of credit." He was actually purchasing cautiously: "I do not bid at auction and I on all suitable occasions declare that I will not pay the prices."[1]

Due to soaring slave values, even small shipments were a heavy investment. A month after sending the coffle overland in 1836, he shipped a small group of twenty-seven people that had cost him $22,246.70. Most were young, what we would think of as college-aged, but leaving for a strange land and a different kind of education. He sent them to Norfolk on September 23 with Boudar, probably on a steamboat down the James River. After a day's wait for Franklin and Armfield's slave ship *Tribune* to arrive, they were loaded on board. Boudar signed the shipping manifest, and the *Tribune* and its cargo "got to sea on the morning of 26th with a stiff north wester."

The group was typical of a carefully chosen lot. Tait had paid the most for men with white ancestry who had gained trust and privileges, such as Aaron Palmer, thirty, "yellow" in color, "a very fine fidler, ostler & coachman, he is very handy with tools and is withall an excellent head man amongst negroes," implying he might be trusted to whip his fellow slaves. James W. Smith, twenty, was "an excellent marksman," proof that he was allowed firearms, the ultimate trust, and "a pretty good cook and also a very smart dining room servant." They had cost $1,100 and $1,150. Bob Powell, a black teenager for whom Tait had paid $900, was showing either pain or resistance. "He contracted the habit of limping since we bought him," Tait reported, expressing no sympathy. "He is in every respect a sound & healthy boy." Dick Cates, twenty, cost only $700. Tait wrote ahead to Ballard and Franklin what could be considered either a recommendation or a caution: he "may be supposed to be inactive but upon trial it will be seen that he can out-run & out-jump any man in your yard." Monarchy Johnson, thirty years old, $675, was the former principal cook at the Bell Tavern. She had been on and off the market since at least 1834, when the creditors of tavern operator Hiram Childs tried to force a sale of some of his assets, including her. An Englishman visiting Richmond reported that the city "is still the great mart of slavery; and the interests of morality and religion suffer from this cause. . . . The sale of slaves is as common, and produces as little sensation as that of cattle." He quoted an ad announcing the sale of Monarchy, five other slaves, and six feather beds as an example of the callous way in which humans were traded like furniture. The sale apparently fell through, because a few months later Monarchy was advertised again, this time along with "fifty feather Beds, with Bedsteads and Furniture complete, all the Tables, Chairs and Bureaus now in the Tavern, . . . one Carriage and pair of dun carriage Horses." That sale also was canceled, but some private arrangement must have been worked out. Two years later Tait made a deal for $675, promising to pay off the $300 to $400 that Henry Clarke still owed on her. The furniture and horses probably went to someone else and were staying in Virginia, but she was headed for the Deep South. The oldest of the twenty-seven on board, forty-five-year-old Betsy Williams, had cost the least, $103.70, but there was work to be gotten out of her yet: the "old woman . . . is a very steady, well disposed woman and is also a tolerable good cook." The youngest were two-year-old Caroline and seven-month-old Frederick, traveling with their mother, Polly Wilkinson, costing $900 for the family.[2] Even after the downturn in trading toward the end of the 1830s, Tait wrote in November of 1838, "unless Boudar & myself are very unfortunate we will make out to ship 150 negroes this winter perhaps 200."[3]

A Larger Jail

As Tait's profits increased, he soon outgrew his jail and began looking for a larger site. On July 6, 1833, after just three years of ownership, he sold his first location to Lewis A. Collier for $5,750, but continued to live there while he sought out a better place. Collier had an overcrowded jail on Shockoe Hill, where he was holding "the rise of one hundred likely young Negroes, consisting of boys[,] young men and girls," but he also was trying to expand, so he planned to keep both jails.[4]

The new site that Tait finally purchased was just three blocks away. The alley that he lived on widened into Wall Street, then Wall Street became Fifteenth, and the new land he wanted was a lumberyard on the southeast corner where Fifteenth crossed Cary Street. It was about the same distance from the Bell Tavern but on the other side, nearer the river—a location at least as advantageous. It was convenient to the slave-trading district, but even nearer the docks where he shipped slaves to Norfolk and from there along the coast southward. This was the Cary Street Jail he would keep through the end of his career. The property did not leave the family until his children sold it in the 1870s. "The neighborhood contained a great many old wooden tenements" (four or five of which had burned down in an accidental fire four years earlier), a livery stable, and a brick tobacco factory, as well as the property that Tait wanted: lot #325, the lumberyard of Whitlock and Wicker. Whitlock was no known relation to the Whitlocks who married into the Lynchburg Tates.[5]

Tait pictured the site as facing Cary, toward the Bell Tavern and downtown, though most of the frontage was along Fifteenth to the side. The lot extended the entire block, back toward what was left of the Old Rock Landing along the James River. The artificially dug boat dock—part of the canal construction that made the James River navigable above the falls—now separated the landing from the actual river. The neighborhood was busy with commerce, in view of the traffic across Mayo's Bridge and close to wharves where boats unloaded their freight. Only cheap structures stood in the lumberyard, so Tait could afford to construct a jail and walled-in areas to suit himself. More importantly, the new lot allowed him to spread out from his current cramped quarters. Over three times as deep and almost twice as wide, it covered more than an acre.[6]

Richard Henry Whitlock and Francis Wicker had no plans to give up the lumber business. Whitlock or his late father, Charles, had operated the yard for at least fifteen years, and twenty years in the future he and his son would still deal in lumber a few blocks away at the corner of Cary and 18th Streets, but he was willing to sell this location now, and Tait was ready to buy. The price was high: $8,000 for the lot, which would need still more invested to fulfill Tait's vision of a perfect slave jail. Part of the value was due to the general rise in real estate prices, part due to the excellent location, and part due to the size.[7]

It would be the largest lot connected to the slave trade in Richmond, but it has been mostly ignored when Richmond's slave history is interpreted. A marker at the corner of Fifteenth and Cary generically mentions slave jails, but fails to note the significance of where the reader is standing, although the site of Lumpkin's jail is marked with its own detailed sign a few blocks away. "Mapping Richmond's Slave Market," developed by the Digital Scholarship Lab at the University of Richmond and Maurie D. McInnis at the University of Virginia, illustrates Richmond's slave-trading spaces in the 1850s. Tait's lot, the farthest detail toward the south, dwarfs all others in size, but it is shown in gray, unlabeled, one of the "buildings not associated with the slave trade," while Bacon Tait's name is attached to a smaller lot nearby that was actually occupied by the warehouse of Wortham, McGruder and Co., later Edwin Wortham.[8]

On February 14, 1834, Whitlock, Wicker, their wives, and Tait concluded the sale. Tait paid in part with a note for $6,000, due in a year and a half, which gave him time to invest his current profits in buildings.[9] When

Tait purchased the lot, the other three buildings sharing the corners of Fifteenth and Cary also held merchandise for sale. Wortham, McGruder and Co.'s grocery and commission business had its two-story brick warehouse on the corner toward the Bell Tavern. Diagonally across stood Ralston and Pleasants' store. The owners, already middle-aged, would become beloved and venerable citizens, living into their eighties. Alongside on Fifteenth Street, Davenport, Allen and Co., auctioneers, sold everything from herrings to Windsor chairs, but there is no record they auctioned slaves. Isaac Davenport Sr. and James Allen were both from Massachusetts, and Davenport had recently brought his nephew, Isaac Jr., down from Maine to assist. Although never a slave trader himself, the nephew would grow wealthy with shipping and banking investments, supported the Confederacy during the war, and in 1872 eventually bought a part interest in Tait's estate.[10]

The New Jail Opens

By the following winter, less than a year later, Tait had developed the property to his liking, creating what he believed was a model slave jail. The neighborhood had been busy with construction that summer. Between the jail and the creek, the Shockoe Manufacturing Company had been expanding also, erecting a foundry that could cast iron and brass for mills and steam engines.

Tait proudly announced his grand opening in the December 1834 *Richmond Whig:*

NOTICE

The commodious buildings which I have recently had erected in the City of Richmond, are now ready for the accommodation of all persons who may wish their NEGROES safely and comfortable taken care of.

The buildings were erected upon an extensive scale, without regard to cost, my main object being to insure the safe keeping, and at the same time the health and comfort of the Negroes who may be placed thereat.

The rooms and yards for the Females are separate from those

for the Males, and genteel house Servants will have rooms to themselves. The regulations of the establishment will be general cleanliness, moderate exercise, and recreation within the yards during good weather, and good substantial food at all times, by which regulations it is intended that confinement shall be rendered merely nominal, and the health of the Negroes so promoted, that they will be well prepared to encounter a change of climate when removed to the South.

These buildings are situated on the lot corner of 15th and Cary streets, between Mayo's Bridge and the Bell Tavern. Apply to

BACON TAIT.

Tait's seemingly innocent enthusiasm was like chum in the water for abolitionists, who subscribed to the Richmond papers and attacked the ad with gleeful sarcasm for months. "Strange that slaves should ever *run away* from such excellent accommodations as those of Bacon Tait!" commented the *Anti-Slavery Record* in its October 1835 edition. "Perhaps they do not relish the *safety* and *comfort* of being *sold*. Would you, reader?"

An abolitionist using the initials "P.H." was probably the first to introduce the ad to the North, in William Lloyd Garrison's December 27, 1834, issue of the *Liberator,* only days after it first appeared in Virginia. Following an initial sarcastic observation comparing Tait to British prison reformer John Howard ("Such a Howard deserves honorable notice from the Prison Discipline Society, for his philanthropic exertions"), the correspondent correctly deduced that Tait's business in particular, and the trade in general, were highly profitable: "It gives one some idea of the extent to which the slave trade is carried on by Virginia, to know that a man, if it be proper to call him so, has a prison built on purpose to confine the victims of the trade, while they are waiting to be carried off. No merchant would build an expensive warehouse for his own use, unless his business were large. We cannot be mistaken, then, in supposing that the kind-hearted Tait, in erecting his jail, must have believed that the business was extensive enough to pay him a good income on his investment." The correspondent also understood that Tait's business, though economically necessary, was an embarrassment to many slave owners: "Tait seems to understand how delicate a subject slavery is. He was not willing to offend the nerves of the Virginia ladies, or to shock their husbands, his customers, by giving the naked truth in his advertisement. He well knew that *hell* was not a place to be mentioned to polite ears."

The writer then crafted his or her own parody of the ad, designed to say what Tait really meant:

> BACON TAIT informs soul-drivers, and others engaged in the domestic slave-trade, that he has lately erected a strong and secure jail in Richmond, where slaves can be sent for safe keeping, preparatory to their being shipped. No danger of escape need be feared, as the windows are all grated with strong iron bars, a good watch is kept, and a large supply of chains, cart whips, thumb screws, and other instruments of torture, are always on hand to restrain and punish refractory slaves.
>
> P.S. Owners wishing to have slaves well flogged can have it done at Tait's Jail, at the lowest prices. He recommends his dungeons as very efficacious in breaking down the spirit of obstinate slaves.
>
> He has some very secure interior rooms, in which negroes, claiming to be free, can be confined, so as to make it impossible for them to communicate with any one out of the jail by voice or letter.

The correspondent concluded seriously: "It almost makes one ashamed of being a man and a christian, when he sees such diabolical miscreants as Bacon Tait boldly avowing and openly pursuing their guilty traffic in a christian land."

The parody was surprisingly accurate. The windows were most likely barred, and though Tait may not have used thumb screws, there were no doubt chains and whips. Sidnum Grady charged 50 cents to whip slaves at the jail during the Civil War, and there is no reason to believe Tait did not offer such a typical service earlier. The best surviving descriptions of either jail that Tait built are of the first one, after Robert Lumpkin purchased it. One local man recalled being sent there in his youth to "the whipping room, and on the floor of that room were rings. The individual would be laid down, his hands and feet stretched out and fastened in the rings, and a great big man would stand over him and flog him."[11]

The *Liberator*'s writer, noting that Tait offered private rooms for "genteel house Servants," speculated that isolation was also available for those claiming to be free, "so as to make it impossible for them to communicate with any one out of the jail by voice or letter." Though recaptured fugitive Anthony Burns could not claim to be legally free, he was confined in 1854 in what had become Lumpkin's jail, and indeed, due to his fame, he was isolated in an attic room and could only communicate with other slaves through a hole he enlarged in the floor or by tossing letters to sympathetic passersby. As his biographer wrote, "The taint of freedom was upon him, and infection was dreaded."[12]

Other Purchases and Sales

At the height of the slave-trading boom, Tait spent his days relentlessly buying people and shipping them to new owners. He held three adults of his own and one or more children to keep his household running smoothly, for there were meals to cook, clothes to be laundered, fires to be tended in winter, and a horse and four-wheeled carryall wagon to be brought round when he needed. In 1837 he was also renting a two-story brick home on Seventeenth Street between Broad and Marshall, five blocks from his jail, that was occupied by "Bacon Tait's slaves," according to an insurance policy. He may have used it as a secondary jail.[13]

Otherwise, he lived the frugal life of a bachelor and, like his father, invested in buildings and land. Most of the real estate sellers—and the buyers, also, as he readjusted his holdings—were what one would expect: white men and an occasional widow, generally slave owners themselves. When land at the foot of his property fronting the James River Canal came up for sale, he bought it, selling some of it later to the City of Richmond in 1850 for $13,200, plus $1 for the use of Dock Street as long as the city kept it open as a public street—a right the city never gave up, as it is still open today.[14] Two transactions, though, showed the complex and contradictory relationships between Tait and the many black people around him. Tait negotiated with real estate buyers and sellers whatever their color.

The Gallegos

Thomas Cowles and Nathanial Charter, justices of the peace, took a black woman alone into a room to examine her as part of a purchase that Bacon Tait wanted to consummate in July of 1833. The interaction was perfunctory, only enough to fulfill a longstanding legal requirement, but it showed the range of ways whites and blacks interacted. Charlotte Ann Gallego, the free black woman, owned some property on Broad Street in Richmond along with her husband, Phillip Gallego. Tait wanted to purchase one of their lots. As required by law, the justices needed to examine her alone, to ask if she agreed freely to the transaction and make sure she was not being coerced to sell by her husband.

Even if only a legal formality, the meeting was an acknowledgment that a married woman—in this case, a black woman—was an individual, whose personhood and right of ownership should be recognized and protected by white men. Yet in their other roles in society, the same white men acted as guardians of the white race, watching for any blacks who might overstep their bounds. That same summer, one of the justices, Thomas Cowles, was struggling to control the slaves under his charge. He advertised a $100 reward for Tom Williams, who had disappeared, while George and Jane were "difficult to manage & in the habit of frequently running away."[15]

By gaining freedom and property, the Gallegos had moved into a different sphere, close enough to glimpse how whites treated other whites. But Virginia still restrained people of color, as the Gallegos understood all too well. They had several children, but Peter, now about nineteen, was chafing the most for a college education, an impossibility where they lived. With the new racial tension after Nat Turner's revolt, the family had decided to seek a better life in Canada. No longer in need of their property and wanting money for the move and college expenses, they sought a buyer, and found one in Tait.

The Gallegos' story stood in contrast to the blacks still trapped in slavery whom Tait dealt with as commodities, yet they were not far removed from that condition. Their success, and their frustration, showed both the possibilities and the limitations that blacks faced in a society that gave men like Tait such absolute power over some of their race. Their last name came from their former owner, Joseph Gallego, a wealthy Spaniard who had developed Richmond's famous Gallego flour mill. In the early 1800s he emancipated Phillip's parents, setting free first his mother, Dilsey, then his father, Hembro. They were already a couple with a son, but as free people they could now legalize their marriage, which they did in 1810.[16]

Their son, Phillip, remained enslaved. The parents worked to raise money—at one point they had an oyster house on Twelfth Street—and in 1814 they purchased Phil and applied to the legislature for permission to emancipate him "from the Shackles of his Parents Successors, and that he may be enabled to inherit, at the Death of Your Petitioners, the property they may possess . . . as tho he had been born originally free."[17] Even after emancipation, Phil had to petition the legislature again to be allowed to remain in Virginia so he could provide "the fostering care and attention . . . and the comfort and affection" to his aging parents.[18] His life had been a struggle to achieve what whites were given by birth: the right to stay with his family, to care for his parents and inherit their property, to be legally married. Once free, though, he kept moving upward.

Almost immediately Phillip wed Charlotte Ann Dunlop, and as his parents had promised, he inherited their property when they died.[19] In preparation now for the move to Canada, he and his wife were selling two adjoining lots on Broad Street, which happened to be near the rental house on Third (now Nineteenth) Street that Tait had owned since the 1820s. They sold one of the lots to Tait for $800 on July 20, 1833, and James M. Winston, a white businessman, bought the other for $1,100 the following month.[20]

With the money, the Gallegos emigrated to the Canadian city of York, soon to be renamed Toronto. In 1837, their son Peter entered Upper Canada College, then attended King's College, became Reverend Peter Gallego, traveled internationally, and campaigned for abolition and fair treatment of blacks in both the newspapers and courts. After the Civil War, he returned to Richmond as a teacher, finally able to pass on his knowledge to a new generation of blacks who were now free to learn.[21] Tait's purchase of the Gallego family's real estate had seemed a good way to invest some of his slave-trading profits, but Phil Gallego's choice to invest the money in his family's future paid off better.

The transaction put Tait on an equal footing with a black man and wife in a real estate transaction at the same time that he was buying and selling others as property themselves. Again, he had to compartmentalize his views of non-whites, and the Gallegos also had to be willing to deal with Tait, knowing how he earned the money they would receive. When the outcome was to their benefit, both looked beyond the broader issues of race.

Isham Ellis

Another dissatisfied free black man in antebellum Richmond was Isham Ellis, a shoemaker active in the local African Baptist Church. He and his wife, Nancy, had been among those who petitioned the legislature to let them form the church in 1823 because "it has been the misfortune of your petitioners to be excluded from the churches, meeting Houses and other places of public devotion which are used by white persons."[22] Unlike the Gallegos, the Ellises stayed past the Nat Turner upheaval, but the situation still rankled. In 1834, Ellis and eleven other petitioners complained unsuccessfully about the law that prohibited free persons of color from preaching alone, "in consequence of which many coloured human beings are inter'd like brutes, their relatives and friends being unable to procure white ministers to perform the usual ceremony in the burial of the dead."[23]

The Gallegos and Ellises had a mutual friend, Hembrey Tompkins, who had signed the 1823 petition and had also acted as bondsman at the wedding of Phil Gallego's parents and therefore was perhaps related to Phil's mother. When Isham Ellis wanted to purchase a home, he too dealt with a man with whom he had little in common: Bacon Tait. The slave trader had bought a small house on Sixteenth Street in November of 1836 for $183. Five months later, he sold it to Ellis for $300, making a quick profit.[24] Ellis lived there with his wife, working as a shoemaker in the slave-trading district and serving as a deacon in the First African Baptist Church until 1854, when, almost sixty years old, he too finally gave up seeking happiness in Virginia and left with family and friends for a better life elsewhere.[25]

Again, Tait dealt with a black man as an equal in a real estate transaction and, perhaps as significant, a free black willingly dealt with him when they could agree on a price. Individually, race relations might proceed differently than they did collectively. But collectively, both the Gallego and Ellis families found that the stigma of being black in Virginia was too great a burden, even if they were free.

Free Men in Jail

Not all of the free blacks in Virginia were outside Tait's jail. Two days before Christmas 1835, a "tall, sallow man . . . with jet-black hair, a restless dark eye, and an anxious, care-worn look" arrived at Fifteenth and Cary with four dark-skinned men in tow—a normal enough occurrence at the year-old jail. Tait might have recognized the white man as John Caphart, a slave catcher from Norfolk. In this case, he was acting as agent for Norfolk's vice consul of Portugal, who had ordered him to capture these men. Caphart stated that they were slaves and "left them with [Tait] for safe keeping." Tait locked them up as requested.

The four were obviously foreigners, but they denied being Portuguese slaves and instead said they were born free on the island of Brava. Their fate was not as hopeless as the *Liberator* correspondent predicted for free men confined in the jail. Apparently Tait let them communicate, because three days later they petitioned the judge of the Henrico County circuit court, who granted a writ of *habeas corpus*. Tait, obedient to the law, showed up in court on January 8, 1836, explaining how he had received them. The court let him keep the men until January 30, when he had to appear again, and once again the court postponed further hearings until February 8. Apparently concluding that repeated court appearances were not worth the profit from jail fees, Tait told the court "his wish that the petitioners should be taken from his possession." The feeling was apparently mutual. On the prisoners' motion, the sheriff took them into custody instead, and Tait ended his involvement in the case.

The four were eventually set free on the testimony of two whites who had accompanied them. They had been among the men who arrived in Virginia seven months earlier on the schooner *Boa Nova*. When the ship put into Norfolk for provisions, the Portuguese consul, Walter de Lacy, demanded their arrest for piracy, claiming they had stolen the ship at Port Praya as part of the revolution occurring there. The entire group from the ship was held until court convened in December, when they were set free, the grand jury failing to find a true bill against them. Because these four were black, de Lacy had apparently made a last-ditch effort to use their race against them, inventing a story that they were escaped slaves belonging to some unknown owners and hiring Caphart to catch them before they left Norfolk. Fifteen years later, slave catcher Caphart remembered them as his only failure. When asked in court, "Are [slaves] not sometimes discharged after you get them?" he answered, "Not often. I don't know that they ever are, except those Portuguese."

Habeas corpus was a right not generally granted to blacks accused of being slaves, but the court allowed it in this case. Rather than making the men wait months in jail for de Lacy to find their Portuguese owners, the court grudgingly turned the men loose without hearing their purported owners' testimony. One judge dissented, noting that a man's being "of African race, is *prima facie* evidence that he is a slave, and puts the *onus* on him to prove that he is free. This is one of the hardships that belong to his condition." The implication was clear: had de Lacy been able to produce some supposed white owners faster, the four free men easily could have disappeared into a life of slavery.[26] What seemed at first to be an example of how wrongfully imprisoned people could use the courts to be freed from Tait's jail showed instead how vulnerable they were to kidnapping and illegal sale into slavery. When men like Tait had a monetary or emotional incentive to treat blacks fairly and well, they did so, but without that incentive the default was to treat them as commodities.

On November 19, 1839, the Henrico County sheriff showed up at Tait's jail. A few days before, Tait had locked up a slave named Manuel Dodson for a trader from Washington who was on his way south. Like the four Portuguese men, Dodson had complained he was being illegally held, but his story was more complicated. Dodson *was* a slave—until 1854, when his mistress had specified in her will that he should be set free. The trader, though, had told him the will had been set aside and he was headed south to be sold as a slave for life.

Dodson managed to get an injunction to prevent either the trader or Tait from transporting him out of Richmond until his complaint could be heard. The sheriff demanded that either Tait post bond of $1,500 or surrender Dodson into his custody to prevent him from being sent south. Tait avoided the legal tangle quickly this time, immediately handing over Dodson, and the sheriff took him to the Henrico County jail. Though Tait avoided the subsequent legal hassle, the sheriff hired Dodson out while the case went through the courts. At first Dodson won, but on appeal to the Virginia Supreme Court the trader regained the right to take him away in 1843, with the trader's promise that he would be set free in eleven years.

It was a lucrative scheme for Thomas Williams, the Washington trader, and for William H. Williams, who was in legal trouble for taking slaves convicted of crimes from Virginia to Louisiana. The two faced the court at least four more times between 1839 and 1845 for trying to sell slaves who felt the conditions of their limited slavery were being ignored. Apparently the scheme worked often enough for them to keep trying it, and jail owners along the way, such as Tait, cared little enough about the legal niceties unless it cost them money.[27]

Rising Prices

Slave prices were clearly soaring in the 1830s, but people disagreed on whether the values were artificially inflated before an upcoming collapse. Tait recalled that he could sell likely young men for $600 in New Orleans in the late 1820s, when he was partnered with Wilkinson and De Ende, but in the summer of 1836 he complained that he was paying far more than that just to purchase them in Virginia: "Men are now fully up to 1200, women nay yearlings at $850."[28]

But as long as the slaves could be sold for even more in New Orleans, he could make a profit. The rising prices actually helped the trade, encouraging planters to migrate to the richer soil of the Deep South to get the most out of their expensive workers. As the planters profited and expanded their holdings, they would need even more slaves to work their land. A correspondent for the *Charleston Courier* explained in the summer of 1835, "Little Negroes must be fed and clothed for fifteen or twenty years before they can do their full share of labor, consequently it is unprofitable to cultivate ordinary lands with valuable Negroes—it is better economy to give away the land, and take the Negroes on to the new soil of the West."[29]

A disastrous wheat crop in Virginia in the summer of 1835 also encouraged migration. "The general cry is 'we cannot make wheat . . . what else can we devote our lands to?' The ready answer is, 'Go to the South: carry your slaves to the South; make cotton and get rich.'"[30]

But some cautioned that the high prices were merely a bubble. The *Richmond Whig* reprinted an article from the June 1835 *Farmer's Register* by a professor of political economy at the College of William and Mary. He attributed the higher prices to more credit being offered by banks, foreign demand for cotton, and emancipation in the British West Indies, predicting: "This rise in prices has already excited a rage for speculation, which will, in all probability, carry up prices still higher." But he warned about an eventual collapse, which would hit the Deep South harder than Virginia: "The high price of negroes and cotton, is now producing a fearful emigration to the South West, where golden harvests will be realized, if present prices can only be kept up. . . . In the mean time, however, let us preserve our sobriety, our industry, and our morality; enjoying the present advantages of high prices, without rushing into schemes and adventures of a wild and reckless character, under the vain belief that these times are to last forever."[31]

Tait also felt that prices would continue to rise before they collapsed, though warning about the imminent collapse was a good way to entice sellers to act quickly.[32] Still wanting to buy, he tried to appeal directly to sellers with an ad in the June 12, 1835, *Richmond Whig*, perhaps hoping to avoid competition with other bidders:

NEGROES WANTED.—I wish to purchase a number of Negroes, field hands, males, from 12 to 25, and females, from 10 to 20 years of age. I also, wish to buy two Carpenters, two Brick-layers, two Black-smiths, four or five male house Servants, and four or five female house Servants and Seamstresses.

It is admitted on all hands that the price obtained for the article of Cotton mainly regulates the value of slave property; the present high prices of cotton have produced corresponding high prices for slaves. Many intelligent dealers in cotton are of opinion that there must be a considerable fall in the prices of that article shortly after the growing crop is gotten into market; it may therefore, fairly be supposed, that the price of slaves will then be greatly reduced below present prices. The present time then, is most favorable for the slave owners in Virginia to dispose of such portion of their stock of ne-groes as has hitherto been unprofitable. Persons in the country who may wish to sell any number of negroes, can communicate with me upon the subject by letters (postage paid.) Prompt attention will be given by me to all such letters, or to personal application.

BACON TAIT,
Corner of 15th and Cary streets,
Richmond, Va.

The boom continued over the winter, though Tait became more cautious. The following summer, in 1836, he wrote Rice C. Ballard, "I never have seen such anxiety to buy as at present . . . I do not bid at auction and I on all suitable occasions declare that I will not pay the prices—yet—between you and me I should like to buy more than I do or can—for I believe that some money can be made on them at present prices—and as I see no prospect of prices coming down."[33] In September of 1836 he wrote, "Choice negroes are very scarce & prices have advanced $50 per head."[34]

The frenzy was only a few months from its end. When cotton prices dropped in the winter of 1836–37, slave prices did the same. In January of 1838, Tait reported from Richmond, "There has been a tolerable number of negroes sold here during the holidays 800 to 850 for men & 600 to 650 for girls," compared to the prices of $1,200 and $850 he had reported a year and a half earlier. The collapse in prices and reduction in credit was hurting business. He added sardonically, "I wish I had money enough to buy even a child's toe." A few days later, as the value of the stock he had already purchased was falling, he confided, "This has been a tough year on all hands but especially so with Boudar & myself who have been all this time spending money without making any and unless there should be some change in our prospects I do not know what will become of us."[35] He discontinued his subscription to the *New Orleans Bee* newspaper, got rid of his carryall wagon, and, the following year, gave up his horse.[36]

Though he preserved his self-deprecating humor, cracking jokes in his letters, Thomas Boudar was openly panicking. In February 1838 he wrote Ballard, his French accent showing through: "I got no money from Mr. Franklin but he had the kindness to say that he would do what he could for me on his return. . . . All I have now to do is to pray to god that he may have it in is [sic] power, for if he has it not, I am ruined thats all."[37]

Tait had some ideas that might carry him through the lean times ahead, but at least when the business had been the most profitable he had made the most of it, investing carefully and avoiding an excess of debt. A decade of slave trading had provided him with some male acquaintances, though apparently no female ones. Loneliness still plagued him.

Chapter 7

I WISH IN MY SOUL I COULD FIND A GOOD WIFE

After the messy partnership with Wilkinson and De Ende, Tait chose not to become a junior partner in anyone else's business. Instead, he always operated as Tait and Boudar. But he allied himself with other successful traders, supplying slaves for them and cooperating in shipping and financing.

Rice C. Ballard

Rice C. Ballard, originally of Fredericksburg, Virginia, had been trading in slaves since at least 1822. That year, the twenty-two-year-old placed an ad in the January 10 *Alexandria Gazette* offering to swap three horses "for young negroes," adding, "also the highest price in cash will be given for 50 or 60 young NEGROES." By 1833, R. C. Ballard and Co. served as the Richmond agent for one of the largest slave-trading firms in the country, Franklin and Armfield. He had his own slave jail two blocks east of Tait's, on Seventeenth Street next to Seabrook's tobacco warehouse. Ballard sold his jail in 1834 to Goodwin and Templeman about the time that Tait was opening his new one at Fifteenth and Cary, so Ballard may have used Tait's jail for a while, although Ballard repurchased his own jail two years later. Before long, he had moved up to become a partner with James Franklin of Franklin and Armfield.

Ballard and Tait cooperated in business, and the two bachelors also became personal friends. Tait's growing connections with influential men in the trade spread to the general cluster of those who supplied Franklin and Armfield, and even circled back to include friends of his cousin Calvin Tate and brother-in-law Linnaeus Dupuy, who were now tobacco and cotton commission merchants in New Orleans. Such networks were vital for sharing news, gossip, advice, and financial support. Lewis Collier, who purchased Tait's first jail, had gained a reputation for dishonesty. Shunned by fellow businessmen, he did not survive the downturn of the late 1830s as well. In 1838, Tait discovered that Collier was almost $57,000 in debt to the Bank of Virginia. Collier soon lost the jail to the bank, which sold it to Robert Lumpkin in 1844.[1] Though Tait's relation with Ballard cooled around 1842, he met another man in the 1830s who would remain a trusted employee for decades.

Sidnum Grady

Rival trader John B. Prentis, revealing his plans to his own agents in the fall of 1832, warned them "not to say one word or whisper the contents of this letter to Graddy the small man, Mr. Tates' agent."[2] The small man was most likely Sidnum Grady. He was thirty-eight in the fall of 1832, just two years older than Tait, and by the end of the decade he would be responsible for the daily running of Tait's jail, managing it in Tait's absence to the point that it was sometimes called "Grady's jail" during the Civil War.

In addition to holding slaves for sale, private jails took in slaves at the demand of individuals, who needed to offer no evidence or reason. An early reference to Grady as manager of Tait's jail was just such a request in 1839: "Mr. Grady will be so good as to take charge of this man Jefferson who will be delivered by Messrs Gibson & Miller—& retain him in custody until further orders—respectfully Wm R. Johnson."[3] An 1840 runaway ad clarified Grady's position, stating a slave had been bought "in Richmond, out of Tate's Jail, sold by Mr. Grady the keeper."[4]

Originally from Rockingham County, Virginia, Sidnum Grady and his younger brother Lorenzo left home for Richmond in the 1830s, according to family history. The family recalled his name as Zephenier Sidnium Willis Grady, but he signed it consistently "Sidnum" in surviving letters and newspaper ads.[5] His brother found a career as a grocery store owner, first at the corner of Seventeenth and I Streets, a few blocks northeast of Tait's jail, then farther west on Brooke Avenue near L Street, where he also lived for many years. Lorenzo married in August of 1833, but Sidnum remained a lifelong bachelor, dedicating himself to the slave trade, a choice that would eventually lead to his death. After the end of slavery left him jobless and destitute, he committed suicide in 1866 by taking an overdose of laudanum at his brother's home on Brooke Avenue.[6]

Thomas Boudar

On the other side of the Virginia capitol building, in the respectable part of the city high above the slave-trading bottom, Tait's closest friend and business partner, Thomas Boudar, rented a quaint little thatched-roof cottage. Located at the northeast corner of Marshall and Fourth Streets, the home was a relic from the eighteenth century and conveniently near the chapel where the Boudar family attended Catholic services. The owner, James Bray, a well-to-do saddler, had lived in the house himself before and would live there again, but while he rented it out he was staying in the dwelling attached to his saddlery shop on Broad Street.[7]

While Tait lived alone beside his jail, the taint of the slave trade did not seem to isolate Boudar. His mother and unmarried sister Mercie moved from Lynchburg to join him and his wife, Mary, and their growing family in Richmond, and all the Boudars were active in the expanding Catholic Church. Joseph Gallego, the Spanish mill owner, had willed property and funds to build a larger church across from where they lived, but after a court disallowed the donation, the church built a new brick structure in 1834, still only a few blocks away at Grace and 8th Streets. In 1836, Thomas's sister Mercie, the last of the local Boudar siblings to wed, was married to Richmond resident George H. Carter by the church's beloved Father Timothy O'Brien.[8] Thomas and Mary Boudar named their first son Joseph after his grandfather, and their second son Thomas after his father, but perhaps out of sympathy that Tait would have no one to carry on *his* name, they named their third son, born in 1837, Henry Bacon Boudar.[9]

Loneliness

The largest known set of Tait's personal papers—a couple dozen letters—is mixed with the correspondence that Rice C. Ballard saved from his many slave-trading colleagues. Historians have studied the collection as evidence of the sexual exploitation of slaves. Edward E. Baptist used them to explore "the passionate desires of [Isaac] Franklin and his partners," pointing out: "More openly than most, these men described the ways in which the sexual history of slaves and masters fogged their vision of enslaved black women with an erotic haze." The letters gave insight into the traders' relationship with their wares: "The trade and consumption of enslaved human beings promised powerful gratifications of the senses and the self, implying psychological and physical—including explicitly sexual—pleasures. . . . [T]he men of the firm of Franklin, Armfield, and Ballard remembered, consciously and unconsciously, the sexual coercion of black women when they spoke or thought about slavery and the slave trade."[10]

Robert H. Gudmestad wrote in *A Troublesome Commerce: The Transformation of the Interstate Slave Trade*: "The private lives of slave traders were scandalous. They joked about the 'one-eyed man,' a euphemism for their sexual organ, and bragged about how they forced sexual relations upon slaves they purchased. [Isaac] Franklin even mused that he would establish a slave whorehouse for the 'comfort' of his agents."[11] Edward E. Baptist also commented on the phrase "one-eyed man": "Like ideas about honor and manhood, independence, and whiteness, the collective sexual aggressiveness enabled and valorized by the slave trade helped form a group identity for slaveowning white men. . . . So greedy were they, in fact, that such men spoke of themselves as if they were animated, erect penises, one-eyed men watching for mulatto women to rape." Steven Deyle also noted that the correspondence was "peppered with sexual innuendos."[12]

Notably missing in such discussions are citations from the interspersed letters of Tait. In contrast to the bawdy allusions, most of the camaraderie in Tait's letters came from gentle ribbing about money or politics. The most sexually explicit reference was in a letter he wrote to Ballard on November 24, 1838, in which he teased Ballard for courting a white woman who owned a plantation, perhaps Ballard's future wife, Louise Berthe, in Louisville. Tait showed that he was well aware of the Franklins' pet phrase, "one-eyed man," but used it as James Franklin had, with its least sexual connotation, to mean a gullible person with perhaps only an overtone of sexuality.[13] Tait also played on the word "forks," referring to the desire for a plantation near the Forks of the Road in Mississippi and Ballard's desire to plant himself in the forks of a woman's legs: "I have recd two letters from you dated at Louisville in both of which you say you was detained there by the low stage of the river and in negotiating for a plantation, all this Ballard does well enough for a one eyed man as Mr. Franklin would say, but to an old cruiser like myself it wont take unless by varying the import of your remarks a little, low water, oh! rather might you have ascribed your delay to your hot blood—you want to buy a plantation near Louisville do you! no no Ballard you want a plantation in the forks but you want to get it without buying it my friend."[14]

He characterized himself as "an old cruiser"—slang that had predatory and sexual connotations. *Cruisers* were "rogues ready to snap up any booty that may offer, like privateers or pirates on a cruise," according to a British vernacular dictionary.[15] But when he continued, "I wish you would come out and tell me what the gal said to you at last," he used his insight to guess that Ballard had been rejected. Rather than add to the other slave traders' reports of conquests, he portrayed himself as experienced with women, but as a failure rather than a success.

Tait certainly treated people of color as commodities, participating in the sadistic exploitation that Edward E. Baptist mentioned. But while his fellow traders used the letters as private confessionals, revealing their sexual conquests and desires, he maintained his persona as a southern gentleman who relished slavery but not sexual immorality. While James Franklin had written Ballard a few years earlier about the "handsome girl" that "has been used & that smartly by a one-eyed man about my size and age," Tait claimed even in this bawdy atmosphere, with a jail of enslaved women whom he kept in private quarters, that he was unwillingly, frustratingly celibate.[16]

There is no evidence to indicate it was strictly true, in the sense of not having sexual relations. In an era when sex and marriage were considered synonymous in polite company, *celibate* might also mean simply unmarried, and that he certainly was. What he actually did with the opposite sex is unknown. His personal letters are so few that the lewd ones may not have survived, or he may have presented a cruder aspect in person than in writing.

At least he must have been aware of Richmond's seamier side. Most of the wealthy business owners in his neighborhood left for their homes else-where at the end of the day, but because he lived beside his jail, Tait got to see the neighborhood after dark. By day it was dominated by the ordinary commerce of shops, warehouses, and a foundry, but "at night, the heart of downtown Richmond became a primarily, though hardly exclusively, working-class leisure scene marked by the mingling of male and female workers, sailors, gamblers, brawlers, thieves, and prostitutes of multiple racial backgrounds and states of bondage," according to Joshua D. Rothman in *Notorious in the Neighborhood.* Tait was within a couple blocks of the gro-ceries and brothels around Fourteenth and Cary, where numerous arrests occurred in the 1830s.[17]

He could have mingled with such people, but if he wanted a white woman for a respectable wife, his profession was an obstacle. Though respectable ladies let him down gently, even polite rejections stung. He could recite the excuses by rote and assumed Rice Ballard heard the same: "I guess when [you] poped [*sic*] the question to her, that she said she was very gratefull for the good opinion you expressed for her and that she would always respect you and would be glad to hear of your marrying some young lady who would make you happy but that she herself had no inclination to marry &c. and a deuce more of such flummery."[18] Flattery no longer fooled him: a rejection was a rejection. The consequences of being labeled a slave trader's wife were real. In Baltimore, visitors learned that slave trader Hope Slatter "was not generally received in respectable society, and that a lady whom he had lately married, was shunned by her former acquaintance."[19]

Slavery's Scapegoat

The stigma came at a time when Virginians realized that rising prices and the ready market in the Deep South meant there was no chance slavery would wither away in unprofitability. The state legislature also had consid-ered, and rejected, ending it for safety's sake in the wake of Nat Turner's rebellion. Resigned to being a slave-raising and slave-selling state, Virgin-ians looked for someone to blame.

They may have encouraged one Swedish visitor, at least, to believe that northerners were at fault. Carl David Arfwedson, observing Richmond on a visit, explained what he was told: "When [northerners] once settle in the South, they are obliged to procure slaves for the cultivation of their land . . . but, unaccustomed to treat them in a proper manner, and never forgetting how much labour a man is able to go through in the North, they require of the slave as much willingness and activity as a free servant. When this disposition is wanting . . . [they] have recourse to the mistaken system of compulsion, in order to force him, by the infliction of corporal punishments and the severest treatment, to work more assiduously."[20]

Slave traders and jail owners were another target because they were most directly responsible for shipping slaves out of state or punishing local ones, even though any sale or incarceration required a cooperative owner. But with scapegoats available, people could maintain the illusion that a *true* Virginian treated his slaves well and kept them from cradle to grave. Traders, of course, were not all shunned. Thomas Boudar had happily wed, as had James Wilkinson, and Hope Slatter's new wife was his second. Isaac Franklin married in 1839 to the daughter of a Presbyterian minister, and Rice Ballard would marry the following year. Such successes may have made Tait feel all the more frustrated at his failures.

The downturn in the market after 1836 placed Tait at the low point of both his personal and professional life since he had begun trading. Nevertheless, he kept his good humor, teasing Ballard in a letter on January 9, 1838, that he told a friend "that you was well and had more money than you knew what to do with. I thought it was as well to say so as not for you know that such will be the case with you in a little while, about which time I shall parade myself before you or about you in beggar's uniform and the Star of Poverty in my cap, singing Poor Billy Barlow. Mr. Franklin [and] myself will instruct you in all the melody of that tune which when you learn perfectly it will be a sovereign panacea against all contageous diseases."

"Billy Barlow," a comic song "sung with unbounded applause at the Western & Southern Theatres," according to the sheet music, was typically performed by a white man in tattered clothes who was lamenting his poverty. There may have been more that resonated with Tait. In one version Billy Barlow sang:

> O dear but I'm tir'd of this kind of life,
> I wish in my soul I could find a good wife,
> If there's any young Lady here, in want of a beau,
> Let her fly to the arms of sweet Billy Barlow.

Billy Barlow pointed out that there was "a nigger" who dressed better than him, either ragged Jim Crow or the well-known black dandy with the "long tail blue" coat, depending on the version. Such songs played with the stereotypes and taboos of the races. Jim Crow in another song was "courting a white gall," while in one version of "Billy Barlow" Billy sang:

> Dinah Rosa, has reported that I've got married
> I wish here she had a little longer tarried
> If she had, I'd caught and choked her ges so,
> She dont know how she has abused Billy Barlow.

Dinah Rosa, or just Dinah, was a black female archetype of the comic stage, perhaps most well known at the time as Dinah Rose, the object of Gumbo and Sambo's affection in Thomas D. Rice's comic play *Oh, Hush!*

The fictional Billy Barlow lived in a theatrical world peopled by blackface personas, and despite being white, his poverty and proximity made him no more than their equal. Tait also shared the neighborhood of Fifteenth and Cary with black people, both enslaved and free, and though he was socially far above those he bought and sold, the song pointed out the uncomfortable truth that fine clothes and wealth were what separated him, as much as color, and that if he were poor, he would be closer to their equals.[21]

Black and White

Whites could justify slavery more easily if they could pretend the two races were inherently different, but as blacks and whites mixed socially and sexually, their offspring gave proof of the opposite. Despite telling each other biblical narratives about the curse of Ham, whites struggled with the plain fact that as much as they wanted to make "negro" a sharply defined social, political, or biological construct, they could not. When the Virginia legislature clamped down after Nat Turner's 1831 rebellion, the new laws highlighted the fact that there were some people who were not exactly white, but who should not be treated as truly black, either. To reconcile the problem, the legislature passed a law in 1833 that attempted, in a vague way, to legislate what was already occurring in reality: "The court of any county or corporation, upon satisfactory proof, by a white person, of the fact, may grant to any free person of mixed blood, resident therein, a certificate that he is not a negro; which certificate shall protect such person against the penalties and disabilities to which free negroes are subject as such."[22] The rarely used law codified what abolitionists said more boldly the same spring: "Set the blacks free, and they will amalgamate with us—keep them in bondage, and still they will amalgamate. Half the people of color now in the United States are of mixed blood."[23]

People like Henry De Ende and Victoire Cavelier had already produced offspring who needed no legislation to move across the color line, but the *Richmond Enquirer* warned its readers in 1835 that British abolitionist George Thompson was coming to America to preach a shocking doctrine, that the races were not distinct. The newspaper revealed what he had been saying in England: "The lying pretence, that Nature herself has drawn the line between the different races, and that an inherent feeling occasions a mutual repulsation, is refuted by the mixed blood and gradations of color, which are seen wherever slavery exists. . . . The assumption of an inferiority in mixed breeds is so entirely at variance, not only with historical facts, but with physiological science, that it must be regarded as either founded on ignorance, or persisted in against better knowledge."[24]

The Richmond paper actually had copied the article from the *Boston (Mass.) Atlas*. Even Bostonians were not ready to hear that whites and blacks should intermarry, but Massachusetts—the future home of Tait and his wife—was still a world ahead of Virginia. There, at least, blacks could legally vote. The state never rescinded the right even when other northern states did, and by 1843 intermarriage of the races legally would be allowed there. Tait apparently never took advantage of the formality of law, perhaps because he and his "wife" already had children when they arrived, so a marriage ceremony would be awkward.

Politics and Economics

At the depths of the economic downturn, Tait considered reorganizing his business. Falling prices eroded the money he invested in slaves awaiting sale, but auctioneers relentlessly took their cut. In January of 1838, he considered dissolving Tait and Boudar as a slave-trading entity and investigated the possibility of entering the auction and commission business himself. From a public tax report, he estimated that John and Samuel Cosby and Exum S. Hubbard "must make from eight to nine thousand dollars *upon their sales at auction* and I think that Cosby makes about one third as much by private sales than he does by publick sales, if so Cosby alone makes from seven to eight thousand dollars per annum."

The Cosbys owned or rented several buildings in the city, including a tobacco factory on Cary Street next to Tait, and dealt in not only slaves but tobacco and other commodities.[25] Tait guessed that if he could get "a fair share of the business, I should make from three to five thousand dollars and my own opinion is that the business might be extended to more than double what it is now—if the present business can be extended and I could get orders to purchase for others I might fairly calculate upon making more than $5000," with less risk of capital than currently required. He would need to construct a building suitable for holding auctions, but he estimated the new construction would cost $2,500 to $3,000—the equivalent of buying four or five slaves—"& the expenses afterwards would only be for the wages of a clerk."

He planned to concentrate initially on what he knew best: "The negroe business would of course be my aim at first but after a little with funds to make advances I might expect consignments of produce from different quarters."[26] With an auction house he could diversify, competing with such firms as Davenport, Allen and Co. across the street, who ran a booming business selling everything *but* slaves. Not only would it protect him from the price fluctuations of a single commodity, it was a path toward respectability. Ballard, Franklin, and other traders retired to managing plantations, but Tait had already tried agriculture briefly before moving to Richmond and apparently realized his strength was in buying and selling. Prices recovered within a few years, though, and there is no record that he actually went forward with the auction plan. He was still sending slaves south to Thomas Boudar into the 1840s, but he also made a business of private sales from the jail locally.

A solid Whig, Tait teased Boudar in January of 1838 for supporting the Jacksonian Democrats and therefore personally bringing about the entire economic collapse. That summer, he happily wrote Ballard, "The Whigs are carrying every thing before them in this state. You and I (I hope you are a good Whig by this time) will have a majority in the legislature the ensuing session." He served on a Jefferson Ward committee for the party's state convention in 1840.[27]

Probably around 1839, Tait wrote an uncharacteristically optimistic and serious letter to Ballard discussing his own economic theory and predictions for the future. Though slave prices were dropping precipitously and would not hit bottom for another five years, his long-term business judgment was sound. Even in the short run, the difference in slave prices between New Orleans and Virginia—the spread that traders made their profit on—remained steady. Although prices sank in both cities to two-thirds or half of what they had been in the heyday of the 1830s, once they reached their low point in the mid-1840s, they would steadily increase until the Civil War.[28]

Tait echoed Adam Smith's belief that labor was the source of wealth, but came to the opposite conclusion from Smith on the question of slavery, endorsing it as vital to economic growth: "The truth is that labour is the actual & certain source of all wealth. It is the basis of all calculations of profit from banks, railroad or other internal improvement stock, for without the product of labour there would be no commerce and without commerce neither bank, railroad nor any other kind of stock would be worth any thing; as you increase banks and internal improvements you at once enhance the value of labour, yes and of Southern or Slave labour more than any other, without the product of Southern Slaves, the Northern part of the Union would be barely able to live without adding to their wealth, in anywise our whole country yea nearly the whole world is blessed with peace & prosperity and with a fair prospect of its long continuance."

He pointed out that slavery had once before seemed unprofitable: "The time was when slave labour was worth but a mere trifle in Virginia & then many persons did sell their slaves for the purpose & with the hope of engaging in something more lucrative than the product of their slaves but have not all such missed the mark?" In hindsight, it was clear that the ones who got rich were "those who strained every nerve to increase their number of negroes." He was so confident that prices would recover "that I would if I could, buy any number of negroes upon a credit even of one year at present prices—nothing but a general War in Europe could prevent me realizing a handsome profit. I would buy at present prices, either here, or in Mississippi. In conclusion, I will remark that such negroes as you now have on hand can not again be bought at similar prices. . . . I am of opinion that investments now in negroes will be more profitable than any kind of stock."

He compared the acquisition of slaves and wealth to a physical contest: "Bear in mind that we here are all eating the bread of idleness against our inclinations. We would like to be in training for when all the horses get upon the track, one only can win the race, bottom is necessary but a good start is absolutely essential—prudence is a virtue, but causeless timidity is weakness." But that reminded him of the other contest that occupied his thoughts: "Apropos—there is a rumor afloat here that Mr. Franklin & yourself each expect to be married shortly."[29] Although he was positioned well for an upturn in the slave market, marriage was a race he was losing among his middle-aged friends.

Chapter 8

DAT DE WAY HE GIT RICH

On the first day of 1840, with Richmond quietly blanketed by a foot of snow, Tait wrote Boudar in New Orleans some bad news: "I have just seen in an extract from a Natchez's News paper that the Fedl court at Jackson Missi lately decided in the case of Hickman vs. Rose that all contracts founded on the sale & purchase of negroes in that state since May 1833 are null & void."

The article from the ironically named *Natchez Free Trader* was making the rounds. The *Pennsylvania Freeman* published it on January 9 with a headline that crowed, "Slave-Traders in Trouble!" Judge Samuel J. Gholson had voided every trader's sale in Mississippi for the last seven years, based on the amended state constitution, which stated: "The introduction of slaves into this State as merchandize or for sale, shall be prohibited from and after the first day of May, 1833." The constitution, approved in the wake of Nat Turner's rebellion, had been designed to prevent the Upper South from dumping its most dangerous slaves, but the law had been ignored by both out-of-state traders and Mississippians because the Deep South needed cheap labor. Now, suddenly, in the wake of *Hickman v. Rose*, the courts would be applying it retroactively. No one seemed to expect that the slaves would be freed or would be returned to their previous masters. Tait and other traders feared purchasers would simply keep them and refuse to pay the money still owed, totaling $2 million in all, according to the article from the Natchez paper.

Tait rightly predicted someone would appeal to the U.S. Supreme Court, but he imagined the worst possible outcome: the court would uphold the ban on the radical grounds that "negroes are not property." He wrote, "I should not apprehend this result of the Supreme Court if the US was composed of such men as John Marshall was but as most of its members are nothing more than political partizans, such decision will be rendered as but subserving non slave holding influence and I may add party purposes." Whigs like Tait felt that the Jacksonian fever for the common man had infected the Supreme Court, to the detriment of the wealthy and their property. All but two of the justices were Jackson appointees. The new chief justice, Roger B. Taney, had been given his position as a reward for helping Jackson defeat the national bank.

Tait worried that such sentiment combined with increasing abolitionism was a dangerous mix: "The crisis is not far distant and as an individual I sincerely hope that a dissolution of the government may be a consequence." Unbeknownst to him, that crisis was still two decades off, and when he considered the problem more realistically, he decided it was not quite so bad: "I can not think that all the citizens of Mississippi will avail themselves of the decision in the case of Hickman vs Rose, but that some of them will there is no doubt, our friends will be greatly incommoded in collections if they do not actually lose by the decision."

Valuable Information

Tait had been selling in New Orleans more than Mississippi, so this would affect his friends more than him, but he realized how he could use the crisis to his advantage. In the confusion, traders would be desperate for information, which would become a valuable commodity. He started his quest to corner the market immediately: "Please let me know whatever you may here [sic] concerning our friends and their Mississippi claims."[1]

After informing Boudar, he wrote Ballard three days later, concerned about the difficulty of getting credit due to the general uncertainty, and fishing again for news: "I ask that you do me the favor to write to me and say how you all come in with collections, and whether or not the judgements which have been obtained can be interfered with now by injunction or otherwise?" He ranted again, though, about the future implications for the country: "It will accelerate the crisis between the North & the South which has been so long anticipated and most probably will produce a dissolution of the Union—The Constitutionality of the Missi law I take for granted will be made a question before the Supreme Court of the US and that court in subserviency to non slave-holding influence and party purposes will decide the law of Mssi to be constitutional upon the ground that *slaves are not property*—then comes the tug of war between the North & the South."[2]

Over the summer he tried to squeeze replies from harried lawyers and politicians, passing to his friends what tidbits he could learn. In September he wrote Ballard and John Armfield that he was "fully aware of the importance of the matter to both of you and I beg you to be assured that nothing but death can prevent me from looking after it and that I will communicate to you frequently whether I have any thing worth saying or not." In October, Richmond trader Thomas McCargo told him that the state courts in Mississippi were indeed refusing to enforce payments of debts. By offering some information, McCargo may have hoped that Tait would return the favor. They were acquaintances in Richmond, and McCargo's New Orleans office faced Boudar's across Moreau Street.

But Tait chose not to reciprocate, wanting to keep his colleagues in debt to him without helping a competitor like McCargo. Tait had also consulted well-known lawyer Chapman Johnson to get more insight, and he wrote Ballard and Armfield: "I must again impress upon you the propriety of keeping Johnson's opinion in every particular to yourselves—I have not let any person here know any thing about it except Mr. Saml Alsop & John A. Rowan. To Freeman & McCargo I have denied having received it."[3]

Tait had reasons for sharing or withholding information from those four men. John A. Rowan of Lynchburg had sold over $10,000 worth of slaves to a Mississippi buyer, who now refused to pay, and Tait must have felt sympathy for him. Rowan and his co-seller, John L. Harris, would eventually win a judgment after taking their case to the U.S. Supreme Court in 1847. Samuel Alsop was a fellow slave trader connected with Ballard and Armfield, and therefore worth helping, but Theophilus Freeman was an aggressive competitor. Tait had informed Ballard the year before that Freeman was "trying to bind all others to him here and elsewhere," so he strategically kept information from Freeman and McCargo.[4]

That fall, Tait planned to go to Natchez to research local court cases firsthand, to see if any were being decided in favor of slave traders, because when trying to collect debts "it will be all important to have a certified copy of such decision or judgement." He needed to visit in person because "I am unwilling to trust any lawyer in your section so far as to let him know any thing upon the subject as far as can be prevented." He planned to leave for Natchez on October 20: "I go by the way of Mobile as being the most certain and expeditious route."[5] Four days later, the *Charleston (S.C.) Courier* reported that B. Tait and "T. Baader" (that is, Boudar) had arrived in that city on the steam packet *Gov. Dudley* from Wilmington, North Carolina, on their way down the coast.[6]

After a winter of strategizing and suspense, slave traders were favored by fortune. The U.S. Supreme Court tested the Mississippi question in *Groves v. Slaughter,* after Robert Slaughter tried to collect almost $15,000 that he was owed in 1835 and 1836 from selling slaves. In a split decision, the court ruled in March of 1841 that such debts *were* collectible, because the Mississippi legislature had not addressed the issue well enough: "When the sale of the slaves in question was made, there was certainly no fixed and settled course of policy which would make void or illegal such contracts." Tait quickly called in the favors he was owed for helping Ballard and his colleagues during the crisis. He wrote on May 6, 1841, to see if Ballard would loan him $20,000 to $30,000, "now that the clouds which have so long darkened the horizon of your fortunes have passed away, and the sunshine of prosperity is shedding its genial influence upon you."[7]

Running a Slave Jail

In 1840, when the census taker stopped at Fifteenth and Cary, he listed a household made up of Tait, another white man in his twenties who was probably an employee, and seven slaves: three adult women, one adult man, and three children under twelve. Throughout the 1840s, Tait paid personal property tax on three or four slaves over age twelve, as well as a gold watch.

Though Sidnum Grady still managed the jail, he resided elsewhere, living and taking his meals in 1843 at the Mansion House, a hotel and boardinghouse on Main Street a block and a half away. He paid tax on a gold watch and, in 1845 only, on one slave.[8] While Tait handled shipments of slaves to Boudar, who sold them in New Orleans, Grady worked diligently making individual sales from the jail. Besides reselling locally those who were not destined for New Orleans, Grady also sold slaves on commission, with expenses paid by the owner. An example was Stephen, sold for John Holdsworth Barlow, a Williamsburg merchant.

Probably working through his lawyer, Barlow sent Stephen to Richmond, where Grady admitted him into the jail on May 30, 1843, charging a flat fee of 50 cents to receive and eventually release him, plus 25 cents a day for keeping him. While there, Stephen became sick. Grady called in Dr. Robert H. Cabell, a respected local physician, who charged $2 for attending him. Shoes, a shirt, and medicine for Stephen added another $1.81. Grady finally sold him for $400 after three weeks on display in the jail and promptly sent a check to Barlow for $385.44, after deducting expenses and his $5 commission.

Along with the check he included a cheerful, chatty salesman's letter, despite the currently depressed prices: "You may tell your friends this is a tip top sale— And although on yesterday I sold a real star fellow such as seldom comes into market at $480 yet I deem it unsafe to quote generally higher than the following lest I might induce those who look to me for information to give too much to sell in this market at a profit— You may consider No 1 young fellows worth about $450 same class young women $350— All others young and likely in same rates. In travelling about among your lower country friends do not forget to mention me to them—and remember the Mansion House where I board."[9]

About this time Tait hired another employee. As a newspaper reported long afterward: "In 1840 Mr. Tait was doing a flourishing business, and had a mart or jail in this city, where he was constantly transacting business in the sale and exchange of slave property.— About this time Solomon Myers . . . who was then a young man, introduced himself to Mr. Tait, and subsequently was engaged as an assistant keeper of the slave jail. Mr. Tait became prepossessed with Myers, took him into his confidence, and was very profuse in acts of friendship towards him."[10] Myers would become another lifelong friend of Tait, and Tait would eventually live with him and die at his home.

Thomas Boudar, like Tait, had seven slaves in his household in 1840, though he also had a white family around him—his wife, his six children, and his widowed mother. In addition to his home in Richmond, he also had an office in New Orleans on Moreau Street in the heart of the slave-trading district, where he received and sold slaves shipped not only directly from Tait but from a network of other Richmond traders—George Kephart, Luther Libby, and David Cume.[11]

Embarrassing Letters

Tait and Boudar's business relationship with George Kephart gave them all some brief infamy long afterward. In 1861, occupying Union troops found letters left on the floor of Kephart's abandoned slave jail in Alexandria, Virginia, and the antislavery *New York Tribune* published them. Dated from 1837 to 1857, the letters provided northerners a fascinating glimpse of the uncensored South. The introduction in the *Tribune* said, "We hear it constantly stated by the glossers over of slavery, that public opinion in the south is opposed to the separation of families, and that such separations are extremely rare. Now, there is scarcely a paper found in this shamble that does not bear witness that such is, on the contrary, the normal usage of slaves in Maryland and Virginia."

The first letter was from Bacon Tait. "After giving an account of certain sales, Mr. Tait gives the following semi-commercial, semi-philosophical observations: 'Mr. Boudor [*sic*] complains a good deal about the negroes he has for sale, and I acknowledge that he has sufficient cause. It was all in all a most wretched lot of negroes when I saw them, and it was perhaps false in me for not advising the sale here of at least 3/4 of them. I assure you, Captain, that inferior negroes are never cheap for the *La.* market. Trash and defective are never permanently profitable. They are very frequently sold at a profit for the time being, yet the sales as often recoil upon the vendor, with detriment more than counterbalancing such profit."

The writer ruthlessly mocked Boudar: "In No. 2 we have a line which gives a neat picture of Mr. Boudor [*sic*], alluded to as complaining in the last letter. This gentleman writes from New-Orleans. . . . 'You ask,' says this glorious gentleman, writing to Kephart the Alexandrian, 'you ask for information about little boys and girls'—kind-hearted, affectionate Kephart! how childhood seems to call out his profoundest interest! Boudor replies, 'All I can say is that they were always ready sale, but they must be purchased right or they do not pay much profit.' Can any one tell us how little boys and girls may be purchased 'right!'"

Even Sidnum Grady did not escape: "No. 8 is from Mr. S. Grady of Richmond, and informs us that 'there is some activity in the market now for young negroes, and they very scarce. I have sold so many negroes lately that there is not now one girl in Jail but what is grown and only two boys—do send me some young negroes—To-day Rachel Lockhart is sold at $587 50. This is the best offer we have had since she was sick affecting her eyes so that she had to be blistered on the back of the neck—and Mr. Tait said I had better let her go. Sophia is laid up again."

The last letter was from Tait again, "who writes to Mr. Windsor: 'Pray do me the favor to hand the enclosed letter *privately* to Mr. Armfield. *Don't take it to him at his house, but seek an opportunity to give it to him when none of his family can see you do so.*'" The author used this final letter as a springboard to bring a happy conclusion to the article: "Thank God, the slave-dealer finds in woman, in the wife and daughter, influences he cannot trust! 'The family,' where face meets face and affections spring, is no place where *his* letters can be safely delivered or his negotiations carried on."[12]

It was not the first time some slave traders' private mail had fallen into the wrong hands. A packet of letters from 1839 and 1840 meant mostly for Theophilus Freeman "found their way into a region which they were never designed to see," and wound up printed in William Lloyd Garrison's *Liberator*. Only one was from Tait, a brief note from February 1840 in which he enclosed a bill of lading "for five negroes, shipped by Mr. Burch." They were going from Richmond to New Orleans on the brig *Orleans* at a shipping cost of $20 each.[13]

"An dat de way he git rich, dat fallow"

After the Mississippi debt-collecting problem ended and Tait had taken the opportunity to ask Ballard for a loan, he wrote Ballard again a few days later on May 9, 1841. The letter is long, contradictory, and puzzling. He repeated his reminder that the Mississippi problem was over and good times were ahead, then invited Ballard to relocate from Mississippi to Richmond. He described in enthusiastic detail the improvements that were being made in the canal, James River, and dock to increase commerce, concluding, "A new era has at length commenced for the prosperity of Virginia at large and for Richmond especially."

He admitted he had personal reasons for the hard sell: "Surely it is natural & fair that I should wish to have my friends around me." Then he offered a cryptic comment about future plans: "But the probability is that I shall ere long take up my abode amongst strangers and therefore my advice is clearly not prompted solely by selfish motives. I will not trouble you with a tedious account of my individual matters further than to say that I must in some manner or other make up the last five years which I regard as even worse than so many blanks in the lottery of my life and whenever I do quit here I shall do so with the utmost regret but with a firm resolve never to return. I may either sell or for the present rent out the property that I have here."

He ended the letter with his usual good humor: "I am told that when my letter announcing the result of Slaughter's suit reached Natchez, Mr. Franklin struck up the tune of 'long time ago,' and that Mr. Armfield & yourself joined in the chorus."[14] The song "Long Time Ago" had a few different sets of words, but Tait probably was not referring to the polite lyrics about the death of a young woman. In the blackface minstrel versions, the central theme involved killing a "nigger," and in one, after killing either the "nigger" or a "coon,"

> He skin him for he hide an tallow
> Long time ago,
> An dat de way he git rich, dat fallow,
> Long time ago.[15]

In a celebratory moment, Tait may have seen himself and his fellow traders as predators who were gleefully exploiting "niggers" for profit, but the reality was more complicated. He was coming near the time when he would give his heart and much of his money to a woman of color.

The last five years had been poor ones, relatively speaking, but whatever plans Tait contemplated for leaving, he apparently did not act on them. Four months later, at the start of the winter 1841–42 shipping season, B. Tait and "T. Bordar" appeared on a list of passengers in the newspaper again, headed south in October on the same packet they had used the year before, along with "T. Freeman," possibly Theophilus Freeman.[16] Tait's life proceeded as it had, except that sometime before May of 1842 he met and fell in love with—or at least had intercourse with—Courtney Fountain, the woman who would change his life.

He continued to buy and sell real estate, and to deal with the usual problems of the slave trade. On September 19, about ten slaves escaped together from his jail.[17] But the danger of his business, and the complex relations that blacks and whites had, were shown dramatically in the rebellion on the slave ship *Creole* in November of that year. Tait's friends and Courtney Fountain's family both reacted to the incident, in opposite ways.

The *Creole*

Tait had no slaves on board this trip, but Thomas McCargo, who had helped with information about Mississippi courts, did, as did Robert Lumpkin, who would soon own Tait's old slave jail. Slaves being shipped from Richmond to New Orleans took over and forced the brig *Creole* to Nassau, where the British government allowed them to remain free. The story gripped the imagination of abolitionists and became an iconic tale of bravery and success, slave versus slave owner, black versus white.

For men like Tait, though, the old lesson came clear again. Those who gained the genuine trust and affection of at least some of their slaves were more apt to survive when disaster struck. Thomas McCargo had sent his young nephew Theophilus on board, along with two personal slaves, Jim and Lewis, who saved Theophilus's life. "Jim and Lewis exclaimed that 'Master Theo. should not be killed,' and clung around him, begging [slaves] Elijah Morris and Ben. Blacksmith, who were then close to him, with knives in their hands, not to kill him; they consented, and ordered him to be taken down to the hold."[18] Two or three slave women saved another white man, William H. Meritt, who had been given free passage in exchange for attending the slaves. He "hid himself in one of the births [sic], and three of the female house servants covered him with blankets, and set on the edge of the birth, crying and praying." The reverse was true as well. At least one slave was saved by a crewman. At the start of the fight, Andrew Jackson, a slave of Thomas McCargo, "jumped into the forerigging, and called to Francis Foxwell, one of the crew, to know where he should go to save his life. . . . Foxwell told him to go into the foretop."

While nineteen slaves actively attacked, the vast majority were inscrutably neutral. The crew recalled, "The other negroes all remained at their regular stations, where they had been placed at the commencement of the voyage." And yet the first mate testified he "saw nothing in their deportment that would induce him to believe they would assist him in re-taking the vessel."[19] After the struggle was over, almost all of the slaves stepped ashore to freedom in the Bahamas, but a few even then chose not to do so. Two of McCargo's had remained in the cabin—Rachel Glover, thirty-four, and Mary Herriggins, eighteen. Rachel also had a nine-year-old son who hid on board. Two others, Elizabeth Murdaugh, eighteen, being shipped by G. H. Apperson, and Lydia Ann Gorden, seventeen, being shipped by Robert Lumpkin, "remained in the hold until all the others had left the vessel, saying that they did not wish such freedom as there was there; they preferred coming to their masters," or so the first mate claimed. They were the only five the *Creole* managed to transport to its original destination, New Orleans.[20]

Trust across the Color Line

Besides protection in case of insurrection, slave owners had many reasons to try to form bonds with the enslaved people who shared so much of their daily life. Such trust and friendship reduced their danger; it made slaves more reliable and therefore easier to manage; it offered a chance of cooperative sexual favors; and it was an outgrowth of the natural human desire to be liked or admired rather than to be hated or ostracized. However, there was a competing social reason to distance oneself from one's slaves: to maintain one's position above them. In addition, a primary psychological reason not to form such bonds was the need to dehumanize them and thereby erase the guilt of enslaving them, with all the attendant control and mistreatment that went with that enslavement. Yet it was impossible to dehumanize all blacks, or all slaves—just as it was impossible for all slaves to dehumanize all whites.

Aboard the *Creole,* Jacob Lietener had assisted McCargo's slave, who was the steward during the voyage. Thus Lietener was known by some of the blacks. When the mutiny began, Elijah Morris, one of the rebellious slaves, "came out, saying, 'Kill every God damn white person on board the vessel, and if none else will, I will!'"

Lietener, who was white, said, "Will you kill me, Morris?"

Morris answered, "No, he should not be hurt."

Enslaved people also had possible motives to shield whites during an insurrection: sympathy to protect any human being from violence, especially a person they knew; genuine friendship or admiration; or a calculated risk, because if insurrection failed they would be in a far better position if they had protected their master. They might also have an internalized sense of duty based on a lifetime of being socialized in the role of a servant. In other words, if they were born to be a servant, they might believe they should become the best servant they could be—which could be clinicalized as either an attempt to be self-actualizing or a lifelong manifestation of Stockholm Syndrome.

If so many whites and blacks could interact outside of the socially prescribed racial and legal categories, it is not surprising that Tait—who had exhausted the possibilities of finding a white wife—would become open to the possibility of a black one. Unfortunately, there is little information about the time when Tait met and began having children with Courtney Fountain. Although she does not appear in the census, she was apparently free, because her older sister "never was a slave" and other members of her family were free. She was about thirty-five years old in 1842, but she apparently had not married before because she was sometimes addressed by her maiden name as late as 1859, and no other last name seems connected with her. Though Tait presented her as his legal wife in Massachusetts, the only clue to how he presented her in Virginia is from a lawsuit after his death, which stated she "held to him the relation of house-keeper."[21]

Courtney Fountain probably worked for Tait or a nearby family for pay. Even free blacks could be dominated and exploited by wealthy and powerful white men. Yet Courtney's family had both white and black abolitionist connections, lived in free states, and she could have turned to them for help if she needed it. She moved near her brother and sister after she married Tait, so her situation was not as vulnerable as that of many of the women Tait might have chosen.

Courtney probably had some white ancestry, because several of her children with Tait were categorized as white in adulthood. At least one had blue eyes and a "fair" complexion, while another had hazel eyes and a dark complexion.[22] If she worked for pay as Tait's housekeeper, he could have thought of her as not a slave, yet also not another white woman who would reject him. She was someone he could not force to love him, yet he had a good chance of success by enticing her with a more luxurious life.

Another son of a Lynchburg merchant who moved to Richmond, George W. Bagby, wrote much later about "the Virginia mulatto": "Why no poem has ever been addressed to one of the most beautiful and useful staples of our State I could never tell. . . . But it is to the softer form of this desirable product that our indebtedness is greatest. What would this world be without a mulatto chambermaid and washerwoman? Nothing, less than nothing. The violence of my feelings will not permit me to say any more on this point."[23]

Though they may have lived near each other in grungy Shockoe Bottom, Tait and Courtney came from backgrounds a world apart. Just as Tait had met at least some of the white slave traders connected with the *Creole*, Courtney's extended family may have met the leader of the rebellion—or at least heard him highly praised.

Reverend Fountain of Utica Takes a Stand

In New York State, the black community hailed the heroic actions of Madison Washington. He had a glorious name, a touching backstory, and exemplified everything good about violent insurrection. Before being shipped south on the *Creole*, he had escaped from slavery to Canada, according to an article in the *Friend of Man*, but was determined to return and free his enslaved wife also. He followed the Underground Railroad south. "As he passed along, he was heard from at Utica and in Albany," eventually arriving in Virginia, where he was captured again. "The next account, he stands a freeman on the deck of the *Creole*."[24]

There is no record of who helped him through Utica.[25] But there is a record of one preacher in Utica who endorsed him. In the summer of 1843, Reverend James Fountain was attending the National Negro Convention in Buffalo. The main speech was an "Address to the Slaves of United States," and it was a fiery one. The speaker, a black minister from Troy, New York, called for widespread insurrection: "Brethren, arise, arise! Strike for your lives and liberties." He hailed Madison Washington as the latest in a line of heroes who included Nat Turner and Denmark Vesey.[26]

Those attending the convention had to decide whether to endorse the speech or distance themselves from it. Although Reverend Fountain had always been free, he came to New York State from Winchester, Virginia, in 1826, so he had seen slavery firsthand.[27] He still had at least one relative in Winchester, John Hatley Fountain, a barber who would be run out of town within the year for helping slaves escape. Other relatives lived in Salem, Massachusetts, where they knew local white abolitionists there. Reverend Fountain likely knew those who helped Madison Washington on his way through Utica, if he was not one of them. And he also had a much younger female relative living in Richmond, probably a niece or cousin, possibly a sister: Courtney Fountain. They were connected so closely that he had named his thirteen-year-old daughter Courtney.

The "Address to the Slaves of United States" polarized those at the convention. A representative from Cincinnati urged the members not to adopt it; he feared for the safety of his constituents, living on the border of a slave state. Others "thought it was time" to advocate insurrection. In the afternoon, Frederick Douglass "made some forcible remarks against its adoption." Finally, after a close vote, the convention refused to endorse the address. Reverend James Fountain, though, voted for it.[28] Reverend Fountain and the rest of the Fountain family were opposite to Tait—in their political views, in their backgrounds, in where they lived, and in their interests—yet within a decade they would become his in-laws and neighbors.

Chapter 9

GOOD AND WORTHY CITIZENS

While men like Tait used the legal system and newspapers to their advantage, documenting each other's lives and leaving a trail for historians, free blacks found little of benefit there. In most cases, they had an incentive to interact with whites as little as possible. They did not consistently register as required, nor did they always let the census taker find them. In their own communities an informal network of family ties, personal acquaintances, and letters long since lost served them well but left few traces. When searching for specific families, a historian can find glimpses, but sometimes little more.

Such is the case with the free black Fountain family of Winchester, Virginia, whose lives would become entwined with Tait's. Courtney Fountain was born in Winchester, 140 miles north of Richmond, probably around 1807. According to her death certificate, she was the daughter of John and Hannah Fountain. She had at least two siblings—Ann, born in 1800, and John, born about 1797—who would later live near her in Massachusetts. Other free black Fountains, originally from Winchester, moved from one community to another and were surely her kin, though the exact relationship is unknown. Just as Tait's white friends over the years shared the slave trade in common, the Fountain family of Winchester shared a different tie: a desire to leave Virginia and to work for black rights and freedom.

The couple's story would be less puzzling had Tait eventually given up dealing in slaves for Courtney's sake, or if Courtney had abandoned her family's racial solidarity for life with a wealthy white man. But neither occurred. Tait continued to own the Cary Street slave jail while living part of the year near Courtney's abolitionist family in Salem. Courtney's choice of husband apparently did not ostracize her from her family, nor is there evidence that she or their children distanced themselves from Tait after they moved among her family. How they reconciled their diverse backgrounds will remain a mystery unless more personal papers come forth.

Free Blacks in Virginia

The Fountains were typical of free blacks in Virginia, who were more apt to reside in cities. The *Richmond Whig* reported in 1840 that 53 percent of Richmond's population was white, 37 percent enslaved, and almost 10 percent "free colored," compared to just 4 percent free colored statewide. The city had a slight excess of males among whites, but a significant excess of females among the free colored population, 124 females per 100 males. Based on raw numbers alone, both white males and free colored women would need to look outside their own demographic if all wanted to find a mate.[1]

Virginia's free blacks survived in a continual condition of probation, as the state did its best to control them: "Every free negro shall, every five years, be registered and numbered in a book to be kept by the clerk of the court."[2] Laws came and went, declaring under what circumstance a free negro convicted of a crime could be sold permanently into slavery and transported out of the state. For the same crime, a white person might serve only a few years in the penitentiary. White men could participate in politics, but people of color could only wait and watch to see what fate white legislators granted them. They could not vote, hold office, sit on juries, or testify as witnesses against whites.

Yet they were vital to everyday life in the city. In an era when being clean-shaven was the fashion, white men regularly allowed free black barbers to hold razors to their throats. Whites sent their laundry to free blacks, purchased from their vendors' carts, employed them as servants, cooks, and nurses, wore clothes they had made, and hired them as bricklayers, carpenters, porters, and factory hands in the booming tobacco business. Free blacks found other ways to extract money in the city also, by theft and prostitution.

Society expected slave owners to keep their servants nearby, so the idea of races segregated into their own communities was not a natural one.

Blacks lived in whites' homes or neighborhoods, cared for their children, and attended their churches to be preached at by white ministers. In fact, whites feared blacks' spending too much time where they could strategize alone. The city had endured the scare of Gabriel's planned Richmond slave rebellion in 1800. In 1831 Nat Turner, seventy-five miles away in Southampton County, reignited white fears. And yet, like the black guides who led British soldiers in the War of 1812 on secret paths, free blacks lived their own surreptitious lives, even when they dwelt within sight of whites.

The Winchester Fountains showed a consistent interest in moving northward and in abolition, they endorsed and probably participated in the Underground Railroad, and they interacted with various notable antislavery figures of the day: Frederick Douglass, Charles Lenox Remond, Charles Torrey, William Lloyd Garrison. Some family members eventually resided near Courtney and Tait in Massachusetts. One even lived in the same household for a time.

Courtney Fountain

Sometime before 1842, Courtney came to Richmond. There is little evidence about her early life. She apparently took no other husband's name before Tait's, and although she was known as Mrs. Tait in Salem, she received a letter addressed to "Cortney Fountain" as late as 1859.[3] No children from any previous marriage appeared in Salem or made any claim on the money that Tait provided. She does not appear by name in any census before the 1855 Massachusetts state census.

Courtney may have been working as a housekeeper for a white family and therefore missed being named as a head of household in the 1840 census. In 1850, though, she and her four children should have appeared in the census in Richmond when all free people were listed by name. It is possible that, because she was living with Tait, the census taker assumed she was one of the many slaves on the Cary Street property. The 1850 slave census listed Tait owning five adults—including a woman within a few years of Courtney's age—an eighteen-year-old, and four children. The four children's ages and sexes were close, but not an exact match. Tait was listed as owning female mulattoes, ages six, four, three, and two, when the children should have been seven, four, four, and two, with one of the twins being a male. In 1850 Tait paid personal property tax on four slaves over age twelve, two less than the number on the census, an indication that perhaps the census taker had assumed Courtney and her children, as well as another adult free black, were his slaves.[4]

Courtney's extended family in Winchester had their own plans for success. In the years before she met Tait and through the end of the war, they gradually moved north and worked for increased rights for blacks, the end of slavery, and northern victory. Although Tait may not have been aware of the details of Courtney's far-flung family when he first met her in Richmond and while their children were young, he surely learned more about them from her over time. She must have made him aware of who he would encounter before suggesting they move to Salem, but his presence as a neighbor apparently did not discourage them, nor did it prevent him from agreeing to the move. Like other slave traders, he had compartmentalized her as being different from the people he bought and sold. But unlike others, he also extended his compartmentalization to her radical family. And they also, aware of how men like him would have treated people of their race on the auction block, accepted him as an in-law rather than as an adversary.

Julia Fountain Washington Williams

Julia Fountain took the same path as Courtney, moving from Winchester to Richmond to Salem, Massachusetts, but a decade earlier. She was the daughter of Edward Fountain of Winchester and probably had been born there before the turn of the nineteenth century, making her just past thirty—a little older than Courtney, perhaps a cousin related through their fathers. Her husband, John Washington, may have come from Winchester also, but they apparently felt that Richmond offered better opportunities.[5] John would die within a few years. Julia and her son, John S. Washington, eventually moved to Salem, Massachusetts, where sometime before 1850 she married a longtime Salem citizen, Abram Williams. Although she came from a slave state to a free one, he had lived through an even more dramatic transformation, having originally come as a slave from Africa.

John Jr. enlisted in the 54th Massachusetts in 1864 and served in the 55th Massachusetts on detached duty at a training center not far from home. Both the *Salem Gazette* and the *Observer* noted his service, as well as that of barber James W. Fountain, another of the Winchester clan: "Among the recent enlistments in Salem, are those of ten or a dozen colored citizens, among whom are . . . Mr. John A. [sic] Washington; Mr. Fountaine, the barber, and others. These are well known in this community as good and worthy citizens." John S. Washington and his wife lived on Porter Street in Salem, a block away from where Tait and Courtney Tait lived in the 1850s.[6]

Reverend James Fountain and Son

Though Reverend James Fountain never left Utica, New York, after abandoning Winchester, his son James Jr. moved to Marblehead in Essex County, Massachusetts, the same county as Salem. The son represented the county along with noted abolitionist Charles Lenox Remond at meetings that were becoming increasingly fiery against slavery and for the rights of people of color. At the July 10–11, 1854, meeting of the Massachusetts State Council for colored residents in New Bedford, James Jr. was named to the committees on finance and business. The members spoke out as citizens of Massachusetts, "repudiating, now and forever, the idea that man can hold property in man," and spoke against the "contribution of funds, by anti-slavery people, towards the purchase of slaves; but, on the contrary, recommend their moneys to be used for under-ground railroad purposes whenever an opportunity presents itself for a chattel to declare its independence of slavery."[7] In 1864, working as a barber in Salem, James Jr. enlisted in the 54th Massachusetts, was immediately transferred to the 55th, and served in South Carolina.[8]

John Hatley Fountain

While Reverend James Fountain and his son were attending meetings with Frederick Douglass and C. L. Remond, John Hatley Fountain stayed in Winchester and became connected with another noted abolitionist: Charles Torrey. Torrey was a white Massachusetts native who established an Underground Railroad network from Washington and Baltimore north, eventually dying in a Baltimore prison in 1846 after being found guilty of slave stealing.

Hatley Fountain narrowly escaped the same fate. A barber who made regular trips to get supplies in Baltimore, in 1843 he was accused of helping Torrey spirit away an enslaved man and the man's free wife and children. He was finally acquitted after spending ten weeks in jail, but had to leave town. He toured the Northeast, meeting noted abolitionists such as William Lloyd Garrison and John Greenleaf Whittier and giving speeches to abolitionist societies to raise money to purchase his enslaved wife and son, whom he had left behind. Finally reunited, they settled in Pennsylvania.[9] Hatley Fountain had had to flee his hometown, but one of the most difficult journeys of a Fountain family member from a slave state to a free state belonged to Courtney's nephew, the son of her older sister Ann, who lived in Salem.

Ann Fountain Marbray Stearns, Courtney's Sister

Ann, born in Winchester in 1800, married Thomas J. Marbray (also spelled Marberry or Marbury) and lived in Alexandria, which was then part of the District of Columbia. Around 1824 they moved to Salem, leaving behind their young son, John, with his grandfather in Alexandria.[10] After her husband died at sea, Ann remarried on November 18, 1844, to William Stearns, a widower and also a seaman from Salem, and they lived on Bridge Street.[11] Meanwhile, her son John's grandfather had died in Alexandria, and in the fall of 1845 John wanted to join her in Salem. The increasing momentum to retrocede Alexandria to Virginia, which would be approved in February of the following year, may have influenced his decision, for most free blacks in Alexandria dreaded becoming residents of Virginia. He was going by the name John Junifer or Juniver now, having taken the last name of his grandfather. Because Ann's father was John Fountain, it is possible that grandfather Juniver was the second husband of either grandmother.

A young male traveling alone out of slave territory, even if he was free, might arouse suspicion, so the family decided to find a white man to accompany him. On October 18, 1845, his mother turned to a local white abolitionist for assistance. John A. Innis was a baker in Salem, rumored to help slaves on the Underground Railroad. She advanced him $50 for the trip, and he left two days later, arriving in Washington on October 24. Unfortunately, the man she had chosen was "a brawling political abolitionst" who was "continually getting into 'hot water,' always ready for a dispute; had frequently interrupted public meetings; and, in short, was one of the most rabid of the abolitionists."[12]

Rather than quietly accompanying her son during the perfectly legal return trip to Salem, he turned it into a cloak-and-dagger mission, using a typical Underground Railroad ruse of smuggling Junifer as his personal slave.

[He] arrived in Washington on the 24th, proceeded to Alexandria, found a colored man by the name of Parry, who knew of John's whereabouts, showed him a ring as a sign, that Parry might place confidence in him, arranged with him to bring John to Washington that evening, and then returned there himself. . . . Entered John on the way bill at the depot as his servant, paid his passage, &c., and arrived at Baltimore. . . . After he had taken his seat in the car [at Baltimore], he was called out and told that John was not a Virginia negro, &c., and with him was taken back to the hotel, and thence before a magistrate. There the clerk of the railroad produced the certificate signed by Innis, in which John was described as his slave. A man stepped up and declared that John was a runaway slave, for whom $100 reward had been offered, and that he should get it.[13]

Rather than immediately explain that Junifer was free, Innis "is said to have made a variety of statements, first that he had bought the negro in Richmond, Va.," then he told the truth, then "finally he declared that he never saw or knew any thing of the negro until Friday night, when he saw him at Washington, and fell in with the negro there." The *Baltimore Sun*'s reporter concluded, "His conversation seems to have been *very much like that of one challenging the martyrdom of the penitentiary*."[14]

Both he and Junifer were taken to jail, Junifer for being a runaway and Innis because he was unable to put up the $2,000 bail for the accusation of stealing a slave. Innis got in touch with lawyers and secured his own release in a few days, but Junifer remained in jail. On November 17, over three weeks later, the *Salem Register* reported he "has been liberated and returned to the District of Columbia . . . but a gentleman of Alexandria, who went to Baltimore and got him liberated, had incurred expenses to the amount of $24.00, which he must first pay, and obtain in addition $12.00 to defray his expenses to Salem. 'He is very anxious to go,' adds the letter, 'and as soon as he can raise the means to get off honorably, he will be off.' We understand that the necessary funds have been sent on from Salem."[15]

John Junifer finally arrived in Salem on December 2. Thanks to the need for fundraising, Innis's natural bragging, and the outrage at an innocent young man being arrested, newspapers reported the incident widely, and it showed up again the next spring when Innis sued a newspaper for libel for calling him a "brawling political abolitionist," among other things. The jury found the newspaper not guilty after numerous witnesses testified that Innis *was* a brawling political abolitionist.[16]

John Fountain, Courtney's Brother

John W. Fountain, age sixty, a laborer, died in Salem of paralysis on November 15, 1857. He was listed as the son of John and Hannah, so although his death record said he was born in Salem, he was most likely Courtney Fountain's brother.[17]

In 1854 he may have been living at 1 Ropes Street in Salem, a couple of blocks from Tait's home on Cedar Street. John Fountain, laborer, was listed as living there in the city directory, along with Abram W. Marbray, who would have been his sister's son. In the 1855 state census, John Fountaine, age fifty, was living with Tait and Courtney in their home. Although his age was several years too young, the census taker made several mistakes, so this John may have been Courtney's brother, moving in with her in the last few years before he died.[18]

Tait and Courtney Become a Couple

There is no evidence for exactly when Tait and Courtney met, but it was no later than May of 1842, nine months before she gave birth to their first child. Their children's names first show up in the 1855 Massachusetts census, but there is no indication Tait changed them between their birth and then. Their names imply he claimed them fully as his own children. The first child, a girl born on February 27, 1843, was Celine C., named after his sister. Next came twins on December 17, 1845, a girl named Constance Rosalie after Thomas Boudar's mother, and a boy named Bacon Cooper after himself and his mother's maiden name. The final daughter, born on April 17, 1848, was named Marie Josephine after Thomas Boudar's sisters.

Such a blatant acknowledgment of paternity was not unusual. Soon, darker-skinned namesakes of other white jail owners arrived. Robert Lumpkin, who had purchased Tait's first jail, sired two girls in 1845 and 1847 by a black wife and named their first boy, born in 1848, Robert after himself. Silas Omohundro, whose jail was near Lumpkin's, fathered Silas Jr. by a black woman in 1849, then continued to have other children with her. Hector Davis also had children with a black woman in the 1850s.[19] To the general public, the various categories of slaves or free people working for Tait in his jail or living with him at Fifteenth and Cary may have been indistinguishable, but to those who knew him, the relationship between Tait, Courtney, and the children with such names must have been unmistakable. Even someone who did not inquire about the children's names may have sensed a subtle difference. A visitor to Franklin and Armfield's slave jail in Alexandria in 1834 noticed in the "cook-room," where trusted slaves worked, "a little boy and girl, five or six years old, who were better dressed than the others. Their complexions were quite light, their features bright and beautiful, and their clothes had an air of neatness and taste, such as free mothers love to impart to their little ones. [The owner] said the mother of these had been with him some time."[20]

Legally, Tait and Courtney could not marry. According to an old law: "Whatsoever white man or woman, being free, shall intermarry with a negro or mulatto man or woman, bond or free, shall, by judgment of the county court, be committed to prison and there remain six months, without bail" and be fined $30. A minister who dared officiate would be fined $250, half to go to the informer.[21]

On August 14, 1842, with Courtney a few months pregnant with their first child, Tait wrote his friend Rice C. Ballard a letter strikingly different in tone from his previous letters. Coolly formal, he wished Ballard the best, but refused to divulge any more business information for free, making clear their partnership had ended and with it any obligation to favor Ballard over his competitors: "My information I have acquired is now complete and would be incalculably valuable to anyone having an interest in the subject but having discharged the duties of my management to the firm and having brought those duties to a close I am not disposed for any thing like the paltry consideration heretofore received to say further on the subject much less am I disposed to impart such information gratuitously I regard the information I have as highly valuable to either side of the question that information & my services in aid of it is now fairly in the market."

He declined an invitation to visit Ballard with the justification "that poor folks like myself can not make visits which cost money." But warming a little at the end, Tait invited Ballard to visit Virginia. He added, "Ballard old fellow, I am done with politics unless I could see that I was to make money by them."[22] He did not stick to that, though perhaps he found political involvement added to his income enough to justify it. As his preschool children played about the Cary Street Jail lot, he increased his influence in Richmond and continued dealing in slaves, meanwhile diversifying his investments further into real estate.

Chapter 10

HE EXPECTS TO LEAVE RICHMOND SHORTLY

During the 1840s Tait concentrated on civic activities, increasing his influence in Richmond. He served as a member of the Richmond Fire Association in 1845, and by 1847 was second assistant foreman of Company Number 6. The following fall, he needed the fire company himself when a small wooden building he owned near the slave jail caught fire one night and was partially consumed.[1] Perhaps recalling the predictions of his uncle Edmund Tate about the future of steam transportation, he promoted railroads, selling subscriptions for the Richmond and Danville Railroad in March 1847, and in November 1847 serving as one of Richmond's delegates to a convention concerning the Richmond and Ohio Railroad that would connect Richmond to Lynchburg and points farther west.[2]

That same year he ran for—and won—a seat representing Jefferson Ward on the Richmond City Council. He used the position to continue promoting railroads for the city, voting for the city to subscribe to two thousand shares of the Richmond and Danville Railroad Company stock. The following summer he served on the council's committee to arrange an "entertainment to be given to the Virginia Regiment of Volunteers just returned from Mexico." When he had been feted at such a banquet over thirty years previously after the War of 1812, he had been at a crossroads, abandoning his military ambitions with perhaps only a vague idea of becoming a storekeeper. But now he had not only a secure business, but a steady love, a growing family, and the political and financial (if not social) respect of his fellow citizens.

In April of 1848 and 1849 he was reelected to the council and continued to push for city improvements, offering a resolution to find a site for the new gas-light works. The *Richmond Enquirer* commented, "We are glad to hear that there are strong indications of a general approval in the Council of lighting the city with Gas." But progress came to a halt while the council fought for most of the year. Whether Tait approved of the final choice for a location is not known. The typically smelly, dangerous process was finally located directly beside Tait's jail, in the adjoining lot to the southeast. In 1850, the superintendent began asking residents to sign up for home gas subscriptions, and the following year the plant began production. After only two years demand outstripped production, so the company purchased a larger lot on the outskirts of town. Operations were moved there by 1856, leaving the massive gasworks framework near Tait's jail abandoned.

Though Tait had consistently promoted the Richmond and Danville Railroad, in October 1849 he asked the council to support an injunction stopping construction on a branch line that would lead to the opposite side of the James River from his Richmond property, because "such branch Road may be seriously detrimental to the interests of this City, by diverting trade to the south side of James River." His support only of railroad construction that would benefit him financially was apparently becoming too obvious. A few weeks later he published a statement in the *Richmond Whig*. Rather than denying the accusations, he announced that they were true:

> Understanding that it is insinuated that my course with regard to the proposed extension of the Danville Railroad . . . has been influenced exclusively by self-interest, I deem it due to myself as an humble individual, and as a member of the Council of Richmond; and for the purpose of relieving others of their troubles in this respect, (done for effect) briefly to state these facts: That I subscribed for stock in the Richmond and Danville Railroad Company, with the expectation of enhancing the value of the property which I own in this city—that as a member of the City Council, I voted in good faith for the appropriation of $200,000 to the Road, believing that, if it were constructed *as then* proposed, the prosperity of Richmond would be advanced thereby—and that I, like any other citizen who has any interest in the city, would receive the benefits which would flow therefrom.[3]

He had taken to heart what he told Ballard in 1842: he would enter politics only if he could make money from it.

Apparently the Jefferson Ward voters liked such refreshing honesty. In March of 1850 Tait announced that after serving four years he would not run again for council, but he wound up running and was reelected the following month. If his constituents knew of his interracial family, they apparently were not discouraged from supporting him. Gustavus Myers, a longtime councilman and president of the council during Tait's service, had fathered a son almost thirty years before with a free woman of color.[4]

Not everyone was pleased with the council. Disgruntled former resident Charles Palmer wrote to his son in March of 1851 about the corruption "in your councils & courts made up of vulgarity Swindlers Gamblers Negro traders & Shavers."[5] But despite his occupation, Tait was becoming trusted in the city. Benjamin Davis consulted with him on a major construction project at the site of the old Bell Tavern, now rebuilt into the City Hotel.[6] In 1842 he helped fellow Richmond resident Charles R. Allen get reimbursed by the government for $211.50 in expenses connected with negotiating a treaty in New York State with the Seneca Indians in 1838. In 1849 he served on the committee to honor the death of former president James K. Polk.[7]

Tait and Boudar's Businesses Continue

Tait continued investing in property. At one real estate auction on June 30, 1848, for example, he spent $19,000 on three lots being sold from Colonel Richard Adams's estate in Richmond. Sidnum Grady handled transactions at the jail, focusing now more on private sales, advertising in 1846: "For Sale.—A likely young Man, a first rate farm hand and good driver, warranted healthy, and sold solely for the purpose of being near his wife, who lives in Richmond. Apply to Mr. Grady, at Bacon Tait's Jail."[8]

The jail's business still required Tait to step in and deal with stickier problems. In 1846 he needed a lawyer in Williamsburg to help defend the title to a slave involved in a trust dispute and to get "the matter adjusted so that I may not hereafter be disturbed about it." His Richmond lawyer referred him to George W. Southall of Williamsburg—a sign of how small the world of slave traders and customers was in eastern Virginia. A couple years before, Southall had purchased a slave through Sidnum Grady, but that slave had run away from Southall's farm and headed back to his previous owner, and Southall had needed to offer a $30 reward for his return.[9]

Though Thomas Boudar still received slaves in New Orleans for other traders who shipped them down the coast, Tait's name gradually disappeared from the surviving manifests of shippers during the 1840s. He was either sending slaves by another route—in coffles overland or by rail—or relying on income from his investments and sales through the jail.

Boudar continued keeping an office in New Orleans as well as a home in Richmond, showing up twice in the 1850 census, once with his wife, children, and four slaves in Richmond, where he owned $500 of real estate. His occupation was listed as "none." A census taker counted him again in New Orleans as a "negro trader" along with his nephew James Dornin, also a negro trader, and fifty-one slaves, most of whom were young adult males presumably awaiting sale. Dornin also appeared twice in the 1850 census, once with Boudar in New Orleans and again as Tait's clerk in Richmond. Single and in his twenties, Dornin owned four slaves himself.

In the 1850 census, Tait was listed as a "trader" with $130,000 worth of real estate, by far the richest man in his neighborhood, which consisted mostly of mulattoes, blacks, and whites working as laborers or shopkeepers. He was still trying to collect the judgment from the Wilkinson and De Ende lawsuit. James Wilkinson, who had helped get the judgment, died in 1845. His widow married Nathaniel Hill, a slave auctioneer who helped administer Wilkinson's estate, and with Tait the only survivor of the original partnership, the collection pressed forward, Tait and Hill on one side, and De Ende's executor John L. Lewis and the heirs on the other.[10]

De Ende's illegitimate children received a few thousand dollars less than De Ende wanted, due to Louisiana laws, so Tait focused on the deeper pockets of De Ende's sisters, who received their own share plus some of the children's. Finally, in 1857, Tait and Wilkinson's estate received a total of $6,000 from De Ende's two living sisters and the estate of the third.[11]

Unlike Tait, Boudar continued to avoid the stigma and the milieu of a slave trader when in Richmond, living in a white neighborhood among prosperous businessmen. When the home where he lived was sold in December of 1850, the advertisement described it as a "valuable and desirably located private residence on the south side of Main street, between 1st and 2d streets, . . . among the most desirable in the city for genteel private residences." By the next summer he was living on Grace Street between Adams and Foushee, where he owned a home with a detached kitchen, worth $4,000. He would live there into the 1860s, when he purchased a farm near Hungary Station in Henrico County.[12]

The Next Generation

Boudar sent his sons to attend school at the College of the Holy Cross in Worcester, Massachusetts, and news soon came back of their achievements. Joseph won a premium in French, while Thomas Jr. earned an award in humanities in 1848. Thomas Jr. earned a silver cross of honor two years later, and both he and Henry Bacon Boudar received more awards the following spring.[13]

Tait's children, younger than Thomas's, were nearing the age when they could begin schooling, but in Virginia he could have no hope of them one day winning awards at a college. Celine, the oldest, was seven in 1850, and the twins turned five by the end of the year, but they could not legally attend school in Virginia, because "if any white person or persons shall assemble with any free negro or mulatto at any place whatsoever, for the purpose of instructing such free negroes or mulattoes to read or write, such white person or persons, shall on conviction thereof be held guilty of a misdemeanor." The punishment was a fine up to $50 and up to two months' imprisonment. If he sent them out of state for education, the law assumed they had emigrated and barred their return.[14]

By mid-century, Tait had achieved more than he had thought possible: he was partnered—if not married—to a woman who apparently loved him and they had a family of four children. He was financially successful, though still living modestly, and had gained as much respect among his peers as a slave trader could. We have no direct insight into what Courtney thought of her situation, but both she and Tait, in separate ways, may have felt that they had reached a plateau higher than they had once expected, but were in a situation where they could not rise much more. She had financial security, an apparently faithful husband, and a tie to him in the children he doted on, but in Virginia neither she nor her children would have the opportunities available to the rest of her family in New York State or Massachusetts. After a long struggle, Salem, Massachusetts, had begun offering racially integrated public schools in 1844.[15] In 1843 Massachusetts repealed its ban on interracial marriages. Though blacks were still socially limited, they had respect there unknown in Virginia.

Courtney undoubtedly pressed for a move to Salem, the specific location where her family was gathering. Tait was apparently amenable to trying out a better life for himself, where he could publicly acknowledge his family with pride and give his children a better chance at a future. Sidnum Grady, with Solomon Myers as an assistant, could operate the jail, and banks and lawyers could handle his other investments with only occasional supervision.

Preparing to Move

At the council's monthly meeting on August 11, 1851, "a letter was laid before the council from Bacon Tait stating that he expects to leave Richmond shortly, to be absent several months and being of opinion that he ought not to hold an office the duties of which he cannot attend to he therefore now resigns." The members then nominated and elected as his replacement auctioneer Nathaniel B. Hill, who had married the widow of Tait's old partner James Wilkinson.[16]

The resignation indicated that Tait planned only to be gone for a few months, not permanently, but over the next decade he split his time yearly between Salem and Richmond. His Salem lawyer later recalled that "though his business and residence were in Richmond, he was in the habit of spending some of his time here, especially in the spring months."[17] He had money to spend for the move, having just received $13,200 the previous October for selling a lot near his jail to the city. With apparently nothing to stand in his way, he and his family headed north.[18]

Into the Heart of Abolition Territory

What must have been a strange and delicate arrival can only be imagined. Tait left no personal papers to indicate how he was accepted in Salem, nor did anything about him appear in the newspapers. In fact, the absence of any information may hint that he deliberately kept his presence low-key. Antislavery people gave no evidence that they remembered the notice about his jail that they had mocked twenty years earlier, nor did they seem to connect him with the "negro sales" offered in the Richmond newspapers, which Grady kept advertising.

Equally unknown is how Courtney was welcomed by her family, considering her husband and the source of her significant wealth. But she and Tait must have integrated successfully, because the following summer Tait purchased a home. In city directories and to census takers, Tait identified himself simply as a merchant, though he did not hide the fact he was a southerner. His lawyer recalled that he openly acknowledged residing in Richmond.[19]

In the summer of 1851 the Taits could read an example in the Salem newspaper of how poorly things might have gone. Former Salem resident Caleb Jones had moved to Richmond in the 1840s to construct a woolen mill. When Salem abolitionist John Innis had helped Courtney's nephew come north, Jones "came to his assistance when he got into difficulty at Baltimore," but even such credentials were not enough to help Jones, now a pro-slavery southerner, when he visited Massachusetts in 1851. Innis invited him to an Essex County antislavery meeting in Danvers, five miles to the north of Salem.

Jones defended slavery in a mild, ten-minute speech to the gathered abolitionists, and "his manner was peculiarly pleasing, entirely devoid of excitement, and his whole appearance gave indication that he was a gentleman." But "during his brief remarks, he was many times coarsely interrupted, and when he had concluded, the house was in a delightful state of excitement; some half dozen were on the floor, and we had serious fears for the gentleman's safety. . . . Mr. Pillsbury made a comparison between their invited guest and a horse-thief, and brought the horse-thief out decidedly ahead. Mr. Garrison ran out the analogy between the same individual and a pirate; and in the parallel for crime the pirate was nowhere. 'Society,' said Mr. G., 'deems the pirate worthy of the gallows; if this be so, this person deserves a greater punishment.'" The next day, Jones "was personally addressed as the vilest of criminals, as a kidnapper, an adulterer, &c."[20]

Although Jones's fate is what one might have expected, Tait's experience shows that he could prevent slave trading from defining him in the North, even while it limited his social relations in the South. There is no record that he legally married Courtney in Massachusetts. Apparently he chose not to draw attention to their unmarried situation, instead presenting himself as her husband and the father of their children. Courtney's motivation for the move seems more obvious. Though still not treated equally to whites, free blacks received far more respect and freedom in Massachusetts, and besides enjoying a better life there, she could also be near relatives. But Tait also took advantage of life in the North. By avoiding mentioning his profession, he found the freedom to raise his family normally without the stigma of being a slave trader with an interracial family. The normalcy he enjoyed was something he had denied hundreds of enslaved blacks, but from his point of view it had also been denied him by the white women who would not associate with him.

He was not unique. Robert Lumpkin and Silas Omohundro also sent their mistresses to free states. A Philadelphian testified, concerning Omohundro, "I have met him and his wife [Corinna] and family in Philadelphia on different occasions; . . . [they] lived together as man and wife; . . . both in public and in private; they were looked upon and regarded as man and wife by those with whom they associated." Omohundro, like Tait, apparently had not made Corinna his legal wife. A judge said in a court ruling, "That [Omohundro] should call her his wife in [Pennsylvania] is not strange. He could not indulge in the practice of concubinage with her in this state, as he had done in Virginia, without subjecting himself to reproach, and perhaps to banishment."[21]

The home that Tait purchased in Salem was located at 29 Cedar Street in the growing area known as South Salem. He bought it from Mary H. Leach on July 6, 1852, for $2,100, and in 1859 he paid $57 for an additional three-foot-wide strip at the edge of the lot.[22] No longer would his children need to play on the city streets of Richmond or in the yard of a slave pen, nor would his wife have warehouses and a slave jail for a view. The home was on a 7,000-square-foot lot, much smaller than his Richmond property, but it was "very pleasantly located, being upon the brow of the hill facing the Mill Pond." The home was the last one on a quiet cul-de-sac, and Mary

Leach agreed to fence the property for him. The two-and-a-half-story house itself contained "thirteen finished rooms, with Gas and Water throughout," and was large enough for two families. Tait spared no expense in furnishing it with "Brussels Carpets, Three-Ply and Common [Carpets]; Mahogany Bedsteads; Mahogany Wardrobes; Marble Top Bureaus; Sofas; Stair Carpets; Parlor and Cook Stoves, &c. &c."[23]

Cedar Street, only a couple of blocks long, contained about two dozen homes and at that time was the last street in the neighborhood, with open fields beyond.[24] Most of the residents of the area were prosperous small-time business owners or tradesmen: a carpenter, a tanner, a shoemaker, a cooper. There were several black families also, including another interracial couple: Edward Cassell, mulatto, from Maryland, and his wife, Margaret, from Ireland. Cassell, just starting on a long and distinguished career as a caterer, lived with his brother, John, a barber, at 12 Cedar Street. The Cassells were family friends of the Fountains. They enlisted in the army together, lived near each other, and their sons probably went to Oregon together after the war. Though they were socially limited to trades deemed appropriate for their race, they had experiences not available to free blacks in Virginia. Edward Cassell was the caterer in 1856 for a rollicking antislavery "Freedom Celebration" led by John A. Innis that was "nothing more nor less than an amalgamation frolic" with "all colors and classes being represented."[25] Six homes down from Tait, on the same side, at 13 Cedar Street, the white Roberts family lived. The daughter, Adeline Roberts, was a teacher and corresponding secretary for the Salem Female Anti-Slavery Society. She regularly corresponded with William Lloyd Garrison, Lucretia Mott, Ralph Waldo Emerson, William Wells Brown, and other abolitionists, inviting antislavery speakers to Salem.[26] Socializing or conducting business in Salem was difficult without running into antislavery connections. Tait was far out of his element.

A Tale of Two Cities

With his wife and children settled in Massachusetts, Tait took care of business in Richmond, traveling there every few months and occasionally visiting New Orleans. Boudar's son Thomas Jr. continued to excel in school, winning a premium in logic on June 29, 1853, at Mount St. Mary's College in Emmitsburg, Maryland, where he was now studying, but by September 3 he passed away at the young age of eighteen. His parents laid him to rest in Richmond's Hollywood Cemetery, in the family lot where they would one day be buried also.[27] Thomas Sr. had never become a U.S. citizen, but on December 12, 1853, he remedied that, renouncing his Spanish citizenship in New Orleans. Tait, presumably in the city on business, served as one of the witnesses, along with an old Lynchburg acquaintance, John D. Murrell.[28]

Though Solomon Myers left Tait's employ within a few years, Sidnum Grady continued loyally managing the jail and promoting sales. In 1852 he was "clerk and manager at Tait's jail," according to the city directory, but living at Terry's Boarding House. With Tait spending much of the year in Salem, the jail needed a full-time manager on-site, so Grady moved in. By 1856 the city directory listed it as the "Cary Street Jail," a name it would continue to have through the end of the Civil War, though the directory still listed Bacon Tait by name at the corner of Fifteenth and Cary.[29]

The jail earned income in two ways, by confining slaves for others, either for convenience or punishment, and by selling, either on commission or from stock owned by the jail. An example of the first was a September 4, 1854, order by Samuel Mordicai, who apparently was dealing with a recalcitrant slave: "Mr. Grady will please discharge John Vaughn, if he promises to go home."[30] Some runaway ads specified what jail the owner wanted his captured runaway confined in, such as an ad Thomas Boudar ran for nineteen-year-old Milly Hill, who ran away from him in December of 1853. He offered a reward of $50 "for her delivery at Cary Street Jail, or lodged in any other Jail, so that I get her."[31] An example of the second way of earning money was the $7.50 commission Grady received for the sale of Martha and her son, Edward, in January 1854 for $650. Joseph Reid Anderson, director of the Tredegar Iron Works, purchased them from the Byrd George heirs. The usual warranty for health was amended: "except that Martha has asthma & therefore she is not warranted either sound or healthy."[32] The usual commission was $5, which included young children with their mothers, but the extra $2.50 may have been for Martha's partially grown son.

Though such transactions were the jail's ordinary source of income, they could be rare personal decisions agonized over by the other participants.

In 1858, storekeeper Mann S. Valentine discovered his slave Washington Winston stealing merchandise and passing it to a free black woman to sell. She was sentenced to be whipped by the court, while Valentine sold Winston south. He paid for Winston to spend a month in Tait's jail and a $5 commission to Grady for the sale. The decision was not easy for Valentine, though, because he had trusted Winston. Discovery of the theft had "come upon me like an attack of life destroying paralysis from which there is no escaping," he wrote, expressing concern for the effect on Winston's mother, China, who had "raised and watched over the existence and wants of every child we have had."[33]

The Cary Street Jail relentlessly transformed such emotionally difficult circumstances into dollars and cents. Not all sales went well. The business of Sneed, Chewning, and Strange of Albemarle County purchased a man named John from "Mr. Grady, trader of Richmond, Va., who sold him for Mr. Ballentine, of Currituck C. H., North Carolina" in March of 1857. Thomas Ballentine had come from North Carolina a few years before and was noted for running one of the best-conducted farms outside of Norfolk. Sneed, Chewning, and Strange put John to work on their farm in nearby Fluvanna County, but a month later they were offering a $50 reward for his return. Apparently he preferred life near Norfolk. "He was seen the day after he left us on the James River Canal, some thirty miles above Richmond, and is probably making his way to the region of country from which he came."[34]

The Valentine, Mordicai, and Sneed transactions show the complexity of what appears on the surface to be a simple business. Mann Valentine complained that he felt pressured by society to deal with Winston as he did. Indeed, there were two conflicting attitudes. Whites could view blacks overall as a mass of people—or even property—to be managed and controlled, but as they dealt one-on-one with blacks, they could not help but take into account their humanity. Society saw Winston as a thief and potential fomenter of insurrection, but Valentine recognized him as a person he had once trusted and the son of someone he knew. Samuel Mordicai accepted that his slave John Vaughn could make a promise to return home and be expected to keep it. The individual who placed the ad for Sneed, Chewning, and Strange realized that John was motivated to return to his former home. Such recognition of humanity did not translate into different treatment for most blacks but it is notable in itself, despite legal and social pressure otherwise.

Late in 1854, Grady began a third money-making enterprise, moving into the lucrative slave-hiring market. He advertised in the *Richmond Whig*: "Negro Hiring.—The subscriber proposes to hire out negroes for others the following year upon the usual terms. He will also continue to sell negroes at private sale as heretofore.—Charge for selling, $5 per head, including small child with the mother." He included a substantial list of references from Richmond and the surrounding counties and mentioned that those wanting to hire slaves could call at his office in "Bacon Tait's Jail near Mayo's Bridge."[35]

Quiet Life in Salem

All of Tait's money came from his southern investments. There is no evidence he invested in real estate or local businesses in Massachusetts, or that he ran for council or gained social influence. In Richmond, he had become trapped by the world that whites like himself had made, unable to acknowledge Courtney as his wife or share public pride in his children. Life in Salem gave him freedom to become a normal husband and father, but with a price: he had to live quietly, keeping secret the truth of his Richmond identity for fear of being ostracized, unable to openly join in white society. The only option for outing himself would be to make a public display renouncing his former advocation of slavery, but that was more than he was willing to do. By traveling between Salem and Richmond, he could have the influence of a businessman and the respect of a husband and father, but not at the same time or in the same place.

The 1855 Massachusetts census taker apparently stopped by the house when Tait was away and spoke to Courtney, or perhaps to the John Fountain who was living in the household at the time. John may have been Courtney's brother, who died two years later of paralysis, and she may have been caring for him. The census taker could see the race of whoever he spoke to, so he did not bother to ask the race of the head of household. He marked "Bacon Taite" and everyone else in the household mulatto.

The census worker may not have even seen the children, because he misreported Josephine as a male named Josephus. Had he seen them alone, without their mother or uncle, he might have thought them white. When Josephine grew to be a young adult, she would be described as having blue eyes, a straight nose, a small mouth, and a fair complexion. Her older brother, Bacon C., had a dark complexion but hazel eyes.[36] In 1855, Celine, the oldest, was twelve, followed by the twins Bacon C. and Constance, nine, and Josephine, seven. Ten years later, the census would reveal their nicknames to be Lena, Bacon, Connie, and Josie and would indicate that their mulatto mother and white father were married—or at least presenting themselves as married.

Tait had friends in Richmond, but as always, they were business colleagues first. Charles W. Purcell, banker and broker, named his third son Bacon Tait Purcell, though Tait outlived the young namesake. The boy drowned at eight years old while learning to swim in 1863.[37] Solomon Myers would move on from being an assistant at the jail to becoming a partner with Albert F. Jahnke, a Prussian jewelry maker. They opened the Myers and Jahnke Jewelry Store on Main Street by the mid-1850s. Tait would remain friends with both throughout his life, eventually dying at Myers's home. Purcell served as one of his executors.[38] But nothing in Richmond offered the affection and pride of his own family.

Chapter 11

THE INEXORABLE JAILOR

In 1860, Tait's name no longer appeared in the Virginia census, nor did he own any people in the slave census. Only the Massachusetts census listed his name. There is little indication that Courtney influenced him enough for him to renounce slave ownership on moral grounds, but there is no record he owned any personal slaves after 1858. The last enslaved man he personally owned, at least based on surviving records, was Henry Banks, a twenty-two-year-old, five-foot-eight mulatto. On October 11, 1858, Tait filed a deed of emancipation for him, giving the reason as "good conduct."[1] It is the only emancipation by Tait that has been found.

A rare description of Banks, as well as Tait's jail and possibly Sidnum Grady, comes from George Teamoh, a man who escaped slavery to Boston. Teamoh and his wife, Sallie, were sold apart, and during one transaction circa 1854, when Henry Banks would have been about eighteen, "she was, on landing of the Richmond boat put in jail at Rockets, not very far from the boat landing." Tait's jail at Shockoe Bottom was a mile or two farther up the James River from Rocketts, but it was also not far from the boat landing compared to all the other slave jails, so Teamoh or his wife easily could have believed she was at Rocketts when she was actually at Shockoe Bottom. Teamoh wrote:

> In this jail was a young man named Henry Banks. . . . He was the jail wagoner, and had considerably to do by way of keeping the slaves orderly &c. His duties were similar to those of [George] Cooper's [the enslaved "whipping master" at Solomon Davis's jail]. Banks, like Cooper did what ever he could to relieve the distressed, and

was highly esteemed by those who know him best. And while it is true that the majority of these colored men, who were stationed as Cooper and Banks, would far exceed their masters in punishing the slaves, these two may be regarded as exceptions; at least in [Sallie's] case. Grief for her children, the cruel tretment [sic] of the Lindsay's [her owners] added to the prison life she was then under going had now reduced her to a mere frame of human bones. Patrons of the auction block swore it to be shameful, that one, so like themselves—complexionally—should even be allowed to stand the usual examination to which females were put in these prison houses of despair. In deed such was her debilitated condition that she could do but little else than looking after her child.

Teamoh then described the jailor, who might have been Tait, but was more likely Sidnum Grady handling the day-to-day sales:

While in this feeble and emaciated condition, the inexorable jailor ordered her, on pain of being lashed, to rise, and like a gymnast, play the part of active health if she had it not. On her [k]nees she besought him to excuse her from being mustered out in common with others at muscular exercise. She informed him of her sufferings, past and present, with which he said he had nothing to do. The friendly Banks now interposes, and through his influence she is released from the shameful exposure. I shall not attempt to discribe [sic] the character, or manner of these examinations and exposures; humanity revolts, the soul sickens, and indeed the whole moral sense of our nature seems to loose its proper channel on contemplating the demon dens where respectable ladies were stripped to be put on exhibition for the speculators in the trafic [sic] . . . While thus undergoing the combined punishments of incarceration, mental and physical infirmities, having also a helpless child to care for, Sallie was again called upon to make a show of good health. In deed, this time she was given the sum of Ten Dollars as an encouragement to the performance of sound health and mind. While the object sought by the Lindsays [her former owners], as stated, was to send her to the "ends of wind and water," that of the speculator was to sell her any where at the greatest profit. . . .

In the midst of her anguish, both mental and physical, her old employer, Rosenfeld made his appearance at the jail, he having previous knowledge of her being again exposed for sale. By their way of doing business under cover of secrecicy [sic], this time, instead of hiring, she was sold to R. by what is termed a private sale.[2]

The description fits Grady's emphasis on private sales at the time, and is a rare glimpse of an enslaved person's view of such sales from Tait's jail. As whites needed sympathetic blacks to act as liaisons between the races, blacks also found they could use the sympathies of someone like Henry Banks. Teamoh mentions Cooper at Davis's jail, who was similar, and Anthony Burns described the kindness of Robert Lumpkin's "yellow" wife at Lumpkin's jail.[3]

Henry Banks seems to have found a neutral position between the races, earning his owner's respect for his "good conduct" while advocating kindness for other enslaved people. The payment of ten dollars to Sallie would be an exorbitant amount, if Grady was selling her on a five-dollar commission. If charged as an expense to the owner, it would be probably the largest single itemized amount. If Grady or Tait had purchased her on speculation, as Teamoh implied, Grady may have judged that such a bribe would raise her value by more than its cost, if she complied. After manumission in October 1858, Banks would have been required to leave the state within a year, but he apparently remained, unofficially. In 1861 he finally applied to stay in Virginia. His petition was granted.[4]

Antislavery Sentiment in Salem

Tait and his family could keep up with the news from Richmond by reading the Massachusetts papers. The editor of the *Salem Register* subscribed to the *Richmond Dispatch* and reprinted selected articles, as many northern papers did, generally to show the evilness of the southerners. On August 4, 1856, after endorsing John C. Frémont and the antislavery Republican party in the presidential election, the Salem paper included good news for

Tait, showing the long slump of the 1840s was over, though it may have dismayed most of Salem's residents: "High Price for Slaves. There has been a greater demand for slaves in this city during the months of May, June and July, than ever known before, and they have commanded better prices during that time. This latter is an unusual thing, as the summer months are generally the dullest in the year for the description of property . . . probably there is not less than $1,000,000 in town now seeking investment in such property.—*Richmond Dispatch.*"

An article in the May 1, 1852, *Salem Observer* described "A Negro Sale" in Richmond, which must have been a curiosity to most readers, though a familiar scene to Tait. Garrison's *Liberator,* published in Boston, even included a familiar name. Decrying how people were sold as livestock, the *Liberator* published a series of advertisements from the *Richmond Enquirer,* including one by owner C. T. Baylor offering a $100 reward if a man named George was "delivered to me in Petersburg, or to Mr. Sidnum Grady, in Richmond."[5]

The *Liberator* also published correspondence from abolitionist journalist James Redpath, who was traveling in the South. In Richmond he talked to an anonymous former slave who explained "how our people are persecuted here, only on account of their color." He listed a series of grievances that the Fountains and Courtney Tait must have been familiar with, and that even Tait realized his children would face if they were raised in Virginia. The complaints were:

"The oath of a colored man, whether free or a slave, is not admissable at courts of justice." A black man could therefore not use the court to collect business debts or to punish shoplifters, and was always vulnerable to extortion by a white man who might make a false complaint and "have the unfortunate object of his malice whipped by the public officers."

"Although free men of color pay all the municipal taxes levied on the white citizens, they are prohibited not only from exercising any influence in elections, but from entering the public square or the cemetery!"

They could not carry weapons, nor could they go abroad after sunset without free papers, or have assemblages of more than five people. "If they are free, but without friends to attend to their interests . . . they are kept in jail for a certain period, and then (God help them!) are sold into slavery to pay for the expense incurred by keeping them incarcerated!"

With a wife and three daughters, Tait would have known: "Women of color are compelled to endure every species of insult. White boys often spit on their dresses as they are going to chapel; and if they meet a colored female out of doors after sunset, they act still more grossly."[6]

Yet even in the Salem newspapers stereotypes of blacks still reigned. While condemning the South's treatment of blacks, the Salem papers posted jokes hinging on the same clichés as in the slave states: "'Say, Pomp, whar you get that new hat?' 'Why, at the shop, of course.' 'What is de price ob such an article as dat?' 'I don't know nigger; *de shop-keeper wasn't dar.*'" The papers announced blackface minstrel shows, though the Alabama Slave Minstrels who came through in 1857 needed no disguise, as they were advertised as *"real negroes, fresh from the plantation,"* who claimed to be "raising money to purchase their freedom—or rather to indemnify their benefactor, who has entered bonds for the payment of the price of their liberty."[7]

But the papers and the community were solidly against slavery and the way it affected them most directly: the Fugitive Slave Act. In 1854, the recapture of fugitive Anthony Burns in Boston raised feelings against slave catchers to a fever pitch. A Salem law student and son of a prominent merchant, Albert G. Browne, was arrested as part of the violent mob. Not many details filtered north at the time about Anthony Burns's experience while jailed in Richmond, but two years later, when Charles Emery Stevens's book about Burns came out, one of the sellers was H. Whipple and Sons in Salem, half a mile from the Taits' home. In the book, residents could read about Burns's imprisonment in the jail of "Robert Lumpkin, a noted trader in slaves. This man belonged to a class of persons by whose society the slaveholders of the South profess to feel disgraced, but with whose services, nevertheless, they cannot dispense." The jail was in fact the first that Tait had built, though no one in Salem would have known that outside his family.[8] Tait was fortunate that Burns had not been taken to the Cary Street Jail.

Two years later, in 1856, more antislavery excitement arose in Salem specifically. A foreigner was arrested in South Salem in a vacant building perhaps half a mile from Tait's house. He gave a garbled story of being a slave trader from Cuba who had buried kegs of coins in the sand. Soon an accomplice from Boston was arrested as well. Officials wavered between believing that the man they had first arrested was either lying or insane, or that he had indeed been connected with transporting slaves into Cuba and had scuttled a ship off Cape Cod. But during the few weeks that officials were desperately seeking information, none apparently realized a genuine interstate slave trader, who might have been able to advise with information on the illegal southern slave market, was living nearby.[9]

Business as Usual in Richmond

Despite the continual outrage in Massachusetts, when Tait returned to Richmond he saw a city steeped in the tradition of slave trading, running as it always had, training a new generation to accept the norm. A visiting foreigner described entering an empty auction room in 1853 Richmond and seeing "nobody in it but three negro children, who, as I entered, were playing at auctioning each other. An intensely black little negro, of four or five years of age, was standing on the bench, or block, as it is called, with an equally black girl, about a year younger, by his side, whom he was pretending to sell by bids to another black child, who was rolling about the floor . . . 'Fifty dolla for de gal—fifty dolla—fifty dolla—I sell dis here fine gal for fifty-dolla,' was uttered with extraordinary volubility by the woolly-headed urchin, accompanied with appropriate gestures, in imitation, doubtless, of the scenes he had seen enacted daily on the spot."[10]

There was discontent, as there had always been. Thomas Boudar's nineteen-year-old slave Milly Hill ran off on December 28, 1853.[11] Sidnum Grady supervised whipping for pay at the jail when owners requested it. The mayor's court heard cases regularly of blacks using insolent language, or worse, toward whites. In 1854, the *Richmond Whig* reprinted an article from nearby Norfolk, pinpointing the problem. "The practice of stealing our slave property is daily increasing. It is now almost a daily occurrence for negroes to escape to the North.—On Tuesday night three more, the property of Mr. Camp, Mr. Dalrymple and Mr. Crowder, editor of the Argus, made their escape. We have urged and urged upon our citizens the precaution of proper vigilance, and the necessity of immediate action in regard to ferreting out the men and means by which our slaves are enticed away."[12] The article praised the citizens of Portsmouth, Virginia, who had established a committee of men who were "determined, regardless of expense or time or means, to bring these abolition thieves to justice."

White southerners may have felt more comfortable blaming abolitionists in general for making their slaves discontent, but specific advertisers recognized other natural motivations. James A. Fore offered a reward if his George was delivered to the Cary Street Jail. "He has a mother in Southampton and a brother in Petersburg, where, I have no doubt, he must be lurking about either one place or the other."[13]

Tait continued investing in real estate, traveling between Massachusetts and Richmond. In 1858, as the city spread, he and others offered "150 building lots in Cullingsworth's Plan, Union Hill, at auction, adjoining Fairfield Race Course." At the edge of the city, they were "lots for building or gardening."[14]

Though Tait had complained of being poor and lived frugally most of his life, he was doing very well. In the winter of 1856–57, he stayed in New York City at the St. Nicholas Hotel, by far the city's finest. It fronted on Broadway, covering one and three-quarter acres, with six hundred rooms, "all well lighted, and provided with hot and cold water," and some had baths and water-closets attached. The white marble building had its own fire department and produced its own gas.[15] He apparently traveled regularly through New York between Salem and Richmond, because the summer before, he had not picked up some mail addressed to him in New York.[16]

His stay that winter was marred by an incident that showed the amount of money he managed. Someone broke into his trunk and stole two notes worth over $12,000 total. They were "drawn by Robert Edmonds to the order of Isaac Davenport, Jun." and endorsed by Davenport and Tait. Isaac Davenport had prospered in the years since 1829, when his uncle by the same name had brought him down from Maine to help with the auction house beside Tait's jail. He partnered with Edmonds, who had come from Vermont to assist an uncle in the stagecoach business. Besides dealing in wholesale groceries, Davenport and Edmonds founded the James River Packet Company, which ran canal boats up to Lynchburg and beyond as well as connecting with stagecoaches. Their biggest moneymaker was a line of barks running from Richmond to South America, taking down flour and cotton and bringing back coffee and sugar. Like Tait, Davenport supported the Richmond and Danville Railroad.[17]

Though Tait lived in Salem only part of the year, there is evidence he was considered a regular resident at the house at the end of Cedar Street, or at least his name was well known as the head of household. He was listed in each Massachusetts five-year census and in the city directories. On November 17, 1859, the local newspaper reported an incident at his house, noting he not only owned it but occupied it: "At a few minutes before 8 o'clock on Monday evening, a fire broke out in the shed connected with the house owned and occupied by Mr. Bacon Tait, at the foot of Cedar street, South Salem. It was soon extinguished, but not till the shed was consumed, and a part of the house occupied by George Farley and owned by Thomas H. Florence, very badly burned. The fire was discovered by Mr. Hamilton who was eeling at the mill-pond." George G. Farley, a cooper born in New Hampshire, was listed next to Tait's family in the 1860 census.

The Taits had settled into a comfortable life in Salem. By 1860, Courtney benefited from an Irish washerwoman, Mary Hodges, age thirty-six, who lived in the household to help with chores.[18] The children were growing up. Celine, the oldest, was seventeen. The twins Bacon C. and Constance were fifteen, and Josephine was twelve. Though there is frustratingly little evidence for the details of Tait's relationship with his family in the 1850s, there is some indication (based on subsequent events) that he doted on the children as they grew up, but that his attention to Courtney waned.

Chapter 12

STATING HE WOULD DIE OF STARVATION

Tait's children, becoming teenagers in the 1860s, were light-skinned enough to appear white, if seen with their father rather than their mother and her relatives. Tait had despaired of a normal marriage to a respectable white woman and instead compromised by choosing Courtney, but a new aspiration now seemed within his grasp. He might be the father of a family of educated, refined white children whom any Virginia sire could be proud of. From what little information is available, in the 1860s his focus seemed to shift more toward being a father to his children than a husband to his wife.

Constance Rosalie—Connie—turned fourteen in December of 1859. Tait paid for her to attend the Spingler Institute in New York City that winter. Called the Abbot Collegiate Institute for Young Ladies before and after it occupied the Spingler building, it was founded by Reverend Gorham D. Abbott of Maine and was attended by refined young ladies from white families both north and south. The year Constance attended, the institute was expanding into the Townsend House at the corner of Fifth Avenue and Thirty-Fourth Street, in addition to the Spingler building on Union Square.

The cost for the collegiate department and board ranged up to $500, plus extras for special studies. The institute advertised: "There is an increasing number of Young Ladies in different parts of the country, whose parents are seeking for them the benefits of a few years of study and instruction in the city of New York. . . . The elevated course of study, the occasional Literary and Scientific Lectures, Musical Concerts of high character, exhibitions of the Fine Arts, and the numerous objects of interest in the city and vicinity, present facilities for expanding the mind, gaining a knowledge of the world, and improving the taste, which are unrivaled in our country."

For whatever reason, Constance attended only one year and thus failed to graduate the two-year course. In the list of young ladies attending, she appeared as Tait, Constance R., of Richmond, Va., though she most likely never lived there. The listing was similar to her sister's at another seminary a few years later, which specified "daughter of Bacon Tait, Richmond, Va."

Tait was claiming the daughters as his own white children. He had seen at the start of his career how Henry De Ende transformed his children from illegitimate mulattoes to refined white young men and women, and now Tait was taking the opportunity to do the same. As he owned the black children of other families, categorizing them as field hands or fancy girls, he now took ownership of Courtney's children, raising them above the status of brave mulattoes demanding equality, such as Charlotte Forten in Salem, and instead recategorizing them as white. He could enroll Constance and later Josephine in schools far from home without mentioning their race, and they would come out educated with the manners and knowledge of any young white ladies. The role was easier for them, and easier for him as well, because it allowed him to integrate them into society's white upper class without needing to become an advocate for racial opportunity or equality.[1]

Elsewhere, Richmond jailers Lumpkin, Omohundro, and Davis were trying to do the same with their light-skinned children. Much of the vast profits of Richmond's slave-trading industry was going not only to benefit white men, as might be expected, but to educate and elevate women and children of color. A very few people of color were becoming well-to-do on the backs of the many. A quote from a correspondent to the *Wheeling (Va.) Intelligencer,* published in the *Salem Register* on January 23, 1860, showed how fine the line was between black and white. Tait and others could be assured that training in good behavior and manners, as much as appearance, was the key to turning their light-skinned children white. On the Orange and Alexandria Railroad outside of Washington, the correspondent

found a negro trader, with half a dozen sons and daughters of the descendants of Ham, whom he had purchased in the State of Maryland, and was on his way with them to the New Orleans market. I was particularly struck by the beauty of a white girl about 17 years of age, whom I was surprised to see sitting beside the negroes; but I concluded that she must be the young and handsome daughter of the trader. I sat myself down beside the stove, smoking my cigar, and took a position where I could see and admire the mingled white and rosy transparent complexion, and the finely chiseled features of the young girl, with her lips like two rose buds, her eyes liquid in their brightness, and her auburn tresses, that Love himself might delight to nestle in . . . when all at once a coarse negro laugh broke out from beneath those pearly teeth and those rose bud lips—called forth by some remark made to her by the swarthy black at her side. That laugh, and that voice of hers, alone betrayed her negro descent—for a negro she was, and a slave, too.

Tait's daughters evidently were just that attractive. His lawyer wrote, "He was apparently very fond of his children, especially of his daughters, and seemed to be, as he well might be, proud of their beauty and accomplishments."[2]

Excitement at a Party

Though the academic year ran from September to June, Constance apparently came home to visit sometime around Christmas or New Year's. She and her sister "had been spending the evening at a neighbors, at a small party of young folks." When the evening concluded, Tait went to escort them home. At the party also was James F. Haley, about twenty-one years old, who lived with his father, master carpenter Shillaber Haley, at 23½ Harbor Street, about four blocks from Tait's. While picking up his daughters, Tait was "offended at some sort of familiarity shewn by Haley to one of the daughters (Miss Constance I think)," according to his lawyer.

Haley was a strapping young sailor who would save a man's life a few years later after almost three hours of powerful rowing at sea. Tait was in his sixties and had never engaged in hard labor. Yet, despite his physical disadvantage, Tait's hot southern blood overcame him and he struck Haley in retaliation. Haley reacted in a way that fit the stereotype of a mercenary, litigious Yankee. Rather than fighting back, he sued for assault.

Tait consulted local lawyer Stephen Bradshaw Ives Jr., a Salem native related to Lucy Gardner Ives, the longtime president of the Salem Female Anti-Slavery Society. Such antislavery connections were almost unavoidable among Salem's leading citizens. By now, Tait apparently had become comfortable treading a line between honesty and concealment. For several years before Ives met him in 1860, Ives "had known by general reputation that a gentleman by that name had a family in that part of the city known as South Salem" though his business was in Richmond. Ives recalled their meetings: "He came with two young ladies, whom he introduced to me as his daughters—one of them was Miss Constance R. Tait:—the other, who was I think older than Miss Constance, I forget the name of, if I ever knew it. . . . I saw him frequently on the subject. The suit was pending for a considerable time, during which he returned to Richmond, & again came to Salem, I think more than once but am not sure. . . . In the conversations, he spoke of himself as residing in Richmond, an account of himself, and of his wife & family who lived in Salem. He always spoke of them as gentlemen ordinarily speak of their family. . . . Mrs. Tait I never saw." A year later, Tait finally settled the suit by agreeing to pay "some small sum as costs" to Haley. He sent his son, Bacon C., now fifteen years old, to deliver a check to Ives, who recalled that the check was from a Richmond bank.

All the while, "the crisis between the North & the South" that Tait had spoken of in an 1840 letter to Rice C. Ballard was impending. Chief Justice Taney, whom Tait had feared would ally with antislavery forces, still sat on the Supreme Court and had been a staunch supporter of the rights of slave owners. But the "dissolution of the Union" that Tait had predicted was now about to happen. In February 1861, Virginia had not yet seceded, but interstate communications would become more difficult soon. Though Celine was his oldest daughter at almost seventeen, Tait trusted Constance more. She served as his "financial agent" and "kept a bank account in her own name of the funds received" from her father.[3]

Dividing His Estate

Inspired perhaps by the death of Thomas Boudar's mother four months earlier, or perhaps by the looming crisis of secession, Tait took the time to write his will while he was in Richmond in March of 1861. He appointed Boudar and John G. Williams, a local lawyer who had handled other estates, as his executors. He divided his significant estate unevenly. To his youngest and oldest daughters, Celine and Josephine, he left $2,000 each, to be paid when they married or reached age twenty-one, whichever came first, as well as $300 a year until that time. To the twins, Constance and Bacon C., he left the rest of his estate, divided evenly, perhaps over $100,000 for each. He left it in trust until they turned twenty-one, with the income used to pay their "maintenance and education" until then. He stated no relationship to the children, merely listing their birth dates for reference.[4]

To Courtney he left nothing, nor was he legally obligated to, despite the longstanding law and tradition of the widow's third. Marriage to her was illegal in Virginia, and in Massachusetts, though he had openly claimed her as his wife for almost a decade, there was no provision for a common law marriage and he had never officially wed her. One could interpret the will as his cold assessment of which persons meant the most to him, Courtney now being merely the means to the end of producing the children he doted on, and the children divided into the best and the common ones.

One could also speculate that Tait tried to deal with the situation as discreetly and simply as possible, expecting that Constance would be experienced at handling money and therefore could care for her mother and siblings with her balance of the estate, while Bacon C. could use his share to continue the Tait fortune. Or it could be that Tait wanted to avoid leaving money directly to Courtney because of the possibility that she would pass some of it on to her family and further the Underground Railroad or similar activities. It is also possible that he passed his estate directly to his offspring in the hopes of avoiding legal challenges that might be harder for Courtney to defend.

In Richmond

Sidnum Grady continued to manage the jail. Tait had been absent so long that many people had forgotten his connection to it and now often called it Grady's Jail, though Grady himself, cognizant of the owner, usually identified it as the Cary Street Jail. Many owners of runaways advertised specifically that they would pay if their slave was taken there. Grady promoted private sales as well as hiring, advertising "a good Female Cook, without encumbrance" and "a No. 1 Carpenter" for sale, or for hire "A good Cook, Washer and Ironer, with one child; also, a good House Girl." There were bargains: "A middle aged Negro Woman; will be sold cheap." But when the merchandise was of high quality, he did not fail to note it: "For Hire—To the last of March, 1862, a genteel woman, some twenty odd years of age, of good manners and disposition, a general house servant, cook, washer, ironer, and seamstress. She has two likely children, one three and the other seven years old. The younger the least trouble of any child I ever saw." He apparently acquiesced to owners' desires not to sell slaves out of state, offering: "To remain in or near Richmond, a fair sized pretty good looking man, (Farm hand and Driver) 42 years old." But Grady was honest about the condition of the wares: "To remain in or near Richmond, a Cheap old Man, who has been accustomed to working in a garden, and is a good hostler."[5]

The abolitionist newspapers that circulated freely in Salem were received differently in Tait's other hometown. In Richmond, "a middle-aged negro fellow, owned by Mr. Wm. Barrett, tobacconist," was accused of being in possession of "an Abolition tract, or newspaper" on March 30, 1861. Confronted, he was unable to give "a satisfactory answer as to how it came in his possession," so Barrett's overseer, Humphrey Miles, tried to take him to the Cary Street Jail for punishment: "I started with the man to Grady's Jail; on the way he suddenly turned and tripped me; he then drew his knife, when I knocked him down." The newspaper reported that the overseer "succeeded in planting a lick on the mutinous darkey's nose, and repeating the blow on the sconce with his stick, succeeded in effectually subduing the evil intentions of the negro, who was carried to jail with a very uncomfortable sensation about the nose and head." In the end, the overseer announced, "There were no abolition documents taken from him; neither had he any, that I was aware of."[6] The man had suffered on mere suspicion of owning abolitionist opinions. White southerners had complained for years about such tracts being sent down from the free states. In its declaration of secession, South Carolina stated that slaves "have been incited by emissaries, books and pictures to servile insurrection," and though Virginia had not yet voted to secede, its interest in keeping its enslaved people controlled was the same as that of the other states of the Confederacy that it would soon join.

Grady had been doing well enough as a trusted manager. He listed a personal estate of $9,170 in the 1860 census, which included a twenty-three-year-old male slave. Thomas Boudar was also succeeding, claiming the occupation of "gentleman" and $2,500 in real estate plus $10,000 in personal property. Though Tait was listed in the Massachusetts census of 1860, which did not include property valuation, his holdings probably dwarfed both of theirs, because by 1870 he would be listed as worth $100,000 in the census, and one estimate of his estate was $250,000.

Tait had continued his friendship with his former salesman at the jail, Solomon A. Myers, who had worked for him in the early 1850s but had soon gone on to partner in a jewelry store with Prussian immigrant Albert Franz Jahnke. As a newspaper summarized later: "Mr. Tait became prepossessed with Myers, took him into his confidence, and was very profuse in acts of friendship towards him; gave the latter a start in business, and he, too, soon began to amass wealth."[7]

Myers did not amass wealth immediately. In the 1860 city directory he was listed as a "watch maker, jeweller and optician" at the corner of Pearl or Fourteenth and Main Streets, though Jahnke had probably brought most of the skills into the business. Myers was single and still not settled. He boarded at the Exchange Hotel in that directory, though in the 1860 census he was listed as living with wealthy merchant James Dunlap. Jahnke was the richer of the two partners at the time, worth $18,000 in real and personal property compared to Myers's $1,000 in the census, but Myers was set to prosper from the war, probably with some investment help from Tait.

Before the war, in February of 1860, Myers was advertising watches, shirt buttons, diamond rings, silver spoons, and all the usual items of a jewelry store. But when war came, he recognized the sudden demand for military brass buttons and switched to focusing on them. The *Richmond Dispatch* actually announced the shortage and indicated it was a want that might be filled profitably: "A correspondent, writing from camp near Norfolk, asks whether there is a button manufactory in any of the Southern States, where a military button might be made by the quantity. We are unable to furnish the information desired."[8]

From the same location at Main and Pearl, the following year Myers advertised "MILITARY BUTTONS. I have on hand a large supply of Virginia and North Carolina BUTTONS, of my own manufacture." By 1862 he had expanded into making "TENTS! TENTS! TENTS! Constantly on hand a large supply of wall and A tents, and will contract for any number to be made at short notice." The business also gave him the advantage of an exemption from the draft, due to being a manufacturer of "munitions of war."[9]

Myers not only profited legitimately from tent making. He also tried a scam where he contracted for North Carolina duck canvas for tents, but instead used cheaper Richmond osnaburg. When charged with the substitution, he admitted it, "but insisted that no harm was done to the interests of the state," and North Carolina quartermaster Lawrence O'Bryan Branch agreed. Such accusations left him unaffected.[10]

Rather than staying at the jail when he came to Richmond, "Mr. Tait retired from business, in order to enjoy, in a quiet way, the immense fortune he had amassed. Age coming upon him apace, he took up his abode with Mr. Myers . . . who then resided at the corner of Main and Fourteenth streets, in which was a jewelry store. . . . In this house Mr. Tait was assigned a room, where he lodged, but took his meals at the Exchange Hotel."[11]

Wartime Richmond bustled with activity, although most of it was managed by younger men like forty-one-year-old Myers.[12] Tait, sixty-five in 1861, was well positioned to continue making money more passively, not only from his jail but by renting out his extensive real estate investments, now the major source of his income. Most of his income came from individuals or businesses, but the Confederate Army quartermaster paid him $25 a month to rent a lot for a wheelwright's shop in 1862, and he received about $16.25 per quarter in rent from a lot at Howard's Grove for a military hospital.

Losing Henry Dishman

Alexandria, Virginia, fell to the Union in 1861, and with it George Kephart's slave jail. But in Richmond, safe for now from the Federal army, jails continued their business unmolested. Sidnum Grady received $2.50 on August 17, 1862, from Dr. W. H. Coffin for "having negro men Warren & Edward flogged"—$2 for the flogging and 50 cents for receiving and releasing them at the jail.

Fifty-six-year-old Dr. Coffin, proud and quick to take offense, was in charge of General Hospital no. 9 in the old Seabrook tobacco factory at Grace and Seventeenth Streets, about four blocks from the jail. In 1862 the receiving hospital took in hundreds, then thousands of patients a month, sending most on to other facilities in the area. Slaves were used as servants and for menial care, but in the bustle of activity mix-ups occurred. Henry Dishman, the slave of a Mr. Davis, was caught by Ward Master Notting stealing money from a patient at Dr. Coffin's hospital. Notting put Dishman in the Cary Street Jail on July 26, 1862, without informing anyone. Notting was then transferred to the army in Maryland. Two months later, someone noticed Dishman was missing and inquired. Dr. Coffin investigated and reported, "the Steward had him delivered as I supposed to the police. This is all I know of the case. I supposed the soldier had appeared against him and know nothing more of the case until it was brought to my notice by some officer who said he was still in prison."

The problem was that the steward or ward master had sent Dishman to a for-profit jail, and Sidnum Grady was demanding payment. Dr. Coffin referred the matter as high as Richmond provost marshal General John H. Winder and Surgeon General Samuel Preston Moore. General Winder replied: "The steward has taken upon himself to confine this negro in an unusual place as you say without authority. He must pay the charges & take him out. A steward has no right to confine anybody. Theft is a crime to be punished by the civil authority this case should have been referred accordingly." The steward was long gone, so the hospital paid the bill that Grady presented: "For board of Henry Dishman from July 26 up to Oct 21st 1862 at $1 per day, 87.00" plus an additional 85 cents for "Soap furnished him."[13]

Support for the War

Both Richmond and Salem contributed men and money to the war. Thomas Boudar served on a committee in November 1862 "to raise money to purchase shoes for such of the soldiers of Gen. Lee's army as might be in need," after the army's grueling Maryland campaign.[14] Boudar's son Henry Bacon

Boudar, one of Tait's namesakes, born in 1837 before anyone thought Tait would have a son of his own, was now twenty-four years old and serving as a clerk at James T. Butler and Co., grocers and commission merchants, on Cary Street a few doors down from the jail. He volunteered at the start of the war as a private in Captain R. M. Anderson's Company of the Richmond Howitzers, serving from April through November of 1861.

Up north, Bacon C. Tait, Tait's son living in Salem, was about the same age in 1861 as his father had been when the War of 1812 started, and young Bacon C. also got to see the stirring of martial sentiment in his hometown, as men in Salem volunteered for the Union Army. Hiram S. Butterfield, listed next to the Taits in the 1860 census, enlisted in the Massachusetts 17th Infantry Regiment in 1861, reenlisted in 1864, and died in a Washington, D.C., hospital in September of 1865. George E. Farley, the son of neighbor George Farley, whose house had been damaged in 1859 when Tait's shed caught fire, was only a few months younger than Bacon C., but he lied about his age in 1862, claimed to be eighteen, and enlisted in Company E of the 48th Massachusetts at the age of sixteen.

As a mulatto, young Bacon C. was not welcome to enlist in the army at the start of the war, even had he lied about his age. When he finally reached eighteen and colored soldiers from Salem, including his relatives, were enlisting, there is no evidence he did. He may already have been suffering from lameness in his left leg, reported when he was twenty-six, that would have made him unfit for the military. For whatever reason, he seems to have avoided deciding between serving the cause of his father's or his mother's family.

A Home in Richmond

Decades earlier, Tait had jokingly identified with the persona of poor Billy Barlow in rags, but now, with his fortune even more secure, he still self-identified as a poor man. Myers claimed that he provided Tait a free room and paid for Tait's meals. In 1863, Myers turned his old jewelry store over to Adolph Gipperich and Henry Wenzel so that he could focus on his military contracts. Two months later, he rented out the two rooms above the store where he and Tait lived.[15]

Myers built a house "on Franklin street, between Seventh and Eighth streets, which he furnished throughout, engaged servants, purchased a horse and buggy," and he and Tait moved there. Tait was no longer living in Salem and traveling to Richmond as needed. He lived in Richmond through the war and until his death in 1871. Myers claimed that he paid for all the expenses himself, though in June Tait deeded him three valuable lots on the corner of Seventeenth and Dock Streets, "considered worth $20,000 in gold." Tait supposedly sold them "for the sum of $67,000 Confederate money, $40,000 cash and the balance at a future time," though the deed stated the price was $1,000. "Among the papers of Mr. Tait [after his death] was found a receipt dated sometime in 1863 in Myers's handwriting and signed by him, for the sum of two thousand dollars in full of all demands."[16] Tait's heirs later claimed that accepting $2,000 as full payment for lots worth ten times that more than compensated Myers for any generosity, and for the most part the courts agreed, awarding Myers only $9,000 in 1871 rather than the $25,000 he wanted.[17]

Prices soared in Richmond to ten times their prewar amounts, and the blockade made many luxuries scarce. By 1863, people commented that the citizens had a poorer look, but Myers and Tait continued to do well. Besides the profits that Tait had invested in real estate over the years, he and Thomas Boudar owned a significant portion of the Virginia Towing Company, as did Solomon Myers.[18] Myers, charged with avoiding the draft in 1864, claimed his position as president of the towing company made him exempt.[19]

Meanwhile, Tait's health declined. "Mr. Tait was subject to fits, several of which he had in the public streets, and which developed itself into paralysis, eventually into an affection [sic] of the brain, which changed his whole character from that of a liberal, whole-souled gentleman to that of a miser, frequently stating he would die of starvation, and refused to afford himself medicines for his recovery to health or even the necessities of life, at the same time having $40,000 in cash to his credit at Maury's banking house, and large revenues from other sources."[20] For those of the working class, Tait's fears of starvation might have sounded reasonable. In July of 1863 a government clerk in Richmond wrote, "I have lost twenty pounds and my wife and children are emaciated to some extent."[21] But high prices should not have affected Tait, as he was at an age where he could afford to spend down his wealth, even if his rent receipts and profits from the jail were not enough for daily expenses.

Tait left the Franklin Street house and moved in with Myers again, where Myers was living "on Leigh street, near Brook avenue."[22] Richmond city directories show Myers, Tait, and Annette Street, the widow of Henry Street, living at 114 West Leigh Street beginning in 1869. Myers does not show up in the 1870 census, but Tait appears as "Baker Tad," worth $100,000 in real estate, $2,100 in personal property, living in Monroe Ward with Anna Street, thirty-five, and her children or other young relatives aged sixteen to seven.

Anna or Annette Street appeared as a widow in the 1860 census, when she was living with her children and Georgiana Allen and two Allen children. While all the Streets and Allens were noted as white, the 1850 census listed Annett and Georgeanna Bertie (or Beltie), about the same age, living together with other young Berties and Margaret Bertie, presumably the mother. If these were the same Annette and Georgiana who would later marry a Street and Allen, they managed to change their race, because in 1850 they were listed as mulatto.

Tait's Generation Dying

Tait's generation of old slave traders and jail owners was starting to pass away. Hector Davis died in Richmond on January 7, 1863, leaving an estate worth $100,000. He bequeathed generously to his "servant woman Ann" and her children, who lived in Philadelphia and had the same relationship to him as Courtney and her children did to Tait. Unfortunately, Ann Davis's money was invested in Confederate securities and stock in a bank that was burned in the 1865 evacuation fire, so Davis's mulatto family wound up with almost none of the wealth he had earned. The following summer, in 1864, Silas Omohundro died. Corinna Hinton, his enslaved woman who had helped him run his jail in Richmond and passed for his wife in Philadelphia, found herself legally not his wife. Though she managed to be financially stable, lawsuits over the will dragged on for decades. Robert Lumpkin survived until 1869, and he too left money to a woman of color he claimed as his wife, Mary F. Lumpkin. Though he provided for her in his will, by March of 1869 she wrote, "I am so worried about money affairs that I hardly know what to do."[23]

Most of the profits from Richmond's slave jails—or at least what was left of them after the war—ironically went to women of color or their mulatto children. Among Davis, Omohundro, Lumpkin, and Tait, Tait was the only one of the four whose fortune passed virtually intact to his interracial children, with only a minor contest to the will by Solomon Myers. Most of his real estate and other investments retained their value through the evacuation fire and the collapse of the Confederacy. Others lost investments in Confederate bonds, failed to invest in real estate that held its value, or had other women or children who felt they deserved a share. Tait's shrewd business sense and faithfulness to one woman protected his children's inheritance.

Selling the Salem House

For a while after secession, mail had been difficult to get north, but soon the problem eased. Still, Tait must have realized that both the war and his ill health might separate him from his Salem family when legal issues required his signature. Specifically, either his wife and children wanted to sell their Salem house or he wanted them to, because on October 27, 1863, he gave Constance R. Tait, his daughter, power of attorney and authorized her to sell any of his real estate in Salem.[24]

Even if it was put on the market immediately, the Salem house did not attract a buyer until March of 1864, when Constance and her mother deeded the property to their attorney, Stephen B. Ives, in preparation for his facilitating a mortgage with the buyer. The deed showed that Bacon and Courtney Tait were considered husband and wife, because it included the standard language: "In witness whereof, I the said Bacon Tait, by my said attorney, together with Courtney Tait, wife of said Bacon Tait. . . ." Both Constance and Courtney signed the deed.[25] Ives granted the property that same month to James C. Thomas, who was willing to offer a mortgage on it.[26] But if they had a buyer arranged at that time, the sale apparently fell through, as the house was offered for sale again at auction on September 26, 1865. The furniture had been auctioned two weeks earlier, on September 12.[27]

The 1865 Massachusetts census, taken in the summer, listed the whole family together, including Tait as a "gentleman," though surely Courtney or someone else only stated his name, because he had not lived at 29 Cedar for several years. By that fall Thomas Still had purchased the house. There is no indication where any of the family moved, except for Bacon C. The 1866 Salem city directory listed him as living at a boardinghouse at 21 Lafayette and working as a coachman at a livery stable at 212 Essex. The rest of the family had other relatives in Salem with whom they might have lived. They are all missing from the 1870 census, as is Courtney's sister, Ann. If the family was living with Ann, the census taker might have missed them all.

After the War

The war had ended. In Richmond, Tait transitioned easily to a life without slavery. His jail, as well as much of his property and the home where he was living, escaped the evacuation fire and retained its value. While most of the city's slave jails clustered around Locust Alley, near where he had built his first jail, he had built his new one separately, close to the dock and where the railroad now passed through. The lot was valuable even if there was no more need for slave jails. Other jailers were not so lucky. A real estate assessor wrote in 1872, "In view of the fact that the slave trade has been abolished, the [Lumpkin] property, [Tait's first jail,] has become of little value comparatively, and is occupied wholly by coloured persons with little prospect of being occupied in future by any better class."[28] In contrast, when Tait's jail lot was sold in 1874, the ad read: "Located in the heart of the heavy business part of the city, with both railroad and water transportation along its line, this property presents advantages as a site for warehouses, manufactories, &c, not equalled by any other in the city."[29]

After the war Tait continued his real estate investing, and his negotiating skills were as sharp as ever. The land at Howard's Grove, which he had rented to Virginia for a Confederate hospital, was sought by a different entity after the war—the Bureau of Refugees, Freedmen, and Abandoned Lands, usually called the Freedmen's Bureau. Created for the benefit of former slaves, the bureau in this case planned to build a lunatic asylum to house people of color who were suffering from mental diseases. Jacob J.

DeLamater, sent down from Washington, D.C., in 1869 to negotiate, said, "I expected to continue the lease at one hundred dollars a year, which was the rent under the former lease, but, finally consented to accept [Tait's] own terms, which were two hundred dollars a year."[30] The Confederate Howard's Grove General Hospital was ordered to close as soon as possible to make room for the new lunatic asylum.

On January 16, 1866, Constance, the twin of Bacon C., married Thomas Moore, a young clerk who would become a civil engineer. She was twenty and he was twenty-three. He was living with his parents in Elizabeth, New Jersey, and was following the profession of his father, a civil engineer who had designed railroads and bridges. During the war Thomas Moore had volunteered for a nine-month Union Army regiment, but he had taken sick and was discharged before his term was up. The *Salem Register* announced the wedding, officiated by Reverend Warren in Elizabeth, New Jersey, naming the bride as "Miss Constance Rosalie Tait of Richmond, Va., formerly of Salem, Mass."[31] Constance may have visited her father in Richmond after the war and there met her husband, if he had come with his father to help with the rebuilding of the city, but she lived the rest of her life with him in Elizabeth, living as white and bearing several children, fitting in well with a middle-class family.

Tait's income continued postwar, but Sidnum Grady, age seventy-one, had lost his modest amount of personal enslaved property as well as his livelihood when freedom came. No longer in charge of the jail, he also lost a place to live and moved in with his brother Lorenzo on Brooke Avenue. In July of 1865 he tried to kill himself, and he finally succeeded in August of 1866, taking an overdose of laudanum. "A note was found pinned on his shirt bosom stating that he had had it in contemplation for some time to take his own life; that he had no means of support; that he did not wish to be a burden to his brother, with whom he was living, and that he had determined on this step to rid himself of his troubles that were greater than he could bear."[32] He was buried in Hollywood Cemetery, Section D, Lot 38.[33]

Because Tait now had a son to carry on his name and fortune, and his real estate's value was intact, one might think he lived his final days after the war in luxury and pride. But he had descended closer to the lives of the people he had enslaved for so long. His heir, Bacon C., was driving, harnessing, and caring for horses, a typically African American occupation, rather than following in the footsteps of his white father and actively investing the family money. Tait himself, although wealthy, lived his final years confined by his health and own mental problems, in fear of starvation, doing without medicine and the "necessities of life," afraid of being out on the streets alone.

In 1871, three closely related deaths occurred within five weeks. Courtney Tait died on May 31, 1871, of inflammatory rheumatism in Salem, where she resided. The death record noted that she was married. When the *Salem Register* printed a brief notice of her death, it added, "Richmond papers please copy."[34] In Richmond two weeks later, Tait died on June 14 at the home of Solomon Myers, 114 West Leigh Street, of "old age & softening of the brain." Dr. Robert G. Cabell of Governor Street pronounced the death and noted that Tait had been sick "about two years." After a funeral at St. Mark's Episcopal Church, he was buried in Hollywood Cemetery on June 16 in Section A, Lot 105. In addition to a notice and open invitation to the funeral in the *Richmond Daily Dispatch*, there was also a brief notice in the *Salem Register*.[35]

In death, Tait and Courtney were treated as any other married couple living apart, but before long, when the will was made public, someone realized something was wrong. A little paragraph began going the rounds of the newspapers within a week: "Bacon Tait, one of the wealthiest residents of this city who died last week, made a will leaving the bulk of his immense fortune, supposed to be $250,000, to four illegitimate children by a colored woman. He had no relatives—at least not in this part of the country." The blurb was even published in the *Utica Weekly Herald*, the editor probably not knowing it was the home of some of the colored woman's relatives.[36]

On July 8, 1871, a month after Tait and Courtney died, Thomas Boudar died also. He had remained in Richmond, "a merchant" as his obituary said, until the end of the war, when he had purchased and moved to a farm in Henrico County near Hungary Station. To the end, he escaped the stigma of the slave trade.[37]

Tait's children apparently also escaped the embarrassment of their parents' circumstances. The brief blurb did not give their names and implied they lived in Richmond, rather than the far-flung cities where they resided. Bacon C. had moved to Cincinnati by 1870. He worked there in an occupation similar to being a coachman in Salem, serving as a driver for the horse-drawn Newport Street Railway Company.[38] Constance remained with her husband in Elizabeth, New Jersey, while Josephine and Celine probably stayed with relatives in Salem. The thousands of dollars that Tait had made from the sale, jailing, and punishment of enslaved people were now in the hands of the next generation, with almost all of the stain of slavery gone.

Chapter 13

FIGHTING THE TIGER AND OTHER KINDRED SPORTS

Upon Tait's death, his children began to deal with his estate and its massive property holdings. Almost immediately, Bacon C. came from Cincinnati to sign papers allowing executor and attorney Charles W. Purcell to sell some of the real estate left to him and Constance "to raise money to pay debts of said father." Bacon C. also requested an advance of $4,000 on his inheritance.[1]

No other illegitimate children or purported wives came forth to contest the estate, despite the tempting money involved. Apparently Tait had been faithful to his Salem family. Only two court battles over the will publicized the awkward situation. Solomon Myers, who pushed for a circuit court trial, claimed he should receive $25,000 for all he had done for Tait in the last years of his life. The trial, in the spring of 1872, caused a little embarrassment in the papers, as the headlines talked about "An Old Slave Dealer's Estate." There was mention of "his illegitimate mulatto children," but the court awarded Myers only $9,000 and the news disappeared from the papers quickly.[2] The Howard's Grove property led to a later, less embarrassing lawsuit hinging on $1,000 in tax liability.

In June of 1872, both Bacon C., who had come to New York temporarily, and Josephine in Boston applied for passports. She requested that hers be sent to New York, as if she planned to meet Bacon C. there to travel abroad with him, but there is no record of their trip. The children gradually sold off more of their father's Richmond real estate over the years. Tait had purchased most of it purely for investment, so there were no memories connected to it, except for one parcel.

The place where Tait earned his fortune, where he first lived with Courtney, and where the children spent their early years—the slave jail at Fifteenth and Cary—was finally sold out of the family in an October

22, 1874, auction. James Gunn expanded his neighboring lumberyard over part of the property, but the lot had more potential than that, being close to both the railroad and the dock. A group of investors bought it, and for the next century it became the site of a series of tobacco warehouses. The Planters and Merchants warehouse, shown on the 1889 Baist map of Richmond, filled the whole lot and probably replaced the jail and other buildings, but that warehouse burned in January of 1900. Philip Morris built a warehouse on the site in 1916, and then a tobacco-curing building in 1948. Those buildings have since been purchased and remodeled into office buildings and a restaurant, as of 2016, under the name Canal Crossing.

Each of the four children had to deal both with their father's unsavory occupation and their mother's prejudicial color. Three of them moved away from Salem and immediately began passing for white, while Celine remained there, accepting that her color would be remembered but still choosing to marry into white society.

Celine

Celine, born in 1840, the oldest of Tait's children, married another Salem resident, Willard Peele Burding, in 1873. He was three years older than her, white, and a widower. There is no record she was married before. He worked at various low-paying jobs both before and during their marriage, as a clerk in a shoe store, a collector, and a horsecar conductor. The 1880 federal census taker marked Burding as white and Celine and their three children as mulatto. The youngest child, born in 1879, was named Agnes Courtney, but none of the children carried a name reflecting Tait or their white paternal line. Celine died in Salem at the age of forty-three on September 24, 1886, of typhoid pneumonia.[3] Although she married into a white family, she was the only one of Tait's children who did not immediately cross the color line herself and who passed on her mother's name.

Constance

Constance and Bacon C. were left as the wealthiest of the four children, splitting the bulk of Tait's fortune. Constance lived out her life in New Jersey, the stigma of both her father's slave trading and her mother's color forgotten. She did not hide her father's name, though. When she died at her home in Elizabeth on April 29, 1907, her death notice in the papers both north and south noted she was the "daughter of the late Bacon Tait."[4]

Her daughter and son, Catherine and Laurence Lane, were interested enough in their grandfather in 1903 to request his War of 1812 service record.[5] Laurence joined the Saint Andrews Society for those of Scottish descent. His paternal line came from Ireland, but he could trace his grandfather Tait's family to Scotland, and that may have been the genealogical line he used. Constance and her family had become comfortable with their paternal, if not their maternal, ancestry.

Josephine

Josephine attended the Moravian Seminary in Bethlehem, Pennsylvania, listed in the class of 1865 as the daughter of Bacon Tait of Richmond. The school was at the peak of its popularity in educating young women, and about half the applicants had to be turned away.[6] Long after the war, Josephine married the wealthiest and most prestigious husband of the Tait sisters, Jean Casper Naegeli, born in 1856 in Zurich, Switzerland. Six feet tall, with light hair and blue eyes, he was a silk merchant who traveled extensively between the United States and Europe. Josephine joined him on his many trips, living the rest of the time in New York City at 28 West Fifty-Ninth Street and later at 381 Central Park West in the early twentieth century.[7]

They married in the 1880s, when he was in his thirties and she was in her forties, but as they grew older she gave her age as only a year or two different from his. She died on November 6, 1917, in Manhattan and is buried alone at New York's historic Green-Wood Cemetery. Her husband died in 1924 in Lyons, France. They apparently had no children. Her husband and her sister Constance's son, Laurence Lane Moore, served as executors of her will.[8] She, too, had become part of white society and, though not bequeathed a large amount, had married well enough to more than compensate.

Bacon C.

Bacon Cooper Tait, twenty-four, moved to Cincinnati and was working as a driver for the Newport Street Railway Company in the summer of 1870.

The horsecar line connected Newport, Kentucky, with Cincinnati, making a circle from Kentucky across the suspension bridge over the Ohio River to Cincinnati and back again. That summer, the stable keeper for the railway, Michael Fitzgerald, "commit[ted] an unprovoked assault" on Bacon C.[9] The stable keeper was fined $15, but soon Bacon C. found himself on the other side of the law.

He began a three-year gambling spree that not only depleted his inheritance, but got him arrested at least twice, and he also managed to pick up the nickname Monkey Todd. In March of 1874, a raid on "Bolly Lewis's gambling-house, at 143 Elm street" in Cincinnati netted the arrest of the "colored" doorkeeper and four presumably white gamblers, including B. C. Tait, who were released on $300 bond.[10] In November of the following year, a police raid at 161 Race Street, a block or so away, caught "B. C. Tait, who was valiantly 'bucking the tiger'" (playing faro), and he put up $500 bond.[11] By then he was working as a hostler for Wallace and Hagan's livery stable, at 22 Patterson according to the Cincinnati city directory. His run-ins with the law must not have put him at odds with the local police socially, because during Cincinnati's 1876 Mardi Gras parade the *Cincinnati Daily Star* asked: "Did you see those lively mouse-colored mules in the parade? Who do you suppose were their riders? B. C. Tait and Ed. Armstrong of the office of the Chief of Police."[12]

Now broke, Bacon C. did not hold a grudge against the gambling operators in the city. Described in 1877 as "a broken down gambler . . . left without a nickel," he became "one of the best-known characters in the city," though one who had wasted his opportunity in life. "He was at one time worth his little $130,000," a policeman explained in 1885, giving a surprisingly accurate estimate of Bacon C.'s share of his father's estate, "and in less than three years blew it against faro. Some men in this town made good fortunes bleeding him. I saw him lose $13,000 in one night several years ago at a gambling-house on Fifth street. He was trying to find the limit. I don't like to say the game was a brace, but it looked very much like it. . . . He came here from Virginia where his folks still live. They are people of wealth, but he never bothers them. . . . Although he now knows that he was bled for all his money, he never squeals. He's a man of nerve—as proud as a peacock."[13]

The policeman told an anecdote showing Bacon C.'s "utter inappreciation of the worth of money" in his wealthier days. Tait handed a package done up in old newspaper to a restaurant owner for safekeeping. The restaurateur thought it was washing and tossed it aside. When Tait picked it up the next day, the package turned out to hold $15,000 in banknotes.[14]

Bacon C.'s 1872 passport includes the handwritten notation "and wife." He apparently married a Cincinnati woman. While the policeman said years later that Tait "married a girl in this city, and was afterward ashamed to go home," a more colorful story circulated in 1877 telling with fictionalized names how Bacon C., or Monkey Todd, lost his wife and fought a duel:

> For several months past there has resided in Cincinnati a broken down gambler known as "Monkey Todd," noted as having spent his patrimony, amounting to some $25,000, in "fighting the tiger" and other kindred sports, until of late he has been left without a nickel, or any other burden, except a handsome wife, who assisted him in making away with his inheritance. There lives in the suburbs of Cincinnati a young man, heir to considerable estates, whom we shall call Ed. Goodson, for want of a better name, who became enamored of Mrs. "Monkey Todd," and on Sunday afternoon escorted her "over the Rhine." Monkey Todd knew nothing of this until late on Sunday night, when he was gravely informed that Mrs. Monkey was faithless. It was but the work of a moment for Monkey to indict a challenge to Goodson and send it by his friend John Smith, being incited thereto by a number of his gambler friends.
>
> The challenge was at once accepted, and Charley Feeney, Goodson's second, informed Mr. Smith that the meeting should take place at once, and that pistols would be the weapons. Accordingly, at an early hour yesterday morning two hack loads of people, the principals, seconds, and two or three friends each, crossed the Suspension Bridge for the sacred soil of Kentucky. They passed through Covington, going to the flats between that city and Latonia Springs, and, driving into the woods, came to a secluded spot, fit for the work of carnage they were bent upon. Here the ground was marked off, the combatants placed, pistols loaded and placed in the hands of the principals. Both were in dead earnest, but not so the seconds.

The pistols were loaded with powder only. After the usual prelim-inaries, the word fire was given. "Monkey" fired first, being a little nervous, but Goodson, to show his magnanimity, and his reluctance to take advantage of an accident, fired his pistol into the air. Still Monkey was not satisfied, and demanded another shot. The pistols were loaded as before, and the firing was simultaneous, but to the great surprise of the principals, neither of them was hit. At this, Monkey got very angry, threw his pistol on the ground, and when it was picked up it was found the tube was filled with earth that could not be picked out. After a short parley, it was decided that the two pistols should be placed beneath a hat, neither principal knowing which was loaded; that they should each draw one, should take their distance and fire, and that it should be the last round of the combat, whether anybody was hurt or not. To this both principals agreed. The loaded pistol (without ball) was drawn by Monkey, although he did not know it, and Goodson swore after the fire that he heard the ball whiz past his ear. The combatants then shook hands, got into the carriages, and came back to the city by the Fifth street ferry for fear they might be arrested in the goodly city of Covington. Neither of the principals knows at the present writing the practical joke that was played upon them. They were both in dead earnest, and con-ducted themselves in the most cool and collected manner. Goodson made his will on Sunday night.[15]

In 1885, "B. C. Tait, alias Monkey Todd, was struck in the head by an unknown person at Plum and Longworth sts. at 3 a.m. Taken to the hospi-tal."[16] By now, he was "a little old man"—though only thirty-nine—scrap-ing by as "a 'finder'—goes about looking for lost jewelry, money, &c., and turning it up when a reward is offered for its return. . . . Mike Coughlin, the well-known saloon man, looks after him. He sleeps in Mike's cellar."[17] Coughlin's saloon was on the corner of Fifth Street and Central Avenue. The 1890–1891 Cincinnati city directory included Bacon C. as a clerk, liv-ing at that address, but in February of 1891, at the age of forty-five, he died of tuberculosis in the Good Samaritan Hospital. Listed as a single white laborer, he was buried alone in St. Joseph New Cemetery, Cincinnati, Section 3, Range 22, Grave 25.[18]

Slave trader Bacon Tait had given half his fortune and his name to his only son, but all had been lost, the money as well as the family pride, what there was of it. "Just think of that!" the policeman was quoted as saying of Bacon C. in 1885. "Once worth $130,000, with everything he could wish for, and now . . . sleeping in a cellar."[19]

EPILOGUE

Today, Bacon Tait's body lies in Hollywood Cemetery in Richmond, an iconic burying place for the South's white elite. Confederate president Jefferson Davis rests there, as do U.S. presidents James Monroe and John Tyler, dozens of Confederate soldiers and officers, and Richmond's favored sons and daughters from before and after the war. Thomas Boudar and Sidnum Grady also are buried there, Boudar near his wife and children. Grady was the first to be buried in his plot, but was soon joined by collateral relatives. The cemetery provides dramatic views of the James River from the high points, but Tait's grave, like his Richmond home and jail in Shockoe Bottom, is in one of the lowest parts. After almost twenty years of enjoying a family, he is alone again. His grave is marked by a plain obelisk, respectable for someone of his wealth, taller than a man, and with a simple inscription giving his name and the dates he was born and died.

Unlike children of war heroes, Underground Railroad conductors, or abolitionists, Tait's descendants could not publicly praise him in the postwar world and expect a favorable reception. The story of his life, like that of many other slave traders, faded into the background. His profession fit neither the narrative of the lost cause that sought to ameliorate slavery, nor the narrative of northern victory that denounced it as evil.

In the decade before the Civil War, Tait had a chance to see something most Richmond residents did not, another world in Massachusetts far away from the interstate slave trade, where free black families mingled with whites, spreading the antislavery gospel. But Tait chose Richmond, even if it meant the loneliness that he had dreaded. A male friend he had met in the slave trade and a hired housekeeper were his companions in his last years. Tait remained at heart a southerner and a slave dealer, and he died in the city where he began his adult life.

Notes

INTRODUCTION

1. Bacon Tait to Rice C. Ballard, November 25, 1838, Rice C. Ballard Papers, Southern Historical Collection, Wilson Library, University of North Carolina at Chapel Hill.

2. Bacon Tait to Rice C. Ballard, August 4, 1839, Rice C. Ballard Papers.

3. For example, Edward E. Baptist, "'Cuffy,' 'Fancy Maids,' and 'One-Eyed Men': Rape, Commodification, and the Domestic Slave Trade in the United States," *American Historical Review* (December 2001): 1619; Robert H. Gudmestad, *A Troublesome Commerce: The Transformation of the Interstate Slave Trade* (Baton Rouge: Louisiana State Univ. Press, 2003), 75; Calvin Schermerhorn, *Money over Mastery, Family over Freedom: Slavery in the Antebellum Upper South* (Baltimore: Johns Hopkins Univ. Press, 2011), 110–11.

4. Bacon Tait to Rice C. Ballard, August 16, 1839, Rice C. Ballard Papers.

5. Joshua D. Rothman, *Notorious in the Neighborhood: Sex and Families across the Color Line in Virginia, 1787–1861* (Chapel Hill: Univ. of North Carolina Press, 2003), 131; Phillip D. Troutman, "'Fancy Girls' and a 'Yellow Wife': Sex and Domesticity in the Domestic Slave Trade," paper presented to the Southern Historical Association, New Orleans, November 10, 2000; Emmanuel Dabney, "Race, Slavery, Diamonds, and Education: The Silas Omohundro Family of Richmond, Virginia," paper presented to the 96th Annual Convention of the Association for the Study of African American Life and History, Richmond, Va., October 4, 2011; Schermerhorn, *Money over Mastery, Family over Freedom*, 111–18.

6. Wendell Holmes Stephenson, *Isaac Franklin, Slave Trader and Planter of the Old South* (Baton Rouge: Louisiana State Univ. Press, 1938); Kari J. Winter, *The American Dreams of John B. Prentis, Slave Trader* (Athens: Univ. of Georgia Press, 2011).

CHAPTER 1.
DOING A GREAT DEAL OF BUSINESS

1. Tait's brother Netherland wrote in 1851 that his "family were originally Scotch, and spelled their name Taite, but the present generation spells it Tate as frequently as Tait." Though all three spellings show up at various times in period records, Bacon Tait most often spelled it *Tait*, while his Lynchburg relatives were more likely to spell it *Tate*. For simplicity's sake, in this work the name is spelled "Tate" for all of the family except Bacon Tait, unless quoting a primary source. Deposition of Netherland Tait, August 23, 1851, Edmund Tate Pension File, R10398, Revolutionary War Pension and Bounty-Land Warrant Application

Files, National Archives and Records Administration, Washington, D.C.; "Henry John Tate," Wikitree, www.wikitree.com/wiki/Tate-609 (accessed November 3, 2012).

2. Homer R. Tate, comp., *The Name and Family of Tate* (Effingham, Ill.: N.p., 1945), http://freepages.genealogy.rootsweb.ancestry.com/~taitandtate/Lin/homer.htm (accessed October 18, 2012); Netti Schreiner-Yantis and Florence Speakman Lee, comps., *Campbell County Personal Property Tax 1787* (Springfield, Va.: Genealogical Books in Print, 1987), 265; *John Dent v. James Callaway & Co.*, 1794-007, Bedford County, Va., Chancery Records, Virginia Memory, Library of Virginia, Richmond, Va., www.lva.virginia.gov/chancery/case_detail.asp?CFN=019-1794-007 (accessed October 18, 2012); "Advertisement," *Lynchburg & Farmers Gazette*, June 13, 1795, 3.

3. Caleb Tait married Nancy Cooper on April 16, 1790, according to Campbell County Register of Marriages Book 1, page 156. Though there were several Caleb Taits in the area, Nancy Cooper is most likely Bacon Tait's mother, because both Bacon and his sister Celine gave their sons the middle name Cooper: Bacon Cooper Tait and Charles Lewis Cooper Dupuy. Celine's son is documented in R. A. Brock, *Documents, Chiefly Unpublished, Relating to the Huguenot Emigration to Virginia* (Richmond: Virginia Historical Society, 1886), 160. In several Lynchburg deeds, Tait's widowed mother is referred to as Ann (for example, Lynchburg, Va., Deed Book L, page 136, Library of Virginia, Richmond, Va.). Nancy was a common nickname for Ann. Nancy Cooper's marriage date also is not contradicted by the fact that Tait's parents had exactly three children over twenty-one in 1815, indicating they were born before 1794 (Lynchburg, Va., Deed Book B, page 302, Library of Virginia, Richmond, Va.).

Complicating the situation is another record listing the marriage of Caleb Tait to Nancy Starke on February 14, 1812, in Lynchburg City Marriage Book 1, page 6. This may be a second marriage by Bacon Tait's father, which would mean that his widow Ann/Nancy was not the same person as Bacon Tait's mother Ann/Nancy, or it may be a marriage record for Tait's brother, Caleb Jr., or another Caleb in the area.

Many genealogists incorrectly list Caleb's wife as Patricia, copying the mistake on page 36 of Ethel Speer Updike's *Tate and Allied Families of the South* (Salt Lake City: Hobby Press, 1971). Updike omits son Patrick from a list of heirs, while including a person named Patricia as his widow—clearly an error in summarizing the heirs. Some genealogists have attempted to reconcile the mistake by listing Caleb's wife as Patricia Ann. Updike's book is also the source for the common error of stating Tait's birth year as 1787.

4. Tait's gravestone in Hollywood Cemetery, Richmond, Section A, Lot 105, gives his birth date as April 13, 1796. His death certificate (Richmond City Department of Public Health, Reel 864, Library of Virginia, Richmond, Va.) lists his age as "75 years & 3 months" at his death on June 14, 1871, indicating he would have been born in mid-March rather than April. Charles H., Bacon, Celine, and Elouisa were described as under twenty-one in 1815, in Lynchburg's Deed Book B, page 302 (Library of Virginia, Richmond, Va.), leaving the remaining children, Netherland, Caleb Jr., and Patrick, as over twenty-one. Charles was probably older than Tait, because the 1810 federal census of Lynchburg, Campbell County, shows a household of Caleb Tait with four males aged sixteen to twenty-five and one male

aged ten to fifteen. If that is the correct Caleb, Tait would be the younger male at fourteen. Charles would have been born circa 1794, barely having reached age sixteen for the census and barely under twenty-one in 1815. The 1810 census also shows an additional female aged ten to fifteen, perhaps a third daughter who died or another relative.

5. This is the clearest connection between the name "Bacon" and the Tate family. There were several Ann(e) or Nancy Tates/Taits in the area, but one was definitely the sister of George Whitlock, whose mother's maiden name was Bacon. An 1805 court record mentions Caleb Tait, his wife Anne, and her slaves, which would default to George Whitlock, Fanny Richardson, and Fanny Bacon Clark upon her death, unless she willed otherwise ("Lynchburg Co. [sic] Virginia Wills, Deeds, Marriages 1807–1831," http://freepages.genealogy.rootsweb. ancestry.com/~taitandtate/Misc/lynchburg.htm [accessed October 18, 2012]). A letter listing siblings includes George Whitlock and "Mrs. Tait," among others (Thomas B. McMurdo to Linnaeus Dupuy, August 28, 1832, Brock Collection, Reel 5069, Frame 19, Box 269, Library of Virginia, Richmond, Va.). "The house nearly adjoining the Methodist Church, was, for many years, the residence of Mrs. Nancy Tait, a sister of the late George Whitelocke, of Petersburg," according to Margaret Anthony Cabell, *Sketches and Recollections of Lynchburg* (Richmond: C. H. Wynne, 1859), 160. In 1839, Ann Tate of Lynchburg (Will Book B, page 348, Lynchburg Circuit Court, Lynchburg, Va.) did indeed leave property to several Clark and Richardson sisters and nieces, including niece Fanny Bacon Clark.

George Whitlock's sister does not appear to be the same woman who married Tait's father, since no Whitlocks, Clarks, or Richardsons are mentioned in any of the records dealing with the estate of Bacon Tait's father; nor are Bacon Tait and his siblings mentioned in the will of George Whitlock's sister. Bacon Tait's father and uncle, Caleb and Edmund, purchased land from Benjamin and Tabitha Clark on Blackwater Creek in 1782, but it is not known if these Clarks were related to the Whitlocks. For more on George Whitlock's ancestry, see Clayton Torrence, ed., *The Edward Pleasants Valentine Papers* (Baltimore: Genealogical Publishing, 1979), 4:2236–38. When other branches of both the Tates and Taits/Whitlocks moved to Georgia, they would intermarry again, separately reintroducing the name Bacon to the Tate/Tait line and puzzling genealogists. "Re: Mr. Tate Married a Bacon in Marietta, Ga," Tate Family Genealogy Forum, http://genforum.genealogy.com/tate/messages/1473.html (accessed October 18, 2012).

6. Thomas Dobson, *Supplement to the Encyclopaedia or Dictionary of Arts, Sciences, and Miscellaneous Literature* (Philadelphia: Thomas Dobson, 1803), 2:353; "On the 2d inst at his own place of residence . . . ," *Lynchburg Press,* September 8, 1814.

7. Caleb Tait estate inventory, Campbell County Will Book 3, pages 323–24, Campbell County Courthouse, Rustburg, Va.

8. W. Asbury Christian, *Lynchburg and Its People* (Lynchburg, Va.: J. P. Bell, 1900), 38; Ted Delaney and Phillip Wayne Rhodes, *Free Blacks of Lynchburg, Virginia, 1805–1865* (Lynchburg, Va.: Warwick House Publishing, 2001), 37–39; "Tobacco Planters' Convention," *Farmers' Register,* April 1, 1837, 748.

9. "Chronicle," *Niles' Weekly Register,* October 28, 1815, 152.

10. Christian, *Lynchburg and Its People,* 59; Delaney and Rhodes, *Free Blacks of Lynchburg, Virginia,* 31.

11. Christian, *Lynchburg and Its People,* 87; "Notice," *New Orleans Commercial Bulletin,* November 1, 1841, 4; *1842 New Orleans City Directory,* USGenWeb Archives Project, Orleans Parish, La., http://files.usgwarchives.net/la/orleans/history/directory/1842cdsz.txt (accessed October 31, 2012); "Messrs. C. & G. B. Tate," *New Orleans Daily Picayune,* March 19, 1854, 4; "Obituary," *Philadelphia Public Ledger,* April 18, 1844, 2; G. B. Tate, Third Representative District, Orleans Parish, La., 1850 U.S. Census, 89; "Died," *Richmond Whig,* August 5, 1856, 4; "Death of a New Orleans Merchant," *Richmond (Tex.) Reporter,* August 2, 1856, 2; "Virginia Manufactured Tobacco," *New Orleans Daily Picayune,* April 1, 1851, 4.

12. *Reports of Cases Argued and Determined in the Court of Chancery of the State of New York* (New York: Banks Gould and Co., 1847), 2:574–81; Benjamin C. Howard, *Reports of Cases Argued and Adjudged in the Supreme Court of the United States, January Term, 1850* (Boston: Charles C. Little and James Brown, 1850), 8:416.

13. "Destructive Fire—Loss of Life," *New Orleans Daily Picayune,* March 16, 1854, 1; "Superb Fire Trumpet," *New Orleans Daily Picayune,* April 26, 1854, 2; A. N. Ogden, *Reports of Cases Argued and Determined in the Supreme Court of Louisiana* (New Orleans: Office of the Louisiana Courier, 1858), 12:160–64; "$100,000 Saved in Herring's Safes," *New Orleans Daily Picayune,* May 28, 1854, 7.

14. G. Brown Goode, *Virginia Cousins* (Richmond, Va.: J. W. Randolph and English, 1887), 78B, 142; "Married," *New Orleans Daily Picayune,* July 16, 1850, 2; Calvin Tate, New Orleans Ward 1, La., 1860 U.S. Census, 100; Wm. Flower, Third Representative District, Orleans Parish, La., 1850 U.S. Census, 77; "Marriages," *Army and Navy Chronicle,* May 4, 1837, 288; "Died," *New York Spectator,* April 17, 1844, 1; "The Courts," *New Orleans Daily Picayune,* July 23, 1872, 2.

15. "C. Tate," New Orleans Ward 1, La., 1840 U.S. Census, 14 (images 339–40 at Ancestry.com); Calvin Tate, New Orleans Ward 1, La., 1860 U.S. Census, 100; Robt. H. Steptoe, Third Representative District, Orleans Parish, La., 1850 U.S. Census, 89; William Hicks, *History of Louisiana Negro Baptists from 1804 to 1914* (Nashville: National Baptist Publishing Board, 1915), 25, 26, 32, 141; Norman R. Smith, *Footprints of Black Louisiana* (Bloomington, Ind.: Xlibris, 2010), 140; "Church Directory," *New Orleans Black Republican,* April 15, 1865, 2.

16. "Will of Henry Tate," The Tait/Tate Families of America, http://freepages.genealogy.rootsweb.ancestry.com/~taitandtate/Wills/willhenry.htm (accessed November 2, 2012).

17. "At the particular request of Mr. Ross," *Richmond Enquirer,* March 4, 1806, 1.

18. For example, "Private Jails," *Liberator* (Boston, Mass.), December 27, 1834, 205.

19. Benjamin Seebohm, ed., *Memoirs of the Life and Gospel Labours of Stephen Grellet* (London: A. W. Bennett, 1860), 1:68–69.

20. "Virginia, Lynchburg, March 15," *New-England Palladium* (Boston, Mass.), April 2, 1811, 4; "Negroes for Cash," *Richmond Enquirer,* February 15, 1811, 4.

21. "Negroes for Cash," *Virginia Patriot* (Richmond, Va.), March 1, 1811, 4; "Negroes for

Cash," *Richmond Enquirer,* February 15, 1811, 4; "Josiah L. Deans," Gloucester County, Va., 1810 U.S. Census, image 7, at Ancestry.com.

22. George William Bagby, "Canal Reminiscences," *Selections from the Miscellaneous Writings of Dr. George W. Bagby* (Richmond: Whittet and Shepperson, 1884), 1:123.

23. Review of "An Historical and Practical Essay on the Culture and Commerce of Tobacco," *Anti-Jacobin Review and Magazine,* February 1801, 177.

24. "The City Board of School Directors," *New Orleans Daily Picayune,* September 17, 1867, 8.

25. "The Lynchburg Star mentions . . . ," *Trenton (N.J.) True American,* December 3, 1810, 2; "Virginia, Lynchburg, Dec. 7," *New-England Palladium* (Boston, Mass.), December 25, 1810, 2; "A Devil Incarnate!" *New York Commercial Advertiser,* January 31, 1811, 3, and other newspapers.

26. "On Friday last the court of hustings . . . ," *Virginia Argus* (Richmond, Va.), February 27, 1810, 2; Ruth Hairston Early, *Campbell Chronicles and Family Sketches* (1927; reprint, Baltimore: Clearfield, 1978), 68; Joseph Tate, *A Digest of the Laws of Virginia* (Richmond: Shepherd and Pollard, 1823), 502.

27. Christian, *Lynchburg and Its People,* 14.

28. "Ten Dollars Reward," *Lynchburg Weekly Gazette,* October 13, 1798, 3.

29. William Wade Hinshaw, *Encyclopedia of American Quaker Genealogy* (Ann Arbor, Mich.: Edwards Brothers, 1936), 6:289–94.

30. John Atkinson, *Centennial History of American Methodism* (New York: Phillips and Hunt, 1884), 175; Early, *Campbell Chronicles and Family Sketches,* 436; Delaney and Rhodes, *Free Blacks of Lynchburg, Virginia,* 50; Christian, *Lynchburg and Its People,* 40.

31. "The Black Preacher," *Salem (Mass.) Gazette,* March 19, 1822, 1–2.

32. *Journal of Lorenzo Dow* (Pittsburgh: Israel Rees, 1849), 123, 127; Delaney and Rhodes, *Free Blacks of Lynchburg, Virginia,* 47–51.

33. Winthrop S. Hudson, "Shouting Methodists," www.spiritjournals.com/Special%20 Sections/Revival%20Fire/Revivals/shoutingmethodists.htm (accessed December 24, 2012).

34. *Historical Sketch of Bedford County, Virginia, 1753–1907* (Lynchburg, Va.: J. P. Bell, 1907), 10–11; Susan R. Beardsworth, "The English Church" (n.p.: Virginia Works Progress Administration Historical Inventory Project, sponsored by the Virginia Conservation Commission, November 23, 1937), Library of Virginia, Richmond, Va., available online at http:// lva1.hosted.exlibrisgroup.com; Christian, *Lynchburg and Its People,* 26, 72.

35. Edmund Tate and Lucy Barksdale were married by "the Revd Mr. Crawford" in Charlotte County on August 2, 1792, according to a statement by Mrs. Lucy Tate on December 2, 1846, in Edmund Tate Pension File, R10398, Revolutionary War Pension and Bounty-Land Warrant Application Files, National Archives and Records Administration, Washington, D.C. There were at least two Reverend Crawfords in the general area of Virginia at that time, though centered in Amherst County closer to Lynchburg, about sixty miles to the north of Charlotte County. They were William and Charles, both Episcopalian. William Meade, *Old Churches, Ministers and Families of Virginia* (Philadelphia: J. B. Lippincott, 1861), 2:51, 57–59.

Tait's sister "Seline" Tate was married to Linnaeus Dupuy by Reverend F. G. Smith, according to the *Lynchburg Virginian,* May 2, 1831, 3. Smith was minister of the Episcopal church in Lynchburg (Cabell, *Sketches and Recollections of Lynchburg,* 341). Tait's first cousin Caleb Tate of Rocky Mount, Virginia, donated $25 to Trinity Episcopal Church there ("Background of Trinity," Trinity Episcopal Church, www.trinityepiscopalrmva.com/backgroundhistory.htm [accessed December 26, 2012]).

CHAPTER 2.
A YOUNG GENTLEMAN OF VERY RESPECTABLE PARENTAGE AND DEPORTMENT

1. "Hon. Powhatan Ellis, of Mississippi," *Southern Literary Messenger,* April 1863, 241; "The Recruiting Service," *Lynchburg Star,* quoted in *Richmond Enquirer,* January 28, 1812.

2. "General Orders, Adjutant General's Office," *Norfolk Gazette and Publick Ledger,* March 24, 1813, 2; W. Asbury Christian, *Lynchburg and Its People* (Lynchburg, Va.: J. P. Bell, 1900), 447; "Camp Holly Springs," http://dls.virginia.gov/GROUPS/1812/meetings/091109/CampHolly.pdf (accessed December 16, 2012); Stuart Lee Butler, *A Guide to Virginia Militia Units in the War of 1812* (Athens, Ga.: Iberian Publishing, 1988), 24.

3. William B. Lynch et al. to Thos Gholson, December 8, 1814, Folder 9593, Roll 0082, Letters Received by the Office of the Adjutant General, 1805–1821, National Archives and Records Administration, Washington, D.C.

4. Letter from R. H. Gray, May 22, 1854, Edmund Tate Pension File, R10398, Revolutionary War Pension and Bounty-Land Warrant Application Files, National Archives and Records Administration, Washington, D.C.; *Journal of the House of Delegates of the Commonwealth of Virginia* (Richmond: Thomas W. White, 1828), 35; Ruth Hairston Early, "Introduction," *Campbell Chronicles and Family Sketches* (Lynchburg, Va.: J. P. Bell, 1927), n.p.; *Journal of the House of Delegates of the Commonwealth of Virginia,* 15, 40.

5. *Acts of the General Assembly of Virginia* (Richmond: Samuel Pleasants Jr., 1808), 2:211; Margaret Couch Cabell, *Sketches and Recollections of Lynchburg* (Richmond: C. H. Wynne, 1858), 335–36; Early, *Campbell Chronicles and Family Sketches,* 510–11. Though Tate died before he could fully develop the springs, the area is still called Tate Springs.

6. Letter from Netherland Taite, August 23, 1851, and appointment of Edmund Tate as lieutenant colonel and commandant of the 53rd Regiment, 12th Brigade, 1st Division, Campbell County Militia, March 17, 1797, Edmund Tate Pension File, R10398, Revolutionary War Pension and Bounty-Land Warrant Application Files, National Archives and Records Administration, Washington, D.C.

7. Statement of Mrs. Lucy Tate, December 2, 1846, Edmund Tate Pension File, R10398, Revolutionary War Pension and Bounty-Land Warrant Application Files, National Archives and Records Administration, Washington, D.C.

8. Statements of Newby Johnson, November 16, 1846, and Mrs. Lucy Tate, December

2, 1846, Edmund Tate Pension File, R10398, Revolutionary War Pension and Bounty-Land Warrant Application Files, National Archives and Records Administration, Washington, D.C.

9. Pension Application Files of Allen Christian and Jacob Woodward/Woodard mentioning their captain, Nathaniel Tate, Revolutionary War Pension and Bounty-Land Warrant Application Files, National Archives and Records Administration, Washington, D.C.

10. Early, *Campbell Chronicles and Family Sketches*, 536–37; "Hon. Powhatan Ellis, of Mississippi," 241; Butler, *A Guide to Virginia Militia Units in the War of 1812*, 231–32.

11. "Hon. Powhatan Ellis, of Mississippi," 242.

12. H. W. Flournoy, ed., *Calendar of Virginia State Papers and Other Manuscripts from January 1, 1808, to December 31, 1835* (Richmond: James E. Goode, Printer, 1892), 10:333, 357–68; "Official," *Norfolk Gazette and Publick Ledger*, July 9, 1814, 2–3, "Richmond, Dec. 7, From Tappahannock," *American Watchman* (Wilmington, Del.), December 14, 1814, 3.

13. Flournoy, ed., *Calendar of Virginia State Papers*, 10:120–22.

14. "Lynchburg, May 12," *Richmond Enquirer*, May 21, 1814, 1.

15. "Lynchburg, August 4," *Richmond Enquirer*, August 13, 1814, 1.

16. Benjamin Watkins Leigh, *Reports of Cases Argued and Determined in the Court of Appeals and in the General Court of Virginia* (Richmond: Cary and Clemmitt, 1867), 6:154–66.

17. Flournoy, ed., *Calendar of Virginia State Papers*, 10:387–88.

18. The heirs eventually sold the Kentucky land to Judge William A. Menzies, but Tait's father had failed to record the original deed and Menzies was reluctant to pay without a clear title, so the Tates spent most of the 1820s fighting to collect, using their lawyer Robert Wickliffe in Kentucky. Tait assigned his share, worth over $2,000 with interest, to his sisters to collect, but Celine's polite letters to Wickliffe achieved only modest results until her new husband, Linnaeus Dupuy, began blasting the lawyer with angry demands for more vigorous efforts, and they finally received the balance, less expenses, in 1832. Wickliffe-Preston Family Papers, Box 35, Tait, Celine, Eloisa and Tait, 1823–1833, University of Kentucky Special Collections.

19. "On the 2d inst at his own place . . . ," *Lynchburg Press*, September 8, 1814, 3.

20. Peachy R. Grattan, *Reports of Cases Decided in the Court of Appeals and in the General Court of Virginia* (Richmond: J. H. O'Bannon, 1898), 6:44–49.

21. Bacon Tait, grantor, February 25, 1841, Lynchburg, Va., Deed Book D, 34, Library of Virginia, Richmond, Va.

22. R. A. Brock, *Documents, Chiefly Unpublished, Relating to the Huguenot Emigration to Virginia* (Richmond: Virginia Historical Society, 1886), 158.

23. "Died," *Lynchburg Virginian*, March 1, 1830, 3; Susan Dabney, Campbell County, Va., 1830 U.S. Census; Margaret Rives King, *A Memento of Ancestors and Ancestral Homes* (Cincinnati: Robert Clarke, 1890), 46; Early, *Campbell Chronicles and Family Sketches*, 387; Tait, Celine, Eloisa and Tait, 1823–1833, Box 35, Wickliffe-Preston Family Papers, University of Kentucky Special Collections.

24. Campbell County Will Book 3, page 320, Campbell County Courthouse, Rustburg,

Va.; Peachy R. Grattan, *Reports of Cases Decided in the Court of Appeals and in the General Court of Virginia* 6:45.

25. Campbell County Will Book 4, page 225, Campbell County Courthouse, Rustburg, Va.; Ann, Celina, and Eliza Tate, Policy #4146, 1822, Mutual Assurance Society, Library of Virginia, Richmond, Va.

26. "Congress of the United States," *Norfolk Gazette and Publick Ledger,* November 26, 1814, 1; Bacon Tait/Taite, *Index to the Compiled Military Service Records for the Volunteer Soldiers Who Served during the War of 1812* (Washington, D.C.: National Archives and Records Administration, 1965); Butler, *A Guide to Virginia Militia Units in the War of 1812,* 91.

27. "Hon. Powhatan Ellis, of Mississippi," 241.

28. Early, *Campbell Chronicles and Family Sketches,* 436.

29. Samuel K. Jennings, *A Plain Elementary Explanation of the Nature and Cure of Disease* (Washington, D.C.: Roger C. Weightman, 1814), 101–4.

30. Bacon Tait's file, Letters Received by the Office of the Adjutant General 1805–1821, National Archives and Records Administration, Washington, D.C.

31. Susan R. Beardsworth, "The English Church" (n.p.: Virginia Works Progress Administration Historical Inventory Project, sponsored by the Virginia Conservation Commission, November 23, 1937), Library of Virginia, Richmond, Va., available online at http://lva1.hosted.exlibrisgroup.com; Zachary F. Smith and Mary Rogers Clay, *The Clay Family* (Louisville, Ky.: John P. Morton, 1899), 84–85; Early, *Campbell Chronicles and Family Sketches,* 376.

32. Bacon Tait's file, Letters Received by the Office of the Adjutant General 1805–1821, National Archives and Records Administration, Washington, D.C.

33. Butler, *A Guide to Virginia Militia Units in the War of 1812,* 47; Christian, *Lynchburg and Its People,* 55.

34. Christian, *Lynchburg and Its People,* 55–56; "Domestic, Lynchburg, November 9," *Richmond Enquirer,* November 15, 1815; "Hon. Powhatan Ellis, of Mississippi," 242; S. Putnam Waldo, *Memoirs of Andrew Jackson* (Hardford: J. and W. Russell, 1819), 279.

CHAPTER 3.

FOUR DOORS BELOW THE BELL TAVERN

1. "Lynchburg," *American Beacon* (Norfolk, Va.), August 12, 1818, 2.

2. Lynchburg, Va., Deed Book D, 112, Library of Virginia, Richmond, Va.; Lynchburg, Va., Deed Book P, 34, Library of Virginia, Richmond, Va.; Margaret Couch Cabell, *Sketches and Recollections of Lynchburg* (Richmond, Va.: C. H. Wynne, 1858), 95; "The Lexington (Va) paper of the 24th inst. says . . . ," *Genius of Liberty* (Leesburg, Va.), August 10, 1819, 3; "To the Editors," *Daily National Intelligencer* (Washington, D.C.), September 27, 1820, 2.

3. "Jordan Dodd," Tennessee Marriages to 1825, Ancestry.com; "Mr. Jasah Staley," *Nashville Gazette,* January 8, 1820, 1; Franklin, Williamson County, Tennessee, 1820 U.S. Census; Maury County, Tennessee, 1830 U.S. Census; *Lewis County Tennessee* (Paducah, Ky.: Turner

Publishing, 1995), 215; *State Papers and Publick Documents of the United States* (Boston: Thomas B. Wait, 1819), 12:481.

4. Lynchburg, Va., Deed Book D, 112, Library of Virginia, Richmond, Va.; Death Certificate of Bacon Tait, Richmond City Dept. of Public Health, Reel 864, Library of Virginia, Richmond, Va.; Lynchburg, Campbell County, 1820 U.S. Census; Order Book 14, Campbell County, Campbell County Courthouse, Rustburg, Va., 372.

5. "Flat-Creek Land," *Richmond Commercial Compiler*, August 4, 1818, and other dates.

6. By 1819, the Richmond directory listed three Kyle family stores between the Bell Tavern and the Market Bridge in Richmond, slightly changed in ownership. The shops of William and David Kyle, J. and J. Kyle, and Hazlett and Robert Kyle all clustered on E Street between Fourteenth and Sixteenth Streets. "Wm. & Jeremiah Kyle," *Richmond Enquirer*, October 9, 1816, 1; *The Richmond Directory, Register and Almanac, for the Year 1819* (Richmond: John Maddox, 1819), 54.

7. "Valuable Coal Lands," *Virginia Patriot* (Richmond), June 24, 1814, 1; "At a Meeting . . . ," *Richmond Commercial Compiler*, June 6, 1818, 3; William Asbury Christian, *Richmond, Her Past and Present* (Richmond: L. H. Jenkins, 1912), 59, 84, 92, 95.

8. *Richmond Commercial Compiler*, December 30, 1817, 1.

9. *The Richmond Directory, Register and Almanac, for the Year 1819*, 50.

10. "Negroes Wanted," *Richmond Commercial Compiler*, September 10, 1817, 4.

11. Cabell, *Sketches and Recollections of Lynchburg*, 273–74.

12. "Joseph Boudar," 1815, Louisiana, Orleans Parish Estate Files, 1804–1846, 90–91, FamilySearch, https://familysearch.org/pal:/MM9.1.1/JJZD-1YZ (accessed January 3, 2013); Lyon Gardiner Tyler, ed., *Encyclopedia of Virginia Biography* (New York: Lewis Historical Publishing Co., 1915), 4:428; *Richmond Directory, Register and Almanac for the Year 1819*, 37; Elizabeth Maulle, Policy #1186, August 18, 1818, and Joseph Marx, Policy #2804, July 20, 1820, Mutual Assurance Society, Library of Virginia, Richmond, Va..

13. Bacon Tait to Rice C. Ballard, January 14, 1838, Rice C. Ballard Papers, Southern Historical Collection, Wilson Library, University of North Carolina at Chapel Hill.

14. Cabell, *Sketches and Recollections of Lynchburg*, 274; "Joseph Boudar," 1815, Louisiana, Orleans Parish Estate Files, 1804–1846, 90–91, FamilySearch, https://familysearch.org/pal:/MM9.1.1/JJZD-1YZ (accessed January 3, 2013); Tyler, ed., *Encyclopedia of Virginia Biography*, 4:428.

15. "Joseph Boudar," 1815, Louisiana, Orleans Parish Estate Files, 1804–1846, 51–52, 91, FamilySearch, https://familysearch.org/pal:/MM9.1.1/JJZD-1YZ (accessed January 3, 2013); Will of C. R. Boudar, City of Richmond Hustings Book 20, 1861, Library of Virginia, Richmond, Va., 639.

16. Cabell, *Sketches and Recollections of Lynchburg*, 273.

17. Tyler, ed., *Encyclopedia of Virginia Biography*, 4:428.

18. "Joseph Boudar," 1815, Louisiana, Orleans Parish Estate Files, 1804–1846, 54, FamilySearch, https://familysearch.org/pal:/MM9.1.1/JJZD-1YZ (accessed January 3, 2013); Tyler, ed., *Encyclopedia of Virginia Biography*, 4:428.

19. Ralph M. Kovel and Terry H. Kovel, *Kovels' American Silver Marks* (New York: Crown Publishers, 1989), 41.

20. Thomas Boudar, July 25, 1808, *Passenger Lists of Vessels Arriving at Philadelphia, Pennsylvania, 1800–1882*, National Archives and Records Administration, Washington, D.C., FamilySearch, https://familysearch.org/search/collection/1908535; "Notarized Sworn Statement, 1809 [*sic* 1808]—Niagara," Mystic Seaport, http://library.mysticseaport.org/initiative/PageImage.cfm?BibID=29290 (accessed January 15, 2013); "Ship News, Port of Philadelphia," *Poulson's American Daily Advertise*r (Philadelphia), July 20, 1808, 3; James Robinson, *The Philadelphia Directory for 1809* (Philadelphia: n.p., 1809); James Robinson, *The Philadelphia Directory for 1810* (Philadelphia: n.p., 1810), 40.

21. Tyler, ed., *Encyclopedia of Virginia Biography*, 4:428.

22. Mrs. Boudar, June 15, 1812, *Passenger Lists of Vessels Arriving at Philadelphia, Pennsylvania, 1800–1882*, National Archives and Records Administration, Washington, D.C., FamilySearch, https://familysearch.org/search/collection/1908535; *Poulson's American Daily Advertiser* (Philadelphia), June 9, 1812, 3; June 13, 1812, 3; June 23, 1812, 2; June 29, 1812, 1; Thomas Boudar, December 12, 1853, *Card Index to Naturalizations in Louisiana*, National Archives and Records Administration, Washington, D.C., available at Ancestry.com as NARA microfilm publication P2087, 20 rolls, Records of District Courts of the United States, National Archives and Records Administration, Washington, D.C.

23. "A List of Letters," *Richmond Enquirer*, April 9, 1814, 4; "Joseph Boudar," 1815, Louisiana, Orleans Parish Estate Files, 1804–1846, 73, 77, FamilySearch, https://familysearch.org/pal:/MM9.1.1/JJZD-1YZ (accessed January 3, 2013).

24. "Married," *Richmond Commercial Compiler*, July 7, 1818, 3; Reverend E. I. Devitt, "The Clergy List of 1819, Diocese of Baltimore," *Records of the American Catholic Historical Society of Philadelphia* (Philadelphia: American Catholic Historical Society of Philadelphia, 1911), 22:241; Tyler, ed., *Encyclopedia of Virginia Biography*, 4:428; William Dornin, Lynchburg, Va., 1850 U.S. Census.

25. Bacon Tait to R. C. Ballard, August 4, 1839, and August 16, 1839, Rice C. Ballard Papers, Southern Historical Collection, Wilson Library, University of North Carolina at Chapel Hill.

26. "What Does Not Happen Every Day," *American Beacon* (Norfolk, Va.), June 26, 1819, 4; "Nuptial," *Weekly Visitor* (New York, N.Y.), January 29, 1820, 208; Benjamin Miles and Sarah Wilson, December 22, 1819, David G. Murrell and Alice Tate, January 19, 1820, Virginia Marriages 1740–1850, Ancestry.com; William D. Reeves, *From Tally-Ho to Forest Home: The History of Two Louisiana Plantations* (Bayou Goula, La.: D. Denis Murrell and David R. Denis, 2006), 79.

27. Bacon Tait to R. C. Ballard, May 9, 1841, Rice C. Ballard Papers, Southern Historical Collection, Wilson Library, University of North Carolina at Chapel Hill.

28. H. W. Flournoy, ed., *Calendar of Virginia State Papers and Other Manuscripts from January 1, 1808, to December 31, 1835* (Richmond: James E. Goode, Printer, 1892), 10:433–36; William Graves Crenshaw III, May Crenshaw Saxton, and Michael Shuler Saxton, "The Crenshaw Family of Virginia," 20, http://familytreemaker.genealogy.com/users/s/a/x/May--mike-Saxton-NJ/BOOK-0001/0007-0001.html (accessed January 26, 2013).

29. "Lynchburg, Dec. 18. Dreadful Occurrence," *American Beacon* (Norfolk, Va.), December 24, 1818, 2; Meredith Lambeth, Campbell County, Va., 1820 U.S. Census; "Edmund West," Family Data Collection—Deaths, Ancestry.com.

30. "Lynchburg, Va. February 19. Murder by Shooting," *Alexandria (Va.) Herald*, March 5, 1819, 2; Cabell, *Sketches and Recollections of Lynchburg*, 71; Joseph Cohen, Lynchburg, Campbell County, Va., 1830 U.S. Census; "Reuben . . . ," *Alexandria (Va.) Herald*, September 17, 1819, 3; Sharon Block, *Rape and Sexual Power in Early America* (Chapel Hill: Univ. of North Carolina Press, 2006), 99; "Lynchburg, Aug. 24. Negro Murders," *New York Evening Post*, August 31, 1821, 2; "Lynchburg, (Va.) Sept. 28. Execution," *Newburyport (Mass.) Herald*, October 12, 1821, 2; "Lynchburg, July 15, Execution," *Baltimore Patriot*, July 26, 1823, 2.

31. William Wirt, *Sketches of the Life and Character of Patrick Henry* (Philadelphia: Henry T. Coates, 1817), 388; "Lynch's Law," *Southern Literary Messenger*, May 1836, 389; Henry Howe, *Historical Collections of Virginia* (Charleston, S.C.: Babcock and Co., 1845), 212.

32. Bacon Tait, grantor, Campbell County Deed Book 11, 530, Campbell County Courthouse, Rustburg, Va.; Cabell, *Sketches and Recollections of Lynchburg*, 95, 245; Fairfax Harrison, ed., *Aris Sonis Focisque Being a Memoir of an American Family, the Harrisons of Skimino* (n.p.: privately printed, 1910), 74–75; S. Allen Chambers, *Poplar Forest and Thomas Jefferson* (Little Compton, R.I.: Fort Church Publishers, 1993), 120.

33. "Joseph Boudar," 1815, Louisiana, Orleans Parish Estate Files, 1804–1846, 51, FamilySearch, https://familysearch.org/pal:/MM9.1.1/JJZD-1YZ (accessed January 3, 2013).

34. Bacon Tate, Lynchburg, Va., 1820 U.S. Census; Thomas Boudare, Richmond, Va., 1820 U.S. Census.

CHAPTER 4.

ANOTHER DEALER IN HUMAN FLESH AND BONES

1. Bacon Tait, Madison Ward, Richmond, Henrico County, Va., 1830 U.S. Census; Samuel Mordecai, *Richmond in By-Gone Days* (Richmond, Va.: George M. West, 1856), 48; Bacon Tate, Policy #7419, December 28, 1829, John Sheppard, Policy #7382, November 5, 1829, John Sheppard, Policy #2850, March 13, 1821, and John Sheppard, Policy #1425, December 16, 1819, Mutual Assurance Society, Library of Virginia, Richmond, Va.; "Falling-Garden Lots," *Virginia Patriot* (Richmond), July 14, 1812, 4. The streets around the house that Tait lived in have now been altered by commercial development, but his home would have been near the corner of Bank Street and U.S. 250/U.S. 360. The house that Tait owned was on the northwest side of Third Street, now Nineteenth Street, between Grace and Broad Streets. It was near the home of John L. Tate, but he was from Goochland County and not a close relation to the Lynchburg Tates.

2. William A. Menzies to Bacon Tait, September 10, 1825, Tait, Celine, Eloisa, and Bacon, 1823–1833, Box 35, Wickliffe-Preston Family Papers, University of Kentucky Special Collections.

3. "Manifest of Negroes . . . taken on board the Schr James Monroe of Norfolk," New Or-

leans, La., Slave Manifests, 1807–1860, Ancestry.com, images 384–85; "Ship News," *Charleston (S.C.) Courier*, March 26, 1828, 3; "Marine Register," *New Orleans Argus*, April 9, 1828, 2. The newspaper listed 186 slaves, but the 6 may have been a misreading of a handwritten o, as the manifest totals 180. One of the enslaved people on Tait's manifest was Courtney, a seventeen-year-old mulatto, approximately the age of his future wife, but there is nothing to indicate she was the same person. This Courtney was originally shipped on the *James Monroe* from Norfolk to New Orleans in March of the previous year by Louisa Marie Titreville, shipped back to Norfolk in May, then sent south again by Tait. Madame Titreville was the widow of Petre G. Titreville, who had died in 1826. The Titrevilles were from Norfolk, not Winchester, where Tait's wife had been born, and there is no evidence that Tait's wife was enslaved.

4. *John G. Daniel v. James P. Wilkinson*, Index Number 1835-024, page 10, Powhatan County Chancery Causes, Library of Virginia, Richmond, Va.

5. James P. Wilkinson, Policy #7533, November 5, 1829, Mutual Assurance Society, Library of Virginia, Richmond, Va.; "Bacon Tait, Admr. of James P. Wilkinson vs. Louisa De Ende, &c.," Index Number 1857-024, page 23, Cumberland County Chancery Causes, Library of Virginia, Richmond, Va.

6. In his 1832 will, Henry De Ende stated he was "a native of Cumberland County, in the State of Virginia, aged about forty eight years," and the report of his half-brother Francis's death said Francis was "a native of the Sate [sic] of Virginia." The De Ende family Bible at the Library of Virginia states that Stair Henry De Ende was born in Chatham, Kent, England, his three sisters in Hesse Cassel, Germany, and a brother who died in infancy in Brooklyn, New York. The family apparently settled in Cumberland County when Henry and his siblings were young.

"Admr. of Henry De Ende vs. Exr. of Stephen W. Trent, &c.," Index Number 1857-012, pages 2, 72, Cumberland County Chancery Causes, Library of Virginia, Richmond, Va.; Francis De Ende, Orleans Parish Estate Files, La., page 4, FamilySearch, https://familysearch.org (accessed February 8, 2013); Stair Henry De Ende, February 22, 1784, England, Births and Christenings, 1538–1975, FamilySearch, https://familysearch.org (accessed February 8, 2013); *John G. Daniel v. James P. Wilkinson*, Index Number 1835-024, page 10; James P. Wilkinson, Policy #7533, November 5, 1829, Mutual Assurance Society, Library of Virginia, Richmond, Va.; *John G. Daniel vs. James P. Wilkinson*, Index Number 1835-024, page 10.

7. "Bacon Tait, Admr. of James P. Wilkinson vs. Louisa De Ende, &c.," Index Number 1857-024, page 20.

8. Ibid., 66.

9. "Coastwise," *New Orleans Argus*, May 3, 1828, 2; "Shipping List," *Baltimore Gazette and Daily Advertiser*, June 2, 1828, 3; "Bacon Tait, Admr. of James P. Wilkinson vs. Louisa De Ende, &c.," Index Number 1857-024, pages 20–24.

10. "Bacon Tait, Admr. of James P. Wilkinson vs. Louisa De Ende, &c.," Index Number 1857-024, pages 22–23, 66; *John G. Daniel v. James P. Wilkinson*, Index Number 1835-024, page 11.

11. *John G. Daniel v. James P. Wilkinson*, Index Number 1835-024, pages 10–12.

12. "Shipping List," *Baltimore Gazette and Daily Advertiser,* September 26, 1828, 2; "Bacon Tait, Admr. of James P. Wilkinson vs. Louisa De Ende, &c.," Index Number 1857-024, page 23.

13. "Bacon Tait, Admr. of James P. Wilkinson vs. Louisa De Ende, &c.," Index Number 1857-024, pages 27–30.

14. Henry De Ende to James P. Wilkinson, July 24, 1829, "Bacon Tait, Admr. of James P. Wilkinson vs. Louisa De Ende, &c.," Index Number 1857-024, page 177.

15. Henry De Ende to James P. Wilkinson, December 11, 1829, "Bacon Tait, Admr. of James P. Wilkinson vs. Louisa De Ende, &c.," Index Number 1857-024, page 181.

16. *John G. Daniel v. James P. Wilkinson,* Index Number 1835-024, pages 5, 29.

17. Henry De Ende to James P. Wilkinson, July 24, 1829, "Bacon Tait, Admr. of James P. Wilkinson vs. Louisa De Ende, &c.," Index Number 1857-024, page 178.

18. For example, "Gen. Jackson's Negro Speculations," *Richmond Enquirer,* September 2, 1828, 1.

19. Louis F. Aulbach, "The Downtown Crypt," *Buffalo Bayou, an Echo of Houston's Wilderness Beginnings,* http://users.hal-pc.org/~lfa/BB38.html (accessed March 10, 2014).

20. "Henry De Ende," Orleans Parish Estate Files, 1804–1846, Louisiana, page 82, FamilySearch, https://familysearch.org (accessed February 24, 2013); "Bacon Tait, Admr. of James P. Wilkinson vs. Louisa De Ende, &c.," Index Number 1857-024, page 33, Cumberland County Chancery Causes; "Admr. of Henry De Ende vs. Exr. of Stephen W. Trent, &c.," Index Number 1857-012, page 2, Cumberland County Chancery Causes; Aulbach, "The Downtown Crypt"; "Orleans Parish Death Index - D," LAGenWeb, http://files.usgwarchives.net/la/orleans/vitals/deaths/index/reel1/nodid.txt (accessed February 24, 2013); "We are authorized . . . ," *Houston Tri-Weekly Telegraph,* July 2, 1862, 2; "Tax Notice," *Houston Tri-Weekly Telegraph,* September 8, 1862, 2; "County Court," *Houston Telegraph,* January 30, 1878, 5.

21. Thirty-three-year-old black female, E. De Ende Donnellan, Houston, Harris County, Texas Slave Schedule, 1850 U.S. Census; forty-year-old black female, F. Dwyer, Houston, Harris County, Texas Slave Schedule, 1860 U.S. Census.

22. C. D. Arfwedson, *The United States and Canada in 1832, 1833 and 1834* (London: Richard Bentley, 1834), 1:323–27.

23. Solomon Northup, *Twelve Years a Slave* (New York: Miller, Orton and Mulligan, 1855), 65. The four enslaved people who were added later to Northup's ship, including Maria, are not listed by name on the manifest, but the name he was given, Plat/Platt, and several others match the manifest for the brig *Orleans,* leaving Richmond for New Orleans on April 27, 1841.

24. Nathaniel B. Hill, Richmond, Henrico County, Va., 1850 U.S. Census; "Deaths," *Richmond Enquirer,* July 1, 1845, 2; William G. Myer, "Hill *v.* Tucker," *Federal Decisions* (St. Louis, Mo.: Gilbert Book Company, 1888), 22:553–58.

25. "For the Enquirer," *Richmond Enquirer,* July 1, 1825, 3.

26. *Proceedings and Debates of the Virginia State Convention of 1829–30* (Richmond: Ritchie and Cook, 1830), 858.

27. Ibid., 225–26.

28. Executive Papers, Archives of Virginia, July 1829, quoted in James Hugo Johnston, *Race Relations in Virginia and Miscegenation in the South, 1776–1865* (Amherst: Univ. of Massachusetts Press, 1970), 134.

29. J. T. Ducatel, "Biographical Notice of L. H. Girardin," *Transactions of the Maryland Academy of Science and Literature* (Baltimore: John D. Toy, 1837), 1:17–23; J. G. Morris, "Maryland Academy of Science and Literature," *Maryland Historical Magazine* (Baltimore: J. H. Furst, 1907), 2:261–63; Meredith Henne Baker, *The Richmond Theater Fire: Early America's First Great Disaster* (Baton Rouge: Louisiana State Univ. Press, 2012), 12, 21, 25, 37, 116; "Married," *Richmond Enquirer*, October 25, 1825, 3; George Holbert Tucker, *Abstracts from Norfolk City Marriage Bonds 1797–1850* (1934; reprint, Baltimore: Genealogical Publishing, 2009), 32; Giles Picot, Policy #7299, November 5, 1829, Mutual Assurance Society, Library of Virginia, Richmond, Va.; Maryland Register of Will Books, Baltimore City, 1821–1827, 12:329, Familysearch.org (accessed March 13, 2013); Tyler, ed., *Encyclopedia of Virginia Biography*, 4:428; "History of Holy Cross," www.holycrosslynchburg.org/history.html (accessed October 20, 2013).

30. James Earl Brown, "Life of Brigadier General John McCausland," *West Virginia History* 4, no. 4 (July 1943): 239–93, available at www.wvculture.org/history/journal_wvh/wvh4-1.html (accessed March 13, 2013); "Married," *Richmond Enquirer*, June 18, 1824, 3.

31. Bacon Tait, grantor, City of Richmond Deed Book 28, 495–97, Library of Virginia, Richmond, Va.; Wm Howlett, Richmond Jefferson Ward, Henrico County, Va., 1830 U.S. Census; William Howlett, Richmond Ward 2, Henrico County, Va., 1840 U.S. Census; William Howlett, Richmond, Henrico County, Va., 1850 U.S. Census; "Swan Tavern," *Richmond Enquirer*, October 16, 1832, 1; "Swan Tavern," *Richmond Enquirer*, October 26, 1832, 1; "Washington Tavern, Richmond. William Howlett, proprietor," *American Constellation* (Petersburg, Va.), July 6, 1838, 3.

32. Robert Lindsey and Sarah Lindsey, *Travels of Robert and Sarah Lindsey* (London: Samuel Harris, 1886), 31.

CHAPTER 5.

A SPACIOUS COMFORTABLE JAIL

1. Some reports listed the passenger's name as Ballas, but most listed him as Balls; he was probably Thomas L. Balls, a grocer who advertised in the Norfolk papers. "From the New Orleans Courier of Dec. 14," *Alexandria (Va.) Gazette*, January 4, 1830, 2; "From New Orleans," *Richmond Enquirer*, January 5, 1830, 2; "New Orleans, Dec. 23," *Daily National Intelligencer* (Washington, D.C.), January 16, 1830, 3; "Items," *Philadelphia Inquirer*, January 28, 1830, 2; "Manifest of Negroes . . . taken on board the Schr Lafayette of Norfolk," New Orleans, La., Slave Manifests, 1807–1860, Ancestry.com, images 463–72.

2. Charles Copland, Policy #6901, December 31, 1829, and #3730, July 10, 1830, Mutual Assurance Society, Library of Virginia, Richmond, Va.; Bacon Tait to Rice C. Ballard, May 1, 1838, Rice C. Ballard Papers, Southern Historical Collection, Wilson Library, University of

North Carolina at Chapel Hill; "Extracts from Diary of Charles Copland," *William and Mary College Quarterly Historical Magazine,* July 1906, 59.

3. City of Richmond Deed Book 29, 14–15, Library of Virginia, Richmond, Va.

4. Matthew R. Laird, "Archaeological Data Recovery Investigation of the Lumpkin Slave Jail Site (44HE1053) Richmond, Virginia," 38, www.dhr.virginia.gov/pdf_files/SpecialCollections/Lumpkin's%20Jail%20data%20recovery%20report%20vol.%201%20(research).pdf (accessed April 2, 2013).

5. Ibid., 40.

6. Ibid., 9.

7. Lewis A. Collier, Policy #8005, July 18, 1833, Mutual Assurance Society, Library of Virginia, Richmond, Va.

8. Laird, "Archaeological Data Recovery Investigation," 9–10.

9. Robert Lumpkin, Policy #16375, May 2, 1851; Lewis A. Collier, Policy #12767, March 19, 1844, #9656, December 5, 1837, #7949, July 21, 1832, Mutual Assurance Society, Library of Virginia, Richmond, Va.; City of Richmond Deed Book 32, 135, Library of Virginia, Richmond, Va.; *Visitor's Guide to Richmond and Vicinity* (Richmond: Benjamin Bates, 1871), 24–25.

10. Kimberly Merkel Chen and Hannah W. Collins, "The Slave Trade as a Commercial Enterprise in Richmond, Virginia," 7, www.dhr.virginia.gov/registers/Counties/Multiple-County/127-6196_Slave_Trade_In_Richmond_MPS_2008_Final.pdf (accessed October 30, 2013).

11. "Bacon Tait, Admr. of James P. Wilkinson vs. Louisa De Ende, &c.," Index Number 1857-024, 28.

12. Ibid., 30, 58, 69, 112.

13. Ibid., 72.

14. Ibid., 169.

15. Ibid., 71–72.

16. *John G. Daniel v. James P. Wilkinson,* Index Number 1835-024, 29, Powhatan County Chancery Causes, Library of Virginia, Richmond, Va.

17. "Bacon Tait, Admr. of James P. Wilkinson vs. Louisa De Ende, &c.," Index Number 1857-024, 162.

18. Ibid., 185–86; Thomas Johnson Michie, "De Ende, &c. v. Wilkinson's Adm'r., Same v. Tait," *Virginia Reports, Jefferson—33 Grattan, 1730–1880 Volumes 1 and 2* (Charlottesville, Va.: Michie Company, 1902), 878–82.

19. "Paul Pascal," Louisiana, Orleans Parish Will Books 1805–1920, 281, FamilySearch, https://familysearch.org/pal:/MM9.3.1/TH-1942-27984-645-59?cc=2019728&wc=M99Q-JK7:n1060449247 (accessed April 22, 2013); "Joseph Boudar," 1815, Louisiana, Orleans Parish Estate Files, 1804–1846, 90–91, FamilySearch, https://familysearch.org/pal:/MM9.1.1/JJZD-1YZ (accessed January 3, 2013); Thomas Curry, *Reports of Cases Argued and Determined before the Supreme Court of the State of Louisiana* (New Orleans: Benjamin Levy, 1837), 10:598; Obituary of Paul P. Pascal, *American Beacon and Norfolk and Portsmouth Daily Advertiser,* February 17, 1836, Bernard J. Henley Papers, Library of Virginia, Richmond, Va.

20. Bacon Tait to Nathaniel Currier, October 4, 1832, Bernard Raux Slave Trade Papers, Houghton Library, Cambridge, Mass.

21. Thomas Jefferson Randolph, quoted in *Slavery and the Internal Slave Trade in the United States of North America* (London: Thomas Ward, 1841), 67–68.

22. *Trials and Confessions of Madison Henderson, alias Blanchard, Alfred Amos Warrick, James W. Seward, and Charles Brown* (St. Louis: Chambers and Knapp, 1841), 14, 17. Though Henderson estimated in 1841 that he was first sold to Ballard's partners when he was twenty years younger, placing his activity with them within a few years of 1821, other evidence indicates it occurred much later. He reported being sold at Orange Court House to James Blakey, a partner with Samuel Alsop, Mr. Ballard, and James Franklin. Those men were actively trading together in the 1830s, rather than around 1820. In September 1834, Isaac Franklin, James Franklin's brother, placed an advertisement in the September 5, 1834, *Alexandria (Va.) Gazette* signed "Orange Court House, Aug. 28, 1834" and offering a reward for a trunk "stolen from the Boot of the Stage, between Robinson's Stand and this place. . . . Any information lodged with Mr. Blakey, of this place, or with Samuel Alsop, near Fredericksburg, either of which gentlemen will pay the reward, and forward the trunk to me; or reference to Franklin & Armfield, Alexandria, D.C." The ad places the men in connection with each other and with Orange Courthouse, and may be evidence that Henderson's sale took place either that year or within a few years of 1834.

CHAPTER 6.
SUCH DIABOLICAL MISCREANTS AS BACON TAIT

1. Bacon Tait to Rice C. Ballard, August 2, 1836, Rice C. Ballard Papers, Southern Historical Collection, Wilson Library, University of North Carolina at Chapel Hill.

2. "Manifest of slaves intended to be transported on board the Brig Adelaide," New Orleans, La., Slave Manifests, 1807–1860, Ancestry.com, images 854–57 (Smith appears with the middle initial "A." rather than "W." on the manifest, and Monarchy Johnson is incorrectly listed as male); Tait, Boudar & Co. to Ballard, Franklin & Co., September 23, 1836, and Bacon Tait to Rice C. Ballard, August 25 and August 2, 1836, Rice C. Ballard Papers; "Trust Sale," *Richmond Whig*, August 1, 1834, 3; "Trust Sale," *Richmond Whig*, December 15, 1834, 3; Andrew Reed and James Matheson, *A Narrative of the Visit to the American Churches, by the Deputation from the Congregational Union of England and Wales* (London: Jackson and Walford, 1836), 1:195.

3. Bacon Tait to Rice C. Ballard, November 15, 1838, Rice C. Ballard Papers.

4. Langhorne, who had recently arrived in Lynchburg, invested in a mill along the Blackwater, as Tait's late father had earlier. Lewis A. Collier, Policy #8005, July 18, 1833, and #7949, July 21, 1832, Mutual Assurance Society, Library of Virginia, Richmond, Va.; "Negroes," *Richmond Enquirer*, May 24, 1833, 4; "This is to inform the citizens . . . ," *Richmond Enquirer*, August 23, 1833, 1; City of Richmond Deed Book 32, 134–37, Library of Virginia, Richmond, Va.; City of Richmond Deed Book 33, 358, Library of Virginia, Richmond, Va.; Margaret Couch Cabell, *Sketches and Recollections of Lynchburg* (Richmond, Va.: C. H. Wynne, 1858),

165; Chris Kraft, "Maurice H. Langhorne," http://worldconnect.rootsweb.ancestry.com/cgi-bin/igm.cgi?op=GET&db=adgedge&id=I1983 (accessed October 23, 2013).

5. "Richmond, March 12, Fire," *New York Evening Post*, March 16, 1830, 2; "Items," *New York Spectator*, March 23, 1830, 4.

6. The size was not listed on the original deed, but the lot is undivided today, Parcel ID #E0000072006 in the City of Richmond, measuring 333.38 by 161.10 feet or 1.223 acres. Micajah Bates, *Plan of the City of Richmond* (Richmond, Va.: n.p., 1835); Bacon Tait, grantee, City of Richmond Deed Book 32, 469, Library of Virginia, Richmond, Va.

7. *Richmond Directory* (Richmond, Va.: John Maddox, 1819), 73, 74; M. Ellyson, *Richmond Directory* (Richmond, Va.: H. K. Ellyson, 1856), 243; Lyon Gardiner Tyler, ed., *Encyclopedia of Virginia Biography* (New York: Lewis Historical Publishing Company, 1915), 5:805.

8. The online map is located at http://dsl.richmond.edu/civilwar/slavemarket.html.

9. City of Richmond Deed Book 32, 469, 472, Library of Virginia, Richmond, Va.

10. "Notice," *Richmond Whig*, October 17, 1834, 3; "Co-Partnership," *Richmond Enquirer*, September 10, 1833, 1; James Wilson, Policy #10289, December 31, 1836, and Wortham & McGruder, Policy #3721, March 30, 1830, Mutual Assurance Society, Library of Virginia, Richmond, Va.; "Death of an Old Citizen," *Richmond Daily Dispatch*, October 14, 1864; Lyon G. Tyler, *Men of Mark in Virginia* (Washington, D.C.: Men of Mark Publishing Co., 1908), 4:82. Davenport, Allen and Co. placed numerous ads in the auction section of the Richmond Whig in the 1830s, but no known ones advertised slaves.

11. Reverend A. M. Newman, quoted in Charles Henry Corey, *A History of the Richmond Theological Seminary* (Richmond: J. W. Randolph, 1895), 50.

12. Charles Emery Stevens, *Anthony Burns: A History* (Boston: John P. Jewett, 1856), 190.

13. 1835 and 1836 Personal Property Tax, City of Richmond, Reel 365, Library of Virginia, Richmond, Va.; Bacon Tait, Madison Ward, Richmond, Henrico County, Va., 1830 U.S. Census; Bacon Tait, Ward 1, Richmond, Henrico County, Va., 1840 U.S. Census; George M. Carrington, Policy #9481, December 30, 1837, Mutual Assurance Society, Library of Virginia, Richmond, Va.

14. City of Richmond Deed Book 34, 234, 511; City of Richmond Deed Book 35, 462; City of Richmond Deed Book 59, 21–22, Library of Virginia, Richmond, Va.; "By virtue of a Deed of Trust . . . ," *Richmond Whig*, November 20, 1835, 4.

15. "$100 Reward," *Richmond Enquirer*, May 17, 1833, 1; "Petition 21683321," Digital Library on American Slavery, http://library.uncg.edu/slavery/details.aspx?pid=15466 (accessed July 1, 2013); City of Richmond Deed Book 32, 137, Library of Virginia, Richmond, Va.

16. Michael E. Pollack, *Marriage Bonds of Henrico County, Virginia, 1782–1853* (Baltimore: Genealogical Publishing, 1984), 62.

17. Dwelling house and oyster house "occupied by Embrew Gallego," insured by Manuel Judah, Policy #1826, December 22, 1815, Mutual Assurance Society, Library of Virginia, Richmond, Va.; "Richmond, Va.—Court—Joseph Gallego, Emancipation of slave Humbro, 10 Feb 1800," http://files.usgwarchives.net/va/richmondcity/court/galego01.txt (accessed November 4, 2013); "Petition 11681407 Details," Digital Library on American Slavery, http://library.

uncg.edu/slavery/details.aspx?pid=2431 (accessed November 4, 2013); "Notice," *Virginia Patriot* (Richmond), April 30, 1814, 1.

18. "Petition 11681408 Details," Digital Library on American Slavery, http://library.uncg. edu/slavery/details.aspx?pid=2432 (accessed November 4, 2013).

19. Phillip Gallego to Charlotte Ann Dunlop, June 14, 1814, Richmond, Va., Virginia Marriages 1740–1850, Ancestry.com.

20. City of Richmond Deed Book 32, 137–39, 150, Library of Virginia, Richmond, Va.

21. George Dickson and G. Mercer Adam, *A History of Upper Canada College, 1829–1892* (Toronto: Roswell and Hutchison, 1893), 297; Natasha L. Henry, *Talking about Freedom: Celebrating Emancipation Day in Canada* (Toronto: Dundurn Press, 2013), 46; "Social Conditions among the Negroes in Upper Canada before 1865," *Ontario's African-Canadian Heritage: Collected Writings by Fred Landon, 1918–1967* (Toronto: Dundurn Press, 2009), 186; Peter Galligo, Richmond, Va., 1870 U.S. Census.

22. "Petition 11682302 Details," Digital Library on American Slavery, http://library.uncg. edu/slavery/details.aspx?pid=2535 (accessed November 4, 2013); Ishan Elles, Richmond, Va., 1850 U.S. Census.

23. "Petition 11683411 Details," Digital Library on American Slavery, http://library.uncg. edu/slavery/details.aspx?pid=2683 (accessed November 4, 2013).

24. City of Richmond Deed Book 36, 304, Library of Virginia, Richmond, Va.; City of Richmond Deed Book 37, 30, Library of Virginia, Richmond, Va.

25. William L. Montague, *Richmond Directory* (Baltimore: J. W. Woods, 1852), 141; Gregg D. Kimball, *American City, Southern Place: A Cultural History of Antebellum Richmond* (Athens: Univ. of Georgia Press, 2000), 131

26. Harriet Beecher Stowe, *A Key to Uncle Tom's Cabin* (London: Thomas Bosworth, 1853), 5–7; Thomas Johnson Michie, "De Lacy, Vice Consul, v. Antoine and Others," *Virginia Reports, Jefferson—33 Grattan, 1730–1880, Volumes 1 and 2* (Charlottesville, Va.: Michie Company, 1902), 686–90; "The Portuguese Insurgents," *Richmond Enquirer*, June 2, 1835, 8; "The Portuguese Pirates," *Alexandria (Va.) Gazette*, July 22, 1835, 3; "The Portuguese Prisoners," *Richmond Whig*, December 8, 1835, 1.

27. Conway Robinson, *Reports of Cases Decided in the Supreme Court of Appeals and in the General Court of Virginia* (Richmond: S. Bottom, 1843), 1:674–88; "Petition 20483804," "Petition 20484002," "Petition 20484304," and "Petition 20484504," Digital Library on American Slavery, http://library.uncg.edu/slavery/ (accessed December 17, 2013). "Criminal Court," *New Orleans Daily Picayune*, February 28, 1841, 2; Merritt M. Robinson, *Reports of Cases Argued and Determined in the Supreme Court of Louisiana* (New Orleans: n.p., 1847), 7:252–315.

28. *John G. Daniel v. James P. Wilkinson*, Index Number 1835-024, 24, Powhatan County Chancery Causes; Bacon Tait to Rice C. Ballard, August 2, 1836, Rice C. Ballard Papers.

29. "Charleston and Its Prospects," *Charleston (S.C.) Courier*, June 27, 1835, 2.

30. "Prospects in Virginia," *Richmond Whig*, June 5, 1835, 1.

31. Thomas R. Dew, "On Prices," reprinted in *Richmond Enquirer*, June 30, 1835, 4.

32. About this time, William Wells Brown reported "a slaveholder by the name of Bacon Tate from the State of Tennessee, came to the north in search of fugitives from slavery." Brown said the incident happened in "the autumn of 1836," though contemporary newspaper reports dated it to the summer of 1835. In the newspaper the slave catcher was identified only as "one Tait, a slave agent from the South." Brown apparently misremembered the slave catcher's first name. The man was a Tait, but not Tait. Charles Bacon Tate, Tait's nephew in Tennessee, was too young to fit the story. William W. Brown, *Narrative of William W. Brown* (London: Charles Gilpin, 1849), 109; "Buffalo Fugitive Slave Case and Riot," *Buffalo Daily Commercial Advertiser*, July 13, 1835.

33. Bacon Tait to Rice C. Ballard, August 2, 1836, Rice C. Ballard Papers.

34. Bacon Tait to Ballard, Franklin & Co., September 23, 1835, Rice C. Ballard Papers.

35. Bacon Tait to Rice C. Ballard, January 9 and 14, 1838, Rice C. Ballard Papers.

36. Bacon Tait to Rice C. Ballard, January 9 and 14, 1838, and Bacon Tait to Thomas Boudar, January 19, 1838, Rice C. Ballard Papers; Bacon Tait, 1836, 1837, and 1838 Personal Property Tax, City of Richmond, 1835–1850, Reel 365, Library of Virginia, Richmond, Va.

37. Thomas Boudar to Rice C. Ballard, February 8, 1838, Rice C. Ballard Papers.

CHAPTER 7.

I WISH IN MY SOUL I COULD FIND A GOOD WIFE

1. "To the Public," *Richmond Enquirer*, October 3, 1834, 3; City of Richmond Deed Book 36, 167, Library of Virginia, Richmond, Va.; Bacon Tait to Rice C. Ballard, May 1, 1838, Rice C. Ballard Papers; Tomoko Yagyu, "Slave Traders and Planters in the Expanding South: Entrepreneurial Strategies, Business Networks, and Western Migration in the Atlantic World, 1787–1859" (Ph.D. diss., University of North Carolina, 2006), 203–5. The Rice C. Ballard Papers include correspondence between Tait and Ballard, between Ballard and other slave traders, and between Ballard and Dupuy, Tate, and Nalle.

2. John B. Prentis to Joseph Prentis, November 5, 1832, quoted in Kari J. Winter, *The American Dreams of John B. Prentis, Slave Trader* (Athens: Univ. of Georgia Press, 2011), 111.

3. William R. Johnson to Sidnum Grady, April 23, 1839, Reel 5071, Box 271, Frame 20, Robert Alonzo Brock Miscellaneous Files, Library of Virginia, Richmond, Va.

4. "Notice—50 Dollars Reward," *Richmond Whig*, August 7, 1840.

5. H. Gamble Grady, *The John Grady I Descendants of Virginia, West Virginia* (Laguna Hills, Calif.: Rossmore Leisure World, 1970), 73, 79.

6. L. Grady, Policy #9504, November 15, 1836, and Policy #11654, October 16, 1843, Mutual Assurance Society, Library of Virginia, Richmond, Va.; "Valuable Real Estate for Sale," *Richmond Whig*, January 31, 1843, 3; Moses Ellyson, *The Richmond Directory and Business Advertiser for 1856* (Richmond: H. K. Ellyson, 1856), 135; "Suicide on Brook Avenue," *Richmond Examiner*, August 29, 1866, 3.

7. "Angle Steel Spring Seated Saddles," *Richmond Whig*, September 8, 1835, 3; Mary Wingfield Scott, *Houses of Old Richmond* (Richmond: Valentine Museum, 1941), 53–54; James Bray,

Richmond, Henrico County, Virginia, 1850 U.S. Census; James Bray, Policy #9553 and #9554, October 19, 1837, Mutual Assurance Society, Library of Virginia, Richmond, Va.

8. F. Joseph Magri, *The Catholic Church in the City and Diocese of Richmond* (Richmond: Whittet and Shepperson, 1906), 51–53; "Married," *Lynchburg Virginian*, July 18, 1836, 3.

9. Henry Bacon Boudar, June 5, 1837–November 8, 1920, gravestone, Hollywood Cemetery, www.webcemeteries.com/Hollywood/ (accessed November 18, 2013).

10. Edward E. Baptist, "'Cuffy,' 'Fancy Maids,' and 'One-Eyed Men': Rape, Commodification, and the Domestic Slave Trade in the United States," *American Historical Review* (December 2001): 1620, 1622.

11. Robert H. Gudmestad, *A Troublesome Commerce: The Transformation of the Interstate Slave Trade* (Baton Rouge: Louisiana State Univ. Press, 2003), 75.

12. Baptist, "'Cuffy,' 'Fancy Maids,' and 'One-Eyed Men,'" 1641; Steven Deyle, *Carry Me Back: The Domestic Slave Trade in American Life* (New York: Oxford Univ. Press, 2005), 127.

13. "I am in hopes that all the fools are not dead yet and some one-eyed man will buy us out yet." James Franklin to Rice C. Ballard, May 7, 1833, Rice C. Ballard Papers.

14. Bacon Tait to Rice C. Ballard, November 25, 1838, Rice C. Ballard Papers.

15. *Lexicon Balatronicum* (London: C. Chappel, 1811), n.p.

16. James P. Franklin to Messrs. R. C. Ballard & Co., March 27, 1832, Rice C. Ballard Papers. See the introduction for more detail about Tait's letters to Ballard in this period.

17. Joshua D. Rothman, *Notorious in the Neighborhood: Sex and Families across the Color Line in Virginia, 1787–1861* (Chapel Hill: Univ. of North Carolina Press, 2003), 94, 107.

18. Bacon Tait to Rice C. Ballard, November 25, 1838, Rice C. Ballard Papers.

19. Joseph Sturge, *A Visit to the United States in 1841* (Boston: Dexter S. King, 1842), 47. He had married Emma D. Clackner, his second wife, on July 10, 1838, in Baltimore.

20. C. D. Arfwedson, *The United States and Canada, in 1832, 1833, and 1834* (London: Richard Bentley, 1834), 1:335–36.

21. "Billy Barlow, A Celebrated Comic Song," Jscholarship, https://jscholarship.library.jhu.edu/handle/1774.2/27924 (accessed November 24, 2013); "Billy Barlow, A Favorite Comic Song 2d Edition," Jscholarship, https://jscholarship.library.jhu.edu/handle/1774.2/16091 (accessed November 24, 2013); "Billy Barlow," *The United States Songster* (Cincinnati: U. P. James, 1836), 206–8; "My Long-Tail Blue," Jscholarship, https://jscholarship.library.jhu.edu/handle/1774.2/8214 (accessed November 24, 2013).

22. *The Code of Virginia* (Richmond: William F. Ritchie, 1849), 468.

23. "Extracts from an Address, Delivered before the N. E. Anti-Slavery Society, by Wm. J Snelling, Esq.," *The Abolitionist*, April 1833, 56.

24. "The Real Object of Thompson's Mission," *Richmond Enquirer*, October 27, 1835, 4.

25. James Wilson, Policy #10289, December 31, 1836, Mutual Assurance Society, Library of Virginia, Richmond, Va.

26. Bacon Tait to Rice C. Ballard, January 31, 1838, Rice C. Ballard Papers.

27. "Whig State Convention," *Richmond Whig*, October 2, 1840, 2; Bacon Tait to Rice C. Ballard, January 16, 1838, and May 1, 1838, Rice C. Ballard Papers.

28. Ulrich Bonnell Phillips, *Life and Labor in the Old South* (Boston: Little, Brown, 1929), 177.

29. Bacon Tait to Rice C. Ballard, Rice C. Ballard Papers. The first page with the date is missing, but it probably is 1839 because Franklin married in 1839 and Ballard married the following year.

CHAPTER 8.
DAT DE WAY HE GIT RICH

1. Bacon Tait to Thomas Boudar, January 1, 1840, Rice C. Ballard Papers.

2. Bacon Tait to Rice C. Ballard, January 3, 1840, Rice C. Ballard Papers.

3. Bacon Tait to "gentlemen," September 1, 1840, and Bacon Tait to Rice C. Ballard or John Armfield, October 14, 1840, Rice C. Ballard Papers. Tait referred several times to "Mr. Johnson" in his September 1, 1850, letter, saying he wrote him in Staunton. Tait also referred to writing "Mr. Leigh." From the context, they appear to be lawyers, and both Benjamin Watkins Leigh and Chapman Johnson were well-known lawyers in the area. Eugenia G. Glazebrook and Preston G. Glazebrook, *Virginia Migrations, Hanover County* (1949; reprint, Baltimore: Genealogical Publishing, 2002), iv; "Negro Bricklayers," *New Orleans Daily Picayune,* January 26, 1840; *1842 New Orleans City Directory,* http://files.usgwarchives.net/la/orleans/history/directory/1842ad-i.txt (accessed December 14, 2013).

4. Benjamin C. Howard, *Reports of Cases Argued and Adjudged in the Supreme Court of the United States, January Term, 1847* (Boston: Charles C. Little and James Brown, 1847), 5:134–41; Bacon Tait to Rice C. Ballard, August 4, 1839, Rice C. Ballard Papers.

5. Bacon Tait to Rice C. Ballard or John Armfield, October 14, 1840, Rice C. Ballard Papers.

6. "Passengers," *Charleston (S.C.) Courier,* October 24, 1840, 2.

7. Bacon Tait to Rice C. Ballard, May 6, 1841, Rice C. Ballard Papers.

8. Sidnum Grady to John H. Barlow, June 20, 1843, Southall Papers, 1807–1904, Earl Gregg Swem Library, College of William and Mary, Williamsburg, Va.; "Mansion House," *Richmond Whig,* July 5, 1841, 3.

9. Sidnum Grady to John H. Barlow, June 20, 1843, Southall Papers.

10. "The City," *Richmond Whig,* March 8, 1872, 4.

11. Boudar's office was at 19 Moreau Street according to the *1842 New Orleans City Directory,* http://files.usgwarchives.net/la/orleans/history/directory/1842ad-i.txt (accessed December 14, 2013), and at 5 Moreau Street according to the *1851 New Orleans City Directory,* http://files.usgwarchives.net/la/orleans/history/directory/1851cdab.txt (accessed December 14, 2013).

12. "Mysteries of a Shamble," *New York Tribune,* July 15, 1861. The same article was printed as a chapter in Moncure Daniel Conway, *Testimonies Concerning Slavery* (London: Chapman and Hall, 1864), implying he was the author of the unsigned article. Conway was a native Virginian who became an abolitionist.

13. "The 'American System,'" *Liberator* (Boston, Mass.), December 2, 1842, 190.

14. Bacon Tait to Rice C. Ballard, May 9, 1841, Rice C. Ballard Papers.

15. *Jim Crow's Vagaries, or, Black Flights of Fancy: Containing a Choice Collection of Nigger Melodies* (London: Orlando Hodgson, 1840).

16. "Passengers," *Southern Patriot* (Charleston, S.C.), October 26, 1841, 2.

17. "Was committed to the jail . . . ," *Richmond Whig*, December 7, 1841, 4.

18. Quotes and information on the *Creole* revolt, unless otherwise noted, are taken from "Protest of the Officers of the Creole," *Niles' National Register*, January 22, 1842, 323–26, and depositions of witnesses published in *Correspondence on the Slave Trade with Foreign Powers . . . from January 1 to December 31, 1842* (London: William Clowes and Sons, 1843).

19. Merritt M. Robinson, "McCargo v The New Orleans Insurance Company," *Reports of Cases Argued and Determined in the Supreme Court of Louisiana* (New Orleans: Samuel M. Stewart, 1845), 1:220.

20. Ibid., 1:217. The names are usually taken from the Louisiana State Supreme Court suit, where only two are noted by name, but all the names are available on the *Creole's* manifest. Historian Walter Johnson also noted the complex cooperation, connections, and signs of mercy between the races that occurred on the *Creole* in the midst of the hostility of insurrection. Walter Johnson, "White Lies: Human Property and Domestic Slavery Aboard the Slave Ship *Creole*," *Atlantic Studies* (August 2008): 237–63.

21. "From the Boston Morning Post, Municipal Court," *Salem (Mass.) Register*, March 16, 1846, 2; "List of letters remaining in the Salem Post Office . . . Cortney [sic] Fountain," *Salem (Mass.) Register*, September 8, 1859, 3; Stephen B. Ives letter, Brock Collection, Miscellaneous Reel 5099, Image 34, Library of Virginia, Richmond, Va.; quit claim deed, Brock Collection, Miscellaneous Reel 5087, Image 82, Library of Virginia, Richmond, Va.; "The City. An Interesting Lawsuit . . . ," *Richmond Whig*, March 8, 1872.

22. Marie Josephine Tait and Bacon C. Tait, Passport Applications, 1795–1905, National Archives and Records Administration, Washington, D.C.

23. George W. Bagby, *Selections from the Miscellaneous Writings of Dr. George W. Bagby* (Richmond: Whittet and Shepperson, 1884), 1:179.

24. *Eighth Annual Report of the Board of Managers of the Mass. Anti-Slavery Society* (Boston: Dow and Jackson, 1840), 38.

25. George Hendrick and Willene Hendrick, *Black Refugees in Canada* (Jefferson, N.C.: McFarland, 2010), 55. The Hendricks say Madison was "in Utica, New York, being helped by the black minister Henry Highland Garnet." Garnet had graduated from Utica's Oneida Theological Institute in 1840, but he had moved to Troy by 1842. Jack Rummel, *African-American Social Leaders and Activists* (New York: Facts on File, 2003), 79.

26. Henry Highland Garnet, *A Memorial Discourse* (Philadelphia: Joseph M. Wilson, 1865), 50–51.

27. Reverend James Fountain was listed as residing in New York for twenty-nine years in the Ward 4, Utica, Oneida County, 1855 New York Census.

28. "Debate Over Garnet's 'Address to the Slaves . . . ,'" 1843, reprinted in *Pamphlets of Protest*, ed. Richard Newman, Patrick Rael, and Philip Lapsansky (New York: Routledge, 2001), 159.

CHAPTER 9.
GOOD AND WORTHY CITIZENS

1. "Census of Richmond," *Richmond Whig*, October 20, 1840, 2. The raw numbers were: 5,435 white males, 5,283 white females, 860 free colored males, 1,065 free colored females, 3,953 male slaves, and 3,556 female slaves.

2. *The Code of Virginia* (Richmond: William F. Ritchie, 1849), 466–67.

3. "List of Letters," *Salem (Mass.) Register*, September 8, 1859, 3.

4. A woman named Courtney, age about thirty, was manumitted along with her four children in Winchester, Virginia, in 1835 by her owner, Margaret Galloway. The last name Peters appears once in the manumission statement, a last name not connected with Courtney Fountain, so she was not the same person connected with Bacon Tait. Deed Book 8, 53, Frederick County Courthouse, Winchester, Va..

5. "John S. Washington," Massachusetts Deaths 1841–1915, FamilySearch, https://familysearch.org/pal:/MM9.3.1/TH-267-11843-133859-79?cc=1463156 (accessed September 27, 2014); "Julie W. (Fountain) Williams," Massachusetts Deaths 1841–1915, FamilySearch, https://familysearch.org/pal:/MM9.3.1/TH-267-11053-188464-62?cc=1463156 (accessed September 27, 2014).

6. According to his obituaries and death certificate, Abram Williams was born in Africa, the son of Dabier and Sah Saul. While a boy, he "was stolen from his home on the Congo river and sold into slavery, becoming the property of an English officer, from whose custody he was released under the most romantic circumstances. He came to Salem with Capt. Christopher Babbage before the year 1800." Later, he "was in Colonel Benjamin Pickman's family from 1806 to the colonel's death, and received his master's house as a reward for his service."

Captain Babbage was most likely the descendant of a long line of men by that name and a master mariner who was born in Salem in 1770 and died there in 1836. Colonel Pickman died in 1819, though neither he nor Captain Babbage listed any nonwhites or slaves in their households in the 1800 census. Abram Williams appeared as a free coloured man in the 1810 census with his first wife and family. By the 1850 census he was married to Julia and employed as a laborer. Her son, John S. Washington Jr., still lived with them, working as a stove polisher.

In 1854, John Jr. married Sara Malysa Blanchard. Though she was from New Hampshire, she was being raised by her aunt in Salem after the death of her father. Even in the 1850s Massachusetts was a world apart from Virginia. John Jr.'s new wife was the daughter of a mulatto husband and his white wife. Her family were friends with Harriet E. Wilson, who may have fictionalized some of them into *Our Nig*, an autobiographical novel about an interracial young woman's life, printed in 1859 by Rand and Avery, the same Boston company that printed *Uncle Tom's Cabin*.

During the Civil War, John, although thirty-five years old, volunteered in September of 1864 for one year of service in the 54th Massachusetts, at a time when colored troops had proved their mettle. Their pay was now the same as white troops and the bounty for enlisting, whether "white or colored," was $100. In November, still in training on Galloup's Island off the coast of Massachusetts, John was transferred to the 55th Massachusetts, though not sent south with them. He spent the war on detached service at the island, where new regiments were continually trained and old regiments mustered out. In May of 1865, at the end of the war, he was discharged and returned home to his wife and children.

The Utica Fountains were entwined in another way with John's mother, Julia. She and his stepfather, Abram, although past middle age, took in two young grandchildren from the Utica clan, James and Courtney Smith, age five and three, after their mother died in 1859.

John prospered in the stove business, eventually having his own store and coal yard. By the 1860s his parents were aging. Abram's sight failed around 1862, and in 1865 he spent a week in the Boston infirmary but was diagnosed with incurable cataracts and remained blind for the rest of his life. Julia died of Bright's disease in 1878 at the age of eighty-eight, and John took in his stepfather, Abram, until Abram's death on September 26, 1880. Abram claimed to have turned one hundred years old in March of that year, though based on earlier reports of his age he was probably a few years younger. He enjoyed visitors and a modicum of celebrity on his birthday for both his age and the story of his rise from African slavery. John outlived his wife and died in Salem at the age of 83 in 1913.

Adams, Sampson and Co., *Salem Directory* (Salem: Geo. M. Whipple and A. A. Smith, 1864), 97, 191; "Among the recent enlistments . . . ," *Salem Observer,* September 10, 1864, 2; "New England News," *Worcester (Mass.) Daily Spy,* March 8, 1880, 4; "Obituary," *Boston Daily Advertiser,* September 27, 1880, 1; Harriet Ruth Waters Cook, *The Driver Family* (New York: John Wilson and Son, 1889), 242; George Francis Dow, *Diary and Letters of Benjamin Pickman (1740–1819) of Salem, Massachusetts* (Newport, R.I.: n.p., 1928); Julia W. Williams, Salem Ward 2, Essex County, Massachusetts, 1850 U.S. Census; "John Washington," Massachusetts Marriages 1841–1915, FamilySearch, https://familysearch.org/pal:/MM9.1.1/N4MP-34N (accessed September 27, 2014); JerriAnne Boggis and Eve Allegra Raimon, *Harriet Wilson's New England: Race, Writing, and Region* (Lebanon, N.H.: Univ. of New Hampshire Press, 2007), 56; P. Gabrielle Foreman and Reginald H. Pitts, "Introduction," *Our Nig; or, Sketches from the Life of a Free Black* (New York: Penguin Group, 2005), xlvii n. 19; "John S. Washington," U.S. Colored Troops Military Service Records, 1861–1865, National Archives and Records Administration, Ancestry.com; Abraham Williams, Salem Ward 2, Essex County, Massachusetts, 1860 U.S. Census; "Courtney Smith," Massachusetts Deaths 1841–1915, FamilySearch, https://familysearch.org/pal:/MM9.3.1/TH-266-11124-143729-5?cc=1463156 (accessed September 27, 2014); Abraam [*sic*] Williams, Essex County, Massachusetts, Schedules of Defective, Dependent and Delinquent Classes, 1880 U.S. Census; "Obituary," *Boston Daily Advertiser,* September 27, 1880, 1; "New England News," *Worcester (Mass.) Daily Spy,* March 8, 1880, 4; "Abraham Williams," Massachusetts Deaths 1841–1915, FamilySearch, https://familysearch.org/pal:/MM9.3.1/TH-266-11816-159960-32?cc=1463156 (accessed September 27, 2014).

7. "Meeting of the State Council, in Behalf of Colored Americans," *Liberator* (Boston,

Mass.), February 24, 1854, 30; "Massachusetts State Council," *Liberator* (Boston, Mass.), July 28, 1854, 119.

8. James Fountain was born about 1787 or 1788, the same generation as Courtney's father, John, and may have been her uncle, cousin, or much older brother. In 1820 he was living with his wife, Eva Kidd Fountain, and seven children in Winchester, Virginia, but in 1826 they left for Utica, New York, where he engaged in activities not possible in Virginia.

A shoemaker by trade, he served as pastor of a black church in Utica. Both he and his son attended conventions demanding rights for blacks, including voting equality for black New Yorkers. He served as chairman at a June 1841 meeting of the "colored citizens of Utica," while his twenty-year-old son James Jr. was appointed a secretary, and the members chose James Sr. as Utica's delegate to the upcoming statewide convention in Troy.

At the Troy meeting, August 25–27, he was selected a vice president, and members voted to hold the next annual meeting in his hometown. "The object of the Convention was to take measures for the repeal of that part of the Constitution of the State, which makes an odious and oppressive distinction between white and colored citizens, by requiring of every colored person real estate to the amount of $250, before he can be allowed to vote; while every drunken vagabond, who is of a white complexion, is exempted from this provision!"

At the statewide meeting in Utica the following year, August 24, 1842, the sixty-five delegates appointed Reverend Fountain vice president and also resolved "that we heartily concur with the Declaration of American Independence that it is a *self-evident* truth that all men are created equal." They demanded once again equal voting rights in New York State.

Though the conventions were less than successful, they gave Reverend Fountain connections with other like-minded people. At the National Negro Convention in Buffalo, New York, in 1843, where he voted in support of violence like the *Creole* insurrection, he met noted abolitionists Frederick Douglass and Charles Lennox Remond. Remond came from Salem, Massachusetts, where some of Reverend Fountain's kin already lived. In a few years, Reverend Fountain's son James would move to the same area. In the 1850s, James Jr. lived in Marblehead, Massachusetts, where his wife, Lucy Brown, and mother-in-law, Lucretia Thomas Brown, owned a tavern. After his mother-in-law died he moved to Salem, where he worked as a barber.

During the Civil War, James Jr. enlisted in the 54th Massachusetts in the fall of 1864, along with John S. Washington, and, like him, was transferred to the 55th Massachusetts. Unlike Private Washington, who remained detached at Galloup's Island, James Fountain Jr. was sent to South Carolina and served in Company F of the 55th at Folly Island and Long Island, South Carolina, before being discharged in August of 1865 at Charleston, South Carolina.

Though James's father, Reverend Fountain, remained in Utica, dying in 1855 at the age of sixty-nine, several of his children besides James Jr. moved to Massachusetts. Catherine Fountain, born in 1819 when the family was still living in Winchester, Virginia, also moved to Essex, in Essex County, Massachusetts, the same county as Salem. She married mariner Charles Richardson there in 1856. Martha, born about 1825, moved to Marblehead, Massachusetts, but died unmarried of consumption at the age of twenty-two. Courtney, born in

1829 and probably named after Tait's future wife, married William Smith and moved to Essex County, Massachusetts, where she died in 1859. Her son, William Jr., born in 1849, claimed he was eighteen in 1864, though he was only fifteen, and enlisted in the 54th Massachusetts at the same time as his uncle, James W. Fountain Jr., serving with him in Co. F of the 55th Massachusetts in South Carolina. Edward, born in 1835, and Felix, born about 1827, both barbers, also moved to Marblehead. George, born about 1837 or 1838, was also a barber, but he remained in New York State, moving 150 miles west to the town of Leroy, Genessee County. The family also had a daughter, Mary, born 1840, and other unidentified children.

James Fountain, Utica City Ward 4, Oneida County, 1855 New York State Census; James Fountain, Winchester, Frederick County, Va., 1820 U.S. Census; "Catherine A. (Fountain) Richardson," Massachusetts Deaths 1841–1915, FamilySearch, https://familysearch.org/pal:/ MM9.3.1/TH-267-11082-191834-72?cc=1463156 (accessed September 27, 2014); "Public Meeting at Utica," *Colored American,* August 14, 1841; "Important Movement," *Liberator* (Boston, Mass.), September 17, 1841, 151; "New York," *Emancipator and Weekly Chronicle* (Boston, Mass.), October 6, 1842, 90; "Died," *Salem (Mass.) Register,* May 28, 1857, 2; James W. Fountain, Marblehead, Essex County, Massachusetts, 1850 U.S. Census; James W. Fountain, Marblehead, Essex County, 1855 Massachusetts State Census; James W. Fountain, Salem, Essex County, Massachusetts, 1860 U.S. Census; "James W. Fountain," Massachusetts Marriages 1841–1915, FamilySearch, https://familysearch.org/pal:/MM9.3.1/TH-267-11617-86131-5?cc=1469062 (accessed September 27, 2014); "James W. Fountain," U.S. Colored Troops Military Service Records, 1861–1865, National Archives and Records Administration, Ancestry.com; "Died," *Boston Courier,* December 24, 1855, 4; "Catherine Fountain," Massachusetts Marriage Records 1840–1915, Ancestry.com; "Catherine Fountain," Massachusetts Deaths 1841–1915, FamilySearch, https://familysearch.org/pal:/MM9.3.1/TH-267-11082-191834-72?cc=1463156 (accessed September 25, 2014); Martha S. Fountain, Marblehead Deaths, Early Vital Records of Massachusetts from 1600–1850, http://ma-vitalrecords.org/ MA/Essex/Marblehead/cDeathsOt.shtml (accessed September 25, 2014); Courtney Smith, Massachusetts Deaths 1841–1915, FamilySearch, https://familysearch.org/pal:/MM9.3.1/ TH-266-11124-143729-5?cc=1463156 (accessed September 25, 2014); "Edward A. Fountain death certificate," Massachusetts Deaths 1841–1915, FamilySearch, https://familysearch.org/ pal:/MM9.3.1/TH-266-12116-16582-64?cc=1463156&wc=12502841 (accessed September 25, 2014); "Felix Fountain death certificate," Massachusetts Deaths 1841–1915, FamilySearch, https://familysearch.org/pal:/MM9.3.1/TH-266-11087-179277-71?cc=1463156 (accessed September 25, 2014); George Fountain, Leroy, Genessee County, New York, 1870 U.S. Census.

9. Born about 1814, he had a barber shop in Winchester, advertising in 1841: "Look at this.—Hatley Fountain has just returned from Baltimore with a new assortment of Fancy Articles," listing shirts, suspenders, shaving brushes and hair tonic. "He continues to carry on the Barbering and Hair Dressing business at the old stand."

His business gave him reason to make regular trips to Baltimore, and though he advertised bringing goods back, he denied ever helping any property leave from Winchester *to* Baltimore. He married—as much as he could marry—an enslaved woman named Eleanor who belonged to a local doctor, Robert Baldwin. Eleanor had "a fair complexion, nearly white, with waving red hair," and was a few years younger than him. About 1840 they had a son, George, who was born the property of Dr. Baldwin like his mother, but the doctor was a benign master who considered Eleanor "a valuable servant," and said that "his children loved her almost as well as they did their mother."

In 1843, Hatley Fountain borrowed $100 from John Templeton of Pittsburgh, Pennsylvania, pledging his property on Market Street in Winchester as security. Templeton had been born a slave in South Carolina and, after being freed in 1813, earned a degree from Ohio University, taught in Ohio, then moved to Pittsburgh in 1836, where he was the principal of a school to educate black children, continuing to work for the cause of abolition. He was not the kind of man to invest randomly in a Virginia barbershop unless the money was to be put to good use.

December 18, the night after the loan was recorded in the Frederick County Deed Book, one of Winchester's leading citizens, Bushrod Taylor, discovered that his slave John Webb was missing. Also gone were Webb's free wife, Emily, and five of their children. Suspicion fell on Hatley Fountain and the white abolitionist Charles Torrey. Taylor never recovered the family, who arrived in Canada. Charles Torrey was not caught and tried for the crime until the next summer, but Fountain, living locally, was easy to locate.

> On the bare suspicion, [Hatley Fountain] was seized, heavily ironed, and imprisoned for ten weeks, during the most inclement part of the winter; and early in the spring, was brought out for trial. Through the kindness of his wife's master, (a gentleman of high respectability,) he was assisted and defended by able counsel; and the designs of his enemies were so far frustrated that he was fully acquitted of the charge laid against him. But, for the sufferings he has undergone, he could have no redress; and while he had been in prison, his business was broken up, and a rival establishment set up in the immediate neighborhood. Under such a pressure of adverse circumstances, he has yielded to the wishes of his friends, and determined to move to a free State, beyond the reach of his persecutors. But alas! his wife and his child may not accompany him!

Dr. Baldwin claimed to have an offer of $800 for Hatley's wife, but proposed to sell her and her son, George, to Hatley for just $400. Hatley traveled through the Northeast in the summer and fall of 1844, speaking to abolitionist societies to raise the money. For example, at a "meeting of the colored citizens of Boston for the relief of Charles T. Torrey," attended by William Lloyd Garrison, "J.N.H. Fountain, an intelligent colored man from Winchester, Va . . . was present, and related, in an affecting manner, his trials and sufferings during his incarceration, and his final expulsion from the place on pain of lynch law, being compelled to leave behind him a beloved wife in slavery." He also met John Greenleaf Whittier when he was in Lowell, Massachusetts. Abolitionists investigated his story, found him to be honest, and donated.

Almost a year after Hatley left Winchester, he wrote William Lloyd Garrison from Philadelphia on December 13, 1844, that his wife "arrived in Philadelphia on the 10th of December; and not withstanding she is much broken by labor and distress the last year, since she began to breathe the air of the free States, she has sensibly revived, and in a short time will, it is thought be perfectly restored. Dear Sir, words are inadequate to express the gratitude that we feel to the people of Massachusetts, New York, and Pennsylvania, for their assistance in raising the one of God's children from the condition of Chattel to that of a human being. We think that, with the aid of Providence, we can take care of ourselves. Yours, in behalf of bleeding humanity, John N.H. Fountain."

A person named Felix Fountain actually went to pay $400 to Dr. Baldwin, who emancipated Eleanor Fountain on December 2, 1844, as agreed. Reverend James Fountain's son Felix would have been only seventeen or eighteen years old, but he may have been the person sent, indicating a closer connection between Hatley and the Reverend Fountain.

By 1850, Hatley, Eleanor, and their son, George, were living in Pittsburgh. He was working as a barber again, and they also appeared to be keeping a boarding house, with several unrelated people living with them. Also in the household were James E. and Robert S. Fountain, thirty and twenty-eight, barbers born in Virginia. They were too old to be Hatley's sons, but were perhaps brothers or cousins. Black abolitionist and educator John Templeton also was still in Pittsburgh, teaching school, and living with him was Richard Fountain, fifteen, born in Virginia, probably another relative of the Winchester Fountain clan, though his connection is not known.

John Hatley Fountain's unusual name, sometimes given as the initials J. N. H. Fountain, offers a tantalizing clue to some relationship the Fountains had with another family. John Hatley Norton (1745–1797) was a wealthy white man and slave owner who lived in Winchester from 1781 until his death. Norton had several children, one of whom was named Courtenay, born in the 1770s and died 1841. Both Hatley and Courtenay/Courtney were family names used many times within the Norton lineage. Though most of the other first names that the Norton family shared with the Fountain family were common, the names Courtney and especially John Hatley are unusual enough that they seem more than coincidence, yet no evidence is available now to indicate why the families shared their names.

A possible reason would be that the Fountains were owned by the Nortons before being freed, or that Courtney Fountain's branch of the family was still enslaved by them. However, Courtney Fountain's older sister, Ann, claimed to be born free. If true, that would mean that Courtney's mother was presumably still free when Courtney was born. It is possible to trace slaves owned by the Nortons from Winchester to Richmond. John Hatley Norton even left an enslaved woman named Hannah, the same name and generation as Courtney's mother, to his wife in his will, "on this express condition that she shall at her death leave them . . . to my child or children which she has or may have by me." The twenty-six slaves that John Hatley Norton left to his wife went to her son, Dr. Daniel Norborne Norton, who received them as a wedding present in 1818. He lived in Richmond and died on January 23, 1842, possibly putting them on the market about the time that Tait is known to have met Courtney, because she became pregnant with their first child in May of 1842. However, the list of slaves in Daniel Norborne Norton's estate inventory included neither a Hannah nor a Courtney. It is therefore unlikely that Courtney belonged to the Nortons or that she was enslaved, and she was probably free like most of the Winchester Fountains. The reason that the free Fountains shared first names with the wealthy white Nortons living in the same city remains a mystery.

"Look at this," *Winchester Virginian,* October 27, 1841, 3; Deed Book 73, 165, Frederick County Courthouse, Winchester, Va.; *Middlesex Standard,* October 10, 1844, quoted in "Network to Freedom," National Park Service, www.nps.gov/subjects/ugrr/community/ shared_stories_details.htm?STORYID=13955 (accessed January 19, 2014); John N. H., Eleanor and George Fountain, Pittsburgh Ward 4, Pennsylvania, 1850 U.S. Census; Deed Book 72, 275, Frederick County Courthouse, Winchester, Va.; Connie and Michel Perdreau, "John Newton Templeton," www.seorf.ohiou.edu/~xx057/john_newton_templeton.htm (accessed January 20, 2014); "C. T. Torrey," *Liberator* (Boston, Mass.), August 9, 1844, 127; "Meeting of the Colored Citizens of Boston for the Relief of Charles T. Torrey," *Emancipator and Weekly Chronicle* (Boston, Mass.), August 28, 1844, 70; "Mass Meeting in Behalf of Torrey and Walker," *Liberator* (Boston, Mass.), September 27, 1844, 155; "John Hatly Fountain Story," National Park Service, www.nps.gov/subjects/ugrr/community/shared_stories_details. htm?STORYID=13955 (accessed January 19, 2014); "A Wife Redeemed!" *Liberator* (Boston, Mass.), December 20, 1844, 203; Deed Book 73, 165, Frederick County Courthouse, Winchester, Va.; "Arrest of a Supposed Abolitionist," *Salem (Mass.) Register,* October 30, 1845, 2; Estate Inventory of Daniel Norborne Norton, Henrico County Will Book 11, Library of Virginia, Richmond, Va., 26–29.

10. In Salem, Ann's husband worked as a cook aboard the brig *Ann,* which limped home from Zanzibar in 1829 after nearly being destroyed in a storm at sea. He received $30 as part of the insurance reward given to the crew and apparently worked on land for a while. In 1835 he advertised that he would "tend to all kinds of job work, including GARDENING; WASHING WINDOWS; Cleaning Cellars, Bottling Wine & Cider, Attending on Parties, Tables, &c &c." But by 1839 he was at sea again, and not so fortunate. As a crew member of the brig *Eagle* he drowned in Para, in South America, on October 17, 1839, at the age of forty-seven.

"Capt. Charles Millet," *Salem (Mass.) Gazette,* June 5, 1829, 1; George Granville Putnam, *Salem Vessels and Their Voyages* (Salem, Mass.: Essex Institute, 1922), 1:52–54; "Deaths," *Boston Traveler,* December 27, 1839, 3.

11. "Vital Records of Salem, Mass. to the end of year 1849," (Salem, Mass.: Essex Institute, 1916), available at http://dunhamwilcox.net/ma/salem_marr_ m1.htm (accessed February 4, 2014).

12. Wilbur H. Siebert, "The Underground Railroad in Massachusetts," *American Antiquarian Society,* April 1935, 56; "The Libel Case—The Testimony of Mr. Innis . . . ," *New York Herald,* 1846, http://fultonhistory.com/Newspaper%2014/New%20York%20NY%20Herald/ New%20York%20NY%20Herald%201846/New%20York%20NY%20Herald%201846%20 -%200512.pdf (accessed September 28, 2014).

13. "From the Boston Morning Post, Municipal Court," *Salem (Mass.) Register,* March 16, 1846, 2.

14. "Arrest of a Supposed Abolitionist," *Salem (Mass.) Register,* October 30, 1845, 2.

15. "John Junifer," *Salem (Mass.) Register,* November 17, 1845, 2.

16. Despite Junifer's fame, he still needed to find work. In February he called at the offices of *The Emancipator* in Boston, which noted, "He is waiting to find permanent employment on a farm, in a garden, or at any other business to which he is accustomed. Who will hire him?" In 1850 he was still living with his mother and siblings, but in 1852 he married Harriet Harris, originally from Nova Scotia, and worked as a mariner and at other jobs until he was killed in a railroad accident in 1862. The other children of Ann Fountain Marbray Stearns married and raised their children in the Salem area. She died of paralysis in Salem in 1873, two years after her sister, Courtney.

"John Junifer . . . ," *Salem (Mass.) Register,* December 4, 1845; "From the Boston Morning Post, Municipal Court," *Salem (Mass.) Register,* March 16, 1846, 2; "Trial for Libel," *Salem (Mass.) Register,* March 19, 1846, 2; "John Junifer," *The Emancipator* (Boston, Mass.), February 25, 1846, 174; "Married," *Salem (Mass.) Register,* December 30, 1852; John T. Junifer, Salem Ward 1, Essex County, 1855 Massachusetts State Census; "Fatal Casualty," *Salem (Mass.) Register,* September 11, 1862, 2; "Ann (Fountain) Stearns," Massachusetts Deaths 1841–1915, FamilySearch, https://familysearch.org/pal:/MM9.3.1/TH-267-11665-47287-60?cc=1463156 (accessed September 27, 2014).

17. "John W. Fountain," Massachusetts Deaths 1841–1915, FamilySearch, https://familysearch.org/pal:/MM9.3.1/TH-267-11828-86252-48?cc=1463156 (accessed September 27, 2014).

18. George Adams, *Salem Directory* (Salem, Mass.: Henry Whipple and Son, 1857), 93, 124.

19. Hannah Catherine Craddock, "Black Female Landowners in Richmond, Virginia 1850–1877," https://digitalarchive.wm.edu/bitstream/handle/10288/17340/Craddock_Thesis.pdf?sequence=1 (accessed October 2, 2014).

20. *Proceedings of the N. H. Anti-Slavery Convention* (Concord, N.H.: Eastman, Webster and Co., 1834), 21.

21. Joseph Tate, *Digest of the Laws of Virginia* (Richmond: Smith and Palmer, 1841), 686.

22. Bacon Tait to Rice C. Ballard, August 14, 1842, Rice C. Ballard Papers.

CHAPTER 10.

HE EXPECTS TO LEAVE RICHMOND SHORTLY

1. "A List of the Members Belonging to the Richmond Fire Association," *Richmond Enquirer,* December 1, 1845, 2; "Richmond Fire Association," *Richmond Enquirer,* March 8, 1847, 2; "Fires," *New York Spectator,* September 7, 1848, 4.

2. "At a meeting of the Commissioners . . . ," *Richmond Whig,* March 23, 1847, 2; "A meeting was held . . . ," *Richmond Enquirer,* November 9, 1847, 1.

3. "The following gentlemen . . . ," *Richmond Enquirer,* April 7, 1847, 2; "The New Council and Aldermen," *Richmond Enquirer,* April 9, 1847, 2; "City Council—Jan. 10," *Richmond Whig,* January 14, 1848, 2; "City Organization," *Richmond Whig,* April 7, 1848, 2; "Our City Council," *Richmond Enquirer,* August 4, 1848, 2; "Election of Mayor, Recorder, Aldermen and

Councilmen," *Richmond Enquirer,* April 10, 1849, 1; "City Council and Light," *Richmond Whig,* November 27, 1849, 2; Jeff Eastman, *Fulton Gas Works Site Development Plan for the National Slavery Museum in Richmond, Virginia* (Richmond, Va.: City of Richmond Department of Community Development, 2008), 10; "At a meeting of the City Council . . . ," *Richmond Whig,* October 12, 1849, 2; "A Card," *Richmond Whig,* October 26, 1849, 1.

4. "To the Citizens of Jefferson Ward," *Richmond Whig,* March 22, 1850; "Municipal Elections," *Richmond Enquirer,* April 5, 1850, 4; Joshua D. Rothman, *Notorious in the Neighborhood: Sex and Families across the Color Line in Virginia, 1787–1861* (Chapel Hill: Univ. of North Carolina Press, 2003), 90. Gustavus Myers was apparently no relation to Tait's employee Solomon Myers.

5. "Municipal Elections," *Richmond Enquirer,* April 5, 1850, 4; Charles Palmer to William P. Palmer, March 3, 1851, Palmer Family Papers, quoted in Gregg D. Kimball, *American City, Southern Place: A Cultural History of Antebellum Richmond* (Athens: Univ. of Georgia Press, 2000), 112.

6. "Proposals," *Richmond Enquirer,* August 6, 1845, 3; "Five Stores for Rent" and "New Auction and Commission House," *Richmond Enquirer,* March 6, 1847, 3; Thomas Johnson Michie, *Virginia Reports, Jefferson—33 Grattan, 1730–1880 Volumes 1 and 2* (Charlottesville, Va.: Michie Company, 1902), 696.

7. U.S. Congress, House of Representatives, "Report No. 410 to Accompany Bill H. R. No. 360," 30th Cong., 1st sess., March 28, 1848; "Public Meeting," *Richmond Whig,* June 29, 1849, 1.

8. "Auction Sale of Real Estate," *Richmond Whig,* July 7, 1848, 4; "For Sale," *Richmond Whig,* November 13, 1846, 2.

9. "Thirty Dollars Reward," *Richmond Whig,* June 17, 1845, 2; Bacon Tait to George W. Southall, March 10, 1846, Southall Papers, 1807–1904, Earl Gregg Swem Library, College of William and Mary, Williamsburg, Va.

10. "Mortuary Notice," *Richmond Enquirer,* July 1, 1845, 2; *Catharine Hill v. Joseph W. Tucker, executor of Abner Robinson,* https://bulk.resource.org/courts.gov/c/US/54/54.US.458. html (accessed March 10, 2014).

11. *Bacon Tait v. Louisa DeEnde, et al.,* Cumberland County Chancery Causes, image 105, http://www.lva.virginia.gov/chancery/full_case_detail.asp?CFN=049-1857-024 (accessed October 2, 2014).

12. "Most Valuable Real Estate," *Richmond Whig,* December 3, 1850, 3; William L. Montague, *Richmond Directory* (Richmond: J. W. Woods, 1852), 24; "School Notice," *Richmond Daily Dispatch,* September 22, 1864, 2; "Death of Thomas Boudar," *Richmond Daily Dispatch,* July 10, 1871, 1; Thomas Boudar, Policy #410, August 13, 1851, Mutual Assurance Society, Library of Virginia, Richmond, Va.

13. Joseph and Thomas Boudar, Worcester Ward 6, Massachusetts, 1850 U.S. Census; "College Commencements," *New York Herald,* July 30, 1848, 1; "Commencement of the Catholic College at Worcester, Mass.," *Mississippi Free Trader* (Natchez), September 4, 1850, 1; "Annual Commencement of the College of the Holy Cross," *Boston Daily Atlas,* July 25, 1851, 2.

14. Chapman Johnson and Robert G. Scott, *Revision and Digest of the Criminal Code of Vir-*

ginia (Richmond: Shepherd and Colin, 1846), 69; John H. Russell, *The Free Negro in Virginia, 1619–1865* (Baltimore: Johns Hopkins Press, 1913), 144.

15. Rebecca R. Noel, "Salem as the Nation's Schoolhouse," in *Salem: Place, Myth, and Memory*, ed. Dane Anthony Morrison and Nancy Lusignan Schultz (Lebanon, N.H.: Northeastern Univ. Press, 2004), 144–49.

16. Richmond City Council Records, 1848–1852, Reel 105, Library of Virginia, Richmond, Va.

17. Stephen B. Ives letter, Miscellaneous Reel 5099, Image 34, Brock Collection, Library of Virginia, Richmond, Va.

18. Bacon Tait, October 23, 1850, City of Richmond Deed Book 59, 22, Library of Virginia, Richmond, Va.

19. Stephen B. Ives letter, Library of Virginia, Richmond, Va.

20. "Anti-Slavery Courtesy," *Salem (Mass.) Register,* July 10, 1841, 2.

21. P. Frazer Smith, *Pennsylvania State Reports* (Philadelphia: Kay and Brother, 1871), 66:115–16.

22. Mary H. Leach to Bacon Tait, July 6, 1852, Salem, Massachusetts, Deed Book 463, 237, Essex County Registry of Deeds, Salem, Massachusetts; Thomas T. Florence to Bacon Tait, August 23, 1859, Salem, Massachusetts, Deed Book 593, 105, Essex County Registry of Deeds, Salem, Massachusetts.

23. "Estate on Cedar Street at Auction," *Salem (Mass.) Register,* September 25, 1865; "Household Furniture at Auction," *Salem (Mass.) Register,* September 7, 1865.

24. H. McIntyre, *Map of City of Salem Mass* (Salem: Henry McIntyre, 1851).

25. John Cassell, Salem Ward 3, Essex County, Massachusetts, 1850 U.S. Census; George Adams, *Salem Directory* (Salem, Mass.: Henry Whipple, 1851), 56; George Adams, *Salem Directory* (Salem, Mass.: Henry Whipple, 1857), 68; James Fountain and James Castell, West Dalles Precinct, Wasco County, Oregon, 1870 U.S. Census; "Up the Columbia," *The Weekly Enterprise* (Oregon City, Oregon), September 11, 1869, 1; "The 'Freedom Celebration,'" *Salem (Mass.) Register,* February 21, 1856, 2.

26. Louis Ruchames, ed., *The Letters of William Lloyd Garrison: From Disunionism to the Brink of War, 1850–1860* (Cambridge, Mass.: Harvard Univ. Press, 1976), 86–87, 213, 223, 245–46, 238; George Adams, *Salem Directory* (Salem, Mass.: Henry Whipple, 1851), 129.

27. "At the Commencement of Mount St. Mary's College . . . ," *American and Commercial Daily Advertiser* (Baltimore), July 4, 1853, 2; "Hollywood Cemetery—Genealogy," www.webcemeteries.com/Hollywood/ (accessed April 7, 2014).

28. "Thomas Boudar," *Card Index to Naturalizations in Louisiana,* National Archives and Records Administration, Washington, D.C., available at Ancestry.com as NARA microfilm publication P2087, 20 rolls, Records of District Courts of the United States, National Archives and Records Administration, Washington, D.C.

29. The 1855 *Richmond Directory* listed S. Grady as a clerk on the north side of Main, between Fifteenth and Locust. That is most likely a mistake, or he may have worked briefly elsewhere.

30. Samuel Mordicia, Reel 5076, Frame 131, Box 276, Brock Collection, Library of Virginia, Richmond, Va.

31. "$50 Reward," *Richmond Whig,* May 23, 1854, 1.

32. "Bill of Sale for Two Slaves, January 25, 1854," Virginia Memory, www.virginiamemory.com/online_classroom/shaping_the_constitution/doc/billsale (accessed April 7, 2014)

33. Kimball, *American City, Southern Place,* 122–23.

34. "$50 Reward," *Richmond Whig,* May 12, 1857; *William S. Forrest, Historical and Descriptive Sketches of Norfolk and Vicinity* (Philadelphia: Lindsay and Blakiston, 1853), 294; "National Register of Historic Places Registration Form—Ballentine Place Historic District," www.dhr.virginia.gov/registers/Cities/Norfolk/122-0829_Ballentine_Place_HD_2003_Final_Nomination.pdf (accessed April 7, 2014).

35. "Negro Hiring," *Richmond Whig,* December 19, 1854, 3.

36. Marie Josephine Tait and Bacon C. Tait, Passport Applications, 1795–1905, National Archives and Records Administration, Washington, D.C.

37. "Was drowned . . . ," *Richmond Daily Dispatch,* August 11, 1863, 2.

38. Moses Ellyson, *The Richmond Directory and Business Advertiser for 1856* (Richmond, Va.: H. K. Ellyson, 1856), 154, 187; Herbert Tobias Ezekial and Gaston Lichtenstein, *The History of the Jews of Richmond from 1769 to 1917* (Richmond, Va.: Herbert T. Ezekial, 1917), 142.

CHAPTER 11.
THE INEXORABLE JAILOR

1. Bacon Tait, grantor, City of Richmond Deed Book 73B, 110, Library of Virginia, Richmond, Va.

2. George Teamoh, *God Made Man, Man Made the Slave: The Autobiography of George Teamoh,* ed. Nash Boney, Rafia Zafar, and Richard L. Hume (Macon, Ga.: Mercer Univ. Press, 1990), 92–94.

3. Charles Emery Stevens, *Anthony Burns, A History* (Boston: John P. Jewett and Co., 1856), 192.

4. "The application of Henry Banks . . . ," *Richmond Daily Dispatch,* June 12, 1861.

5. "Refuge of Oppression," *Liberator* (Boston, Mass.), September 29, 1854, 153.

6. "Colored Contentment in Virginia," *Liberator* (Boston, Mass.), August 11, 1854, 128.

7. "Varieties," *Salem Observer,* March 26, 1864, 4; "The Alabama Slave Minstrels . . . ," *Salem (Mass.) Register,* June 1, 1857, 2.

8. "New Publications," *Salem (Mass.) Register,* October 2, 1856, 2; Charles Emery Stevens, *Anthony Burns, A History* (Boston: John P. Jewett and Co., 1856), 187.

9. "The Arrest of Suspected Slave-Traders in Boston," *New York Times,* December 1, 1856; "The Slave Trade Case," *Boston Traveler,* December 2, 1856, 2; "The Slaver Case Once Again," *Salem (Mass.) Register,* December 22, 1856, 2.

10. William Chambers, quoted in Willie Lee Rose, ed., *A Documentary History of Slavery in North America* (Athens: Univ. of Georgia Press, 1999), 144.

11. "$50 Reward," *Richmond Whig*, May 9, 1854, 3.

12. "More Runaway Slaves," *Norfolk Beacon*, quoted in *Richmond Whig*, April 28, 1854, 1.

13. "Thirty Dollars Reward," *Richmond Enquirer*, December 10, 1858, 3.

14. "150 Building Lots . . . ," *Richmond Whig*, June 11, 1858, 3.

15. "A New York Hotel," *Gentleman's Magazine and Historical Review* (November 1856), 627.

16. "List of Letters . . . ," *New York Herald*, July 4, 1856, 6.

17. Lyon G. Tyler, *Men of Mark in Virginia* (Washington, D.C.: Men of Mark Publishing, 1908), 4:82–86; "Notice.—Were Stolen From My Trunk . . . ," *New York Herald*, January 12, 1857, *Richmond Whig*, February 10, 1857, and other dates.

18. Bacon Tait, Salem, Massachusetts, 1860 U.S. Census.

CHAPTER 12.

STATING HE WOULD DIE OF STARVATION

1. Gorham D. Abbott, *The Abbot Collegiate Institute for Young Ladies* (New York: C. A. Alvord, 1861–62), 27, 29, 30; "The Spingler Institute," *New York Evening Post*, August 24, 1859, 2.

2. Letter by Stephen B. Ives Jr., March 16, 1875, Image 23, Brock Miscellaneous File 5099, Library of Virginia, Richmond, Va.

3. Letter by Stephen B. Ives Jr., March 16, 1875, Image 23, Brock Miscellaneous File 5099, Library of Virginia, Richmond, Va.; Adams, Sampson and Co., *Salem Directory* (Salem: G. M. Whipple and A. A. Smith, 1861), 104; James F. Haley, Salem Ward 5, Essex County, Massachusetts, 1860 U.S. Census; "Praiseworthy," *Salem (Mass.) Register*, March 22, 1866, 1; "Saving Life at Sea," *Salem (Mass.) Register*, July 4, 1866, 2; Julie Roy Jeffrey, *The Great Silent Army of Abolitionism* (Chapel Hill: Univ. of North Carolina Press, 1988), 71; William Richard Cutter, ed., *Genealogical and Personal Memoirs Relating to the Families of Boston and Eastern Massachusetts* (New York: Lewis Historical Publishing Company, 1908), 4:1948–49.

4. Will of Bacon Tait, Chancery Court Reel 846, Richmond City, page 99, on microfilm at Library of Virginia, Richmond, Va.

5. *Richmond Daily Dispatch*, November 12, 1860; November 22, 1860; December 29, 1860; January 7, 1861; February 27, 1861.

6. "Local Matters," *Richmond Daily Dispatch*, April 2 and April 4, 1861.

7. "An Interesting Law Suit," *Richmond Whig*, March 8, 1872.

8. "Military Buttons," *Richmond Daily Dispatch*, May 29, 1861.

9. "Watches, Jewelry . . . ," *Richmond Daily Dispatch*, February 11, 1860; "Military Buttons," *Richmond Daily Dispatch*, October 3, 1861; "Notice.—Tents!" *Richmond Examiner*, March 10, 1862; "City Intelligence," *Richmond Examiner*, March 17, 1862, 3.

10. Harold S. Wilson, *Confederate Industry: Manufacturers and Quartermasters in the Civil War* (Jackson: Univ. Press of Mississippi, 2002), 74–75.

11. "An Interesting Law Suit," *Richmond Whig*, March 8, 1872.

12. Myers's age is based on his self-reported age in "Confederate Applications for Presidential Pardons, 1865–1867," Ancestry.com.

13. Records of Bacon Tait and Sidnum Grady, Confederate States of America, Fold3 .com; "Information about General Hospital #9 in Richmond, VA during the Civil War," Civil War Richmond, www.mdgorman.com/Hospitals/general_hospital_9.htm (accessed Oct. 23, 2014); "A Card," *Richmond Whig,* June 14, 1861.

14. "Shoes for the soldiers," *Richmond Daily Dispatch,* November 11, 1862.

15. "Notice," *Richmond Examiner,* January 7, 1863; "Rooms for Rent," *Richmond Daily Dispatch,* March 4, 1863.

16. "An Interesting Law Suit," *Richmond Whig,* March 8, 1872. The evidence points to Myers and Tait moving into the house around 1863, though Myers contracted a "house containing two tenements" to be built starting in February 1866. However, "the building [was] on Seventeenth street, where the sugar refinery was recently carried on," and therefore was not the house on Franklin Street where Tait and Myers lived. Thomas Johnson Michie, *Virginia Reports, Jefferson-33 Grattan* (Charlottesville, Va.: Michie Company, 1901), 536; "The Courts," *Richmond Daily Whig,* March 14, 1873, 3.

17. "Circuit Court," *Richmond Whig,* March 12, 1872.

18. "A General Meeting . . . ," *Richmond Dispatch,* February 8, 1864.

19. "In the case of Solomon A. Myers . . . ," *Richmond Dispatch,* February 9, 1864.

20. "An Interesting Law Suit," *Richmond Whig,* March 8, 1872.

21. J. B. Jones, *A Rebel War Clerk's Diary* (Philadelphia: J. B. Lippincott, 1866), 1:381.

22. Ibid.

23. Mary F. Lumpkin to Charles Corey, March 23, 1869, quoted in Hannah Catherine Craddock, "Black Female Landowners in Richmond, Virginia, 1850–1877" (Master's thesis, College of William and Mary, 2012), 28.

24. Salem, Massachusetts, Deed Book 670, 158, Essex County Registry of Deeds, Salem, Massachusetts.

25. Ibid., 158–59.

26. Ibid.

27. "Estate on Cedar Street at Auction," *Salem (Mass.) Register,* September 25, 1865, 3; "Household Furniture at Auction," *Salem (Mass.) Register,* September 7, 1865, 3.

28. Statement filed November 29, 1872, *Lukin Ext. v. Kelsey & Co.,* quoted in Craddock, "Black Female Landowners in Richmond, Virginia, 1850–1877," 31.

29. "Auction Sales—Future Days," *Richmond Whig,* October 20, 1874.

30. "Petition of Bacon Tait's Ex'ors and Others," pamphlet at University of Virginia, Charlottesville, Va., 18.

31. "Married," *Salem (Mass.) Register,* January 22, 1866, 2.

32. L. Grady, Policy #9504, November 15, 1836, and Policy #11654, October 16, 1843, Mutual Assurance Society, Library of Virginia, Richmond, Va.; "Valuable Real Estate for Sale," *Richmond Whig,* January 31, 1843, 3; Moses Ellyson, *The Richmond Directory and Business Advertiser for 1856* (Richmond: H. K. Ellyson, 1856), 135; "Suicide on Brook Avenue," *Richmond Examiner,* August 29, 1866, 3.

33. "Hollywood Cemetery," hollywoodcemetery.org/genealogy/burial-records.

34. Courtney Tait, May 31, 1871, Massachusetts Death Records, Familysearch.org; "Died," *Salem (Mass.) Register,* June 1, 1871, 2.

35. "Died," *Richmond Daily Dispatch,* June 16, 1871; "Died," *Salem (Mass.) Register,* June 19, 1871, 2; Bacon Tait, Richmond City Department of Public Health Death Certificate, Reel 864, Library of Virginia, Richmond, Va.

36. "Bacon Tait . . . ," *Petersburg (Va.) Index,* June 20, 1871; "Bacon Tait," *Utica Weekly Herald,* June 27, 1871.

37. "Death of Thomas Boudar," *Daily State Journal* (Alexandria, Va.), July 10, 1871, 1.

38. "Esquire Payne . . . ," *Cincinnati Daily Enquirer,* June 2, 1870.

CHAPTER 13.
FIGHTING THE TIGER AND OTHER KINDRED SPORTS

1. City of Richmond Deed Book 96A, 276, 482, Library of Virginia, Richmond, Va.

2. "An Interesting Law Suit," *Richmond Whig,* March 8, 1872; "Circuit Court," *Richmond Whig,* March 12, 1872.

3. Celine Tait Burding, "Massachusetts Deaths 1841–1915," FamilySearch, http.familysearch.org.

4. "Moore," *New York Herald,* April 30, 1907; "Funeral of Mrs. Moore," *Richmond Times Dispatch,* May 4, 1907.

5. Image 2056, "United States Index to General Pension Office, 1889–1904," FamilySearch, familysearch.org.

6. William C. Reichel and William H. Bigler, *A History of the Moravian Seminary for Young Ladies* (Bethlehem, Pa.: Published for the Seminary, 1901), 266, 531.

7. "SS Kaiser Wilhelm der Grosse," Immigrant Ships Transcribers Guild, http:immigrantships.net; "Jean C. Naegeli," New York City Directory 1894 and 1911, Ancestry.com.

8. "Marie J. Naegeli," New York, New York, Death Index 1862–1948, Ancestry.com; "Naegeli—Jean C.," *New York Times,* Historical Newspapers Birth, Marriage and Death Announcements 1861–2003, Ancestry.com; "Naegeli, Marie Josephine," *New York Tribune,* May 20, 1918.

9. "Esquire Payne . . . ," *Cincinnati Daily Enquirer,* June 2, 1870.

10. "Haul of Gamblers," *Cincinnati Daily Enquirer,* March 15, 1874, 1; "Twelve Gamblers Caught at Play," *Cincinnati Daily Gazette,* March 16, 1874, 8.

11. "In the Police Court . . . ," *Cincinnati Daily Times,* November 4, 1875, 1; "James Arnold . . . ," *Cincinnati Daily Enquirer,* November 5, 1875, 8.

12. "Mardi Gras Notes," *Cincinnati Daily Star,* March 1, 1876.

13. "A Practical Joke," *Cincinnati Daily Gazette,* April 17, 1877, 2; "A Man of Nerve," *Canton (Ohio) Repository,* March 16, 1885, 7.

14. "A Man of Nerve," *Canton (Ohio) Repository,* March 16, 1885, 7.

15. "A Practical Joke," *Cincinnati Daily Gazette,* April 17, 1877, 2. A similar story with different names and less accurate information about Tait ("B. C. Tait, alias Charley Todd, New

York") appeared as "A Bloodless Duel," *Albany (N.Y.) Daily Times,* April 17, 1877, and other papers.

16. "City News," *Cincinnati Post,* March 30, 1885.

17. "A Man of Nerve," *Canton (Ohio) Repository,* March 16, 1885, 7.

18. "Cincinnati Birth and Death Records 1865–1912," University of Cincinnati Libraries, https:drc.libraries.uc.edu; St. Joseph New Cemetery, stjoenew.com/search.html. Records conflict on his exact date of death.

19. "A Man of Nerve," *Canton (Ohio) Repository,* March 16, 1885, 7.

Index